American Cars
of the
1960s

John Gunnell

©2005 John Gunnell

Published by

kp books

An Imprint of F+W Publications

700 East State Street • Iola, WI 54990-0001
715-445-2214 • 888-457-2873

Our toll-free number to place an order or obtain

a free catalog is (800) 258-0929.

Library of Congress Catalog Number: 2005906843

ISBN: 0-89689-131-3

Designed by Elizabeth Krogwold

Edited by Tom Collins

Printed in the United States of America

Contents

Beautiful

Abbreviations

ABS	Antilock Braking System	Lbs.	Pounds
AM	Audio Modulation	Lbs.-Ft.	foot-pounds
Cam	Camshaft	LWB	Long-wheelbase
CB	Citizens Band	MK	Mark
Cc	cubic centimeters	Mpg	miles per gallon
CID	cubic inch displacement	Mph	miles per hour
Co.	Company	N/A	not available
DOHC	double overhead camshaft	Rpm	revolutions per minute
Dr	door (2d, 4d)	SAE	Society of Automotive Engineers
DRL	daytime running lights	SBR	Steel-belted radial
EPA	Environmental Protection Agency	SOHC	single overhead camshaft
FM	Frequency Modulation	SUV	sport utility vehicle
Ft.	Feet	THM	Turbo-Hydra-Matic
Hp	horsepower	U.S.	United States
I6	inline six-cylinder	WSW	white sidewall
In.	inches	WWII	World War II
Inc.	Incorporated	2+2	Four seater

Parameters

A number of choices were made to help organize this book. In the compact car section, cars with wheelbases up to 110 in. are generally considered compact, cars with wheelbases of over 100 in. are considered senior compacts or mid-size, wheelbases over 118 in. standard-size or limousine. Cars generally classified as pony cars (as well as the Avanti and the Corvette) are not included in the compact car section, despite wheelbase size. In the muscle car section, the focus is on mid-size cars with 300+ cid V-8s. (Compacts and pony cars with muscle car options are covered in compact or pony car sections.)

1960 Thunderbird convertible **Cappy Collection**

The Cars of the 1960s

The first 1960 cars to be introduced were Oldsmobiles and Pontiacs. Both of these General Motors Divisions unveiled their new models on October 1, 1959. Chevrolets and Cadillacs appeared in showrooms the following day. Fords and Buicks were introduced on October 8 and Dodges came out a day later. Mercurys, Lincolns and Edsels made their bow on October 15, the same day that the new-for-1960 Studebakers arrived. Plymouth was the last to bring out its line, on October 16. A new decade in the history of the automobile had begun.

The 1960 Pontiac Ventura, an example of the option-laden, sporty cars with the Pontiac styling touches. **David Lyon**

1 9 6 0

Compact American cars from the Big 3 automakers (Chevrolet, Ford and Plymouth) highlighted the year's automotive news. They were hatched in 1957, when the American economy hit a recession and small, economical foreign cars started catching on. American Motors' Rambler in 1958 and Studebaker's Lark in 1959 started the new trend. The Chevrolet Corvair, Ford Falcon, Plymouth Valiant and Mercury Comet arrived for 1960. With the arrival of these cars, imported car deliveries in the U.S. dropped 18.8 percent.

Chrysler made industry headlines with a revival to a 14 percent market share, although it wasn't enough to save the De Soto beyond 1960. For the industry as a whole, this was the first 1,000,000-unit new-car dealer inventory year and the first time in several years that all makers showed a profit. An 8.9 percent rise in combined domestic and import car sales made 1960 the second best year in automotive history. It was the first time since 1950 that sales increased two model years in a row.

In addition to an improved national economy, a number of factors fueled the rise in car sales. One was the resumption of the National Automobile Show at Cobo Hall in Detroit, Michigan. Another, at Ford Motor Company, was the first 12,000-mile/12-month new-car warranty. (Prior to 1960, most cars came with a warranty for just three months or 4,000 miles.) A third factor was factory sales incentives and inventory rebates. These programs moved carryover inventory very late in the 1960 model year and cost over $100 million dollars.

HOW TO BE A CORVETTE OWNER: 1960 EDITION!

In 1960, Chevrolet told people how they could be Corvette owners. **Phil Hall**

1960 Cadillac Series 62 two-door hardtop. **David Lyon**

The cars of 1960 were either compact or enormous. There was practically nothing in the middle. The hot-selling Rambler American was a revived '50s car with bigger doors and windows. The 1960 Cadillac was a memorable design and the first sign of shrinking interest in tail fins. Other luxury makers like Lincoln and Imperial were still "stuck in the 1950s." The Chrysler looked fast standing still – and was in its 300-F "Letter Car" format.

Of the compacts, the Corvair was radical, the Falcon was conventional and the Valiant was a unique Virgil Exner design that had a hard job catching on with buyers. The Comet "baby Merc" was a midyear entry. Like the Falcon, full-size Ford products had a "custom car" look and were considered style leaders in their time—though not so much today. You could tell Ford designers had spent time checking out the "lead sleds" on the West Coast. The last Edsel tried to steal Pontiac's trademark split-grille look, but went nowhere with it.

Chevrolet—with 1,873,567 sales—was America's most popular brand and shared its low, long, wide look with other cars in the GM stable including the heavily-sculptured Buick, the slabby-looking Oldsmobile and the take-me-racing-please Pontiac. Like other Mopars, Dodges and Plymouths had unique looks, but their styling was more about the past than the future. That wasn't the way to go in 1960, if you wanted to excite buyers.

As for Studebaker, it was "all Lark all the time," unless you were lucky enough to sneak a Hawk out of the showroom. The Hawk reflected a sporty-car trend that would blossom in the 1960s, but at its core it was a throwback to the 1953 Raymond Loewy design, with some Brooks Stevens updating.

Sixties light commercial vehicles were utilitarian, but the decade brought several new types of "sport trucks" that started the ball rolling towards the truck-dominated market we know today. Chevy's full-size El Camino was in its second and last season, but other models worth watching were the new IHC Scout and the small Falcon Ranchero.

Big 3 U.S. Automobile 1960 Model-Year Production

General Motors		Ford		Chrysler		Other Companies	
Buick	253,999	Ford	911,034	Plymouth	242,725	AMC Rambler	458,841
Cadillac	142,184	Falcon	435,676	Valiant	187,814	Studebaker	125,800
Chevrolet	1,404,095	Edsel	2,846	Dodge	42,517		
Corvair	250,007	Mercury	155,000	Dodge Dart	306,603		
Pontiac	396,716	Comet	116,330	DeSoto	23,832		
Oldsmobile	347,141	Lincoln	24,820	Chrysler	72,951		
		Thunderbird	92,843	Imperial	17,707		

Notes:

Chevrolet includes some 10,300 Corvettes.

1960 Dodge Dart is not a compact.

Chrysler includes some 1,200 Chrysler 300F Letter Cars.

Studebaker includes some 4,300 Hawks.

1 9 6 1

Every one of the five major American automakers showed a profit in 1961 for the second year in a row. Late in August, American Motors became the first car company to share its good fortune with its workers through a stock and profit-sharing plan. GM, Ford, Chrysler and Studebaker-Packard signed three-year labor contracts with the United Autoworkers Union to keep the assembly lines humming. Overall imported car sales continued to fall in reaction to the new domestic compacts, but no one seemed to be watching as Volkswagen sales leaped to 177,308 units (or 46.8 percent of the import market). Pontiac capped its move into the youthful, high-performance market—begun in 1957—by capturing third place in U.S. car sales behind Chevy and Ford. Better yet, Pontiac would hold that slot throughout the 1960s.

Most 1961 American cars were similar to their 1960 counterparts. For the most part, innovations were limited to the new compacts—the Buick Special, Dodge Lancer, Olds F-85 and Pontiac Tempest.

Though not a new trend, another growth area in 1961 was the increased sale of options and accessories used to make a standard car more luxurious, sporty or performance oriented. Luxury features that were catching on included

1961 Thunderbird convertible **Cappy Collection**

power seats, power windows and air conditioning. As far as sports-car-like features, bucket seats were installed in 330,708 American cars, 225,701 of them compacts. Almost 53 percent of all 1961 models carried a V-8 engine and 15.6 percent of them had over 250 hp. Some extras were now being sold in packages such as Chevrolet's first Super Sport (or SS) kit.

An exciting new sporty truck for 1961 was the Corvair 95 in Corvan, Loadside and Rampside models, all of which reflected innovative thinking. Dearborn designers came up with the Ford Econoline, a cab-forward model based on the Falcon platform and available in van, pickup and station bus models. The full-size Chevrolet El Camino was gone, although the name would return in 1964 on a smaller, more popular mid-size version.

Big 3 U.S. Automobile 1961 Model-Year Production

General Motors		Ford		Chrysler		Other Companies	
Buick	189,982	Ford	791,498	Plymouth	198,444	AMC	377,902
Buick Special	87,444	Falcon	489,323	Valiant	133,487	Studebaker	65,260
Cadillac	138,379	Thunderbird	73,051	Dodge	14,032		
Chevrolet	1,193,980	Mercury	120,088	Dodge Dart	167,678		
Corvette	10,937	Mercury Comet	197,263	Dodge Lancer	74,773		
Corvair	297,881	Lincoln	25,164	Chrysler	87,372		
Oldsmobile	242,323			De Soto	12,249		
Oldsmobile F-85	76,446			Imperial	3,034		
Pontiac	239,852						
Pontiac Tempest	100,783						

Notes:

1961 Dodge Dart is not a compact.

Chrysler includes some 1,700 Chrysler 300G Letter Cars.

Studebaker includes 3,708 Hawks.

After a two-year movement towards compact cars and smaller "big" cars, the American auto industry did a partial about-face in 1962 and stretched its full-size cars back to their 1950s proportions. This change in thinking reflected improvements in the U.S. economy, which was now just humming along. Two manufacturers—Plymouth and Rambler—did not follow the new trend. The Rambler Ambassador had its wheelbase reduced from 117 to 108 inches, while the Plymouth shrunk from 118 to 116 inches. Dodge reinstated the 112-inch wheelbase Custom 880 that it had dropped in mid-1961.

Numerous styling changes included a flatter deck lid for the Mercury Comet and a new roof line for some Cadillac, Chevrolet and Pontiac hardtops that looked like a raised convertible top. A hit of the year was the new Pontiac Grand Prix, another Bill Mitchell design. In-between-size models Chevy II, Ford Fairlane and Mercury Meteor were new in '62. They were conventionally-engineered vehicles that were larger than a compact and smaller than a full-size car. Ford said the Fairlane, despite its 111.5-inch wheelbase, had more interior room than a 1959 Ford on a 118-inch wheelbase. Something new for the Chevy II was its single-leaf rear spring arrangement.

Cars continued to get better as Detroit strived to increase the durability and serviceability of its products. The majority of front chassis no longer had grease fittings as the 32,000-mile "lube" became the standard of the industry. Self-adjusting brakes were another technical improvement. Chevrolet got some laws changed to make two-ply tires legal in all states and introduced them as standard equipment. A new Powerglide transmission with an aluminum case replaced the trouble-prone Turboglide automatic.

Chevrolet dropped its 348-cid engine, Ford introduced a 212-cid six, Pontiac added a convertible version of the Tempest and Chevrolet decided it did not have a big market for the car-style Lakewood station wagon after the Corvan arrived. American compacts continued to get sportier with models like the Corvair Monza, Tempest LeMans, Valiant Signet and Falcon Futura coming out as packages that included bucket seats, consoles and sporty wheel covers.

So called "sports-personal" versions of big cars like the Thunderbird Sport Roadster and the newly-de-finned Chrysler 300 "Letter Car" applied the same concept to larger automobiles.

The horsepower-and-cubic-inches race continued to expand, with 57.9 percent of all new cars carrying V-8 engines. Of those, 10.2 percent had above 300 hp. Chevrolet built 15,019 cars with the legendary "409" V-8 (up from 142 in 1961), Ford built 162,189 cars with a 390-cid V-8 and 8,384 cars with the 406 V-8 and Chrysler made 39,426 cars with a 413. Both AMC and Studebaker built over twice as many big-V-8 cars in 1962. By the end of the year, Pontiac one-upped everybody with a rare 421-cid "Super Duty" V-8. Many of these big-block V-8s used in Chevys, Pontiac, Fords and Mopars went into so-called "factory lightweight" race cars that had aluminum sheet metal, Plexiglas windshields, stripped interiors and even drilled-out "Swiss Cheese" frames. Can you say "muscle car?"

Big 3 U.S. Automobile 1962 Model-Year Production

General Motors		Ford		Chrysler		Other Companies	
Buick	245,683	Ford	704,775	Plymouth	172,134	AMC	442,346
Buick Special	154,467	Fairlane	297,116	Valiant	145,353	Studebaker	94,731
Cadillac	160,840	Falcon	414,282	Dodge & Dart	165,861		
Chevrolet	1,424,011	Thunderbird	78,011	Dodge Lancer	64,271		
Corvette	14,531	Mercury	107,009	Chrysler	118,539		
Chevy II	326,618	Mercury Comet	165,305	Imperial	14,337		
Corvair	306,023	Mercury Meteor	69,052				
Oldsmobile	353,026	Lincoln	31,061				
Oldsmobile F-85	94,568						
Pontiac	378,740						
Pontiac Tempest	143,193						

Notes:

1962 Dodge Dart is not a compact.

Chrysler includes some 600 Chrysler 300H Letter Cars.

Studebaker includes 8,800 Hawks.

1 9 6 3

The 1963 American cars broke new ground for the auto industry in styling, equipment and technology. Three "classic 1960s" designs came from Detroit styling studios this year—the Buick Riviera designed by Bill Mitchell, Raymond Loewy's Studebaker Avanti sports car and the Corvette Sting Ray that Bill Mitchell dreamed up during a fishing trip.

Sports-personal two-door-only cars like the Ford Thunderbird, the Chrysler 300 K and the Oldsmobile Starfire and the Pontiac Grand Prix combined sportiness, luxury and high-performance in glitzy packages that appealed to the "Jet Set." In such models, bucket-style front seats and floor-mounted gearshift levers were standard or commonly added as options. Studebaker's handsomely refined GT Hawk coupe fit into the same segment. These were all beautiful cars that had that something-special look when you saw them parked on the street.

GM's Tilt-Away steering wheel was introduced in 1963 and the Avanti offered disc brakes. While neither of these features was "all new," the 1960s versions were refined to work better and attract buyers in much larger numbers. Ford introduced the industry's first fully-synchronized three-speed manual transmission.

Other important manufacturing innovations of 1963 included the Buick Riviera rear window, which needed no weather stripping. AMC started stamping Rambler door frames out of galvanized steel, the Corvette revived retractable headlights and Pontiac adopted a new bake-sand-bake painting process. The venerable Chevy six got a cast iron crankshaft and a seven-main-bearings design that started a new trend.

Aluminum engines didn't fare well in 1963, with Pontiac dropping its alloy V-8 and Chrysler discarding its aluminum Slant Six right after production started. The cubic-inch race continued and the number of cars built with 144 to 200-cid engines fell 26 percent, while the number of cars with engines of over 400 cubic inches rose to double what it had been in 1961. Chevy made 3,670 of its 409s, Pontiac turned out 3,670 big-block 421s, Chrysler Corporation produced 2,130 wedge-head 426s and Ford produced 4,978 of its 427-cid high-performance V-8s.

With the economy picking up steam, the compact car market began to shift in an important way. Overall sales of compacts were up because car sales were up in general and there were now 11 compacts to choose from: Chevy II, Corvair, Tempest, F-85, Special, Falcon, Comet, Valiant, Dart, Rambler and Lark. The small cars' share of the total market actually declined from 35.2 percent to 32.9 percent, meaning they were *losing* popularity. It is important to note that sporty compacts were selling much better, with sales of small two-door hardtops up two percent and sales of compact convertibles up nearly 12 percent. This was a trend that the Mustang would tap into quite successfully, in 1964 and 1965.

1963 Corvette Sting Ray coupe **Tom Glatch**

1963 Buick Riviera two-door hardtop

Many small engineering refinements made in 1963 were more important than they seemed to the average person. Cadillac's five-joint drive shaft, with one single joint and two double joints, didn't seem too exciting until you felt how smooth the car rode even if a slight misalignment existed. Oldsmobile mounted its V-8 flatter and further ahead in the chassis to help reduce the height of the drive tunnel and increase roominess. On the other hand, the sports trend towards floor shifts and consoles turned many coupes and convertibles (and even a few sedans and wagons) into five-passenger cars.

Big 3 U.S. Automobile 1963 Model-Year Production

General Motors		Ford		Chrysler		Other Companies	
Buick	269,068	Ford	845,292	Plymouth	244,395	AMC	464,126
Buick Special	149,538	Fairlane	343,887	Valiant	198,399	Studebaker	76,146
Buick Riviera	40,000	Falcon	345,972	Dodge	209,841		
Cadillac	163,174	Thunderbird	63,313	Dodge Dart	153,921		
Chevrolet	1,571,730	Mercury	121,048	Chrysler	118,862		
Chevy II	375,626	Mercury Comet	134,623	Imperial	14,108		
Corvair	266,564	Mercury Meteor	50,775				
Corvette	21,513	Lincoln	31,233				
Oldsmobile	357,942						
Oldsmobile F-85	118,811						
Pontiac	458,617						
Pontiac Tempest	131,490						

Notes:

The 1963 Dodge Dart is a new compact car replacing the Lancer.

Studebaker includes some 3,900 Hawks.

The "big car" was back in vogue in 1964, as full-size cars like Chevy's Impala SS, Ford's Galaxie 500 XL and Pontiac's new Catalina 2+2 chased the youth market. GM compacts, with the exception of the Corvair, became "senior compacts" and rode on a three-inch-longer wheelbase. They also switched from unit-body to body-on-frame construction.

Most '64s stayed away from major "rehabs" and took a quick trip to the beauty parlor, but the Rambler American and Chrysler Imperial went all the way while Fords got major sheet metal tailoring. Plymouths and Dodges were setting the performance pace and got a cantilevered hardtop roof line to make them look faster. AMC followed Chevy into the seven-main-bearings camp with a much-improved in-line six.

So many headline makers arrived in '64 that it's hard to pick the winner. It's easier to list them in chronological order, as they all arrived at different times of the year. The Pontiac GTO—America's first mid-size muscle car—came first. It arrived in October 1963 and was selling quite well by the end of that calendar year. On February 23, 1964, three Hemi-powered Plymouth Belvederes and one of their Dodge cousins swept the field at the Daytona 500 and finished 1-2-3-4. In order to "legalize" the Hemi for NASCAR racing, Chrysler had to make 6,359 (Hemi and Wedge) 426-cid engines and put them in both Plymouth and Dodge production cars.

In the spring of 1964, the first Dodge coupe with a complete, factory-installed, Maximum Performance package left the assembly line. It had skinny front tires and real mag wheels. With such machines, the factory-backed "Ramchargers" drag racing team drew crowds, set records and sold Dodges. On April first, the Ford Mustang arrived, beginning the "pony car" market segment and quickly becoming the best-selling new car in history and stealing many sales from Chevy's sporty Corvair, despite its larger 164-cid air-cooled six. The Plymouth Barracuda arrived right behind the Mustang, but the fish car didn't sell as well as the pony.

Other new-for-'64 models included Chevrolet's Chevelle (with an El Camino truck version) and Buick and Oldsmobile mid-size wagons with train-like "observation windows" built into a raised rear roof section. Buick's was called the Sport Wagon and Oldsmobile's was dubbed a Vista Cruiser.

With the emphasis on bigger cars the spotlight was placed on reliability, performance and deluxe styling. Cadillac upped its engine to 429 cubes, big Buicks used aluminum front brake drums, Oldsmobile introduced a new thin-wall V-8 and GM launched two brand new automatic transmissions more like those available from other automakers. For the first time in history, GM got Corvette bodies from more than one source.

There were some notable departures in 1964. Mercury dropped its Meteor line and Studebaker disappeared completely, at least from the United States. In a last-ditch attempt to save the brand, car production was moved to a Canadian factory, while ZipVans for the U.S. Post Office Department continued to be built at Studebaker's birthplace in South Bend, Indiana.

Big 3 U.S. Automobile 1964 Model-Year Production

General Motors		Ford		Chrysler		Other Companies	
Buick	288,320	Ford	923,232	Plymouth	275,689	AMC	393,859
Buick Special	185,688	Fairlane	277,586	Barracuda	24,552	Studebaker	33,150
Buick Riviera	37,658	Falcon	317,437	Valiant	200,693		
Cadillac	165,959	Thunderbird	92,465	Dodge	280,409		
Chevrolet	1,574,468	Mustang	121,541	Dodge Dart	195,263		
Chevy II	191,691	Mercury	110,342	Chrysler	131,129		
Corvair	200,063	Mercury Comet	189,942	Imperial	23,285		
Corvette	22,229	Lincoln	36,297				
Chevelle	338,286						
Oldsmobile	368,494						
Oldsmobile F-85	177,618						
Pontiac	480,135						
Pontiac Tempest	235,126						

1 9 6 5

Three distinct styling themes came through on American cars in 1965. Most GM cars adopted design motifs that originated with the Buick Riviera including smooth sculptured lines and gracefully contoured rear quarters with a fastback roof line. Ford products took on a boxy-but-sculptured appearance. Chrysler products stressed crisp body lines.

1965 Buick Riviera two-door hardtop **Elton McFall**

Large cars continued to be popular and several grew in size a bit. Models with major changes included the Ford Galaxie, all Mercurys, full-size Chevys and Pontiacs, Buicks, Cadillacs, Oldsmobiles, Chrysler, Dodge Polara and Plymouth Fury and AMC's Rambler Ambassador. At midyear, Chevy released the Caprice Custom Sedan package for the Impala four-door hardtop. In addition to a beefed-up frame, it added special trim features that were like a Cadillac.

GM and Ford products went to perimeter frames and Cadillac had a new load-leveling suspension. Telescopic steering wheels were offered in Cadillacs, Corvairs and Corvettes. Low-section two-ply tires were introduced. Nine or more cars got front disc brakes (standard on T-Birds and Lincolns), while four-wheel disc brakes were used on all Corvettes. More automakers went to three-speed automatic transmissions and Chrysler dropped its old push-button gearshift. Olds replaced its 394-cid V-8 with a 425 that weighed less.

Car buyer choices were expanded again with more engines, transmissions, convenience options and accessories than ever before. Ford station wagons could now be ordered with dual center-facing rear seats. Of the 8,842,700 U.S. cars built in model-year 1965, 6,486,300 had a V-8 under the hood. Chevrolet introduced a 396-cid V-8 and offered it in a special SS 396 Chevelle aimed at the muscle car niche. Ten percent of all 1965 model year cars had engines over 400 cubic inches.

For the first time, the two-door hardtop became America's leading car body style. Exactly 33.8 percent of U.S. models were Sport Coupes, compared to 26.4 percent the previous year. The popularity of the convertible fell over half a percent and stood at 5.7 percent compared to 6.6 in 1962 and 6.3 in 1963. The drop of the "drop-top" was said to be due to increased use of air conditioning and vinyl roof coverings, that provided the comfort and look of a convertible without the hassle.

Big 3 U.S. Automobile 1965 Model-Year Production

General Motors		Ford		Chrysler		Other Companies	
Buick	330,593	Ford	978,519	Plymouth	303,203	AMC	391,366
Buick Special	234,969	Fairlane	223,954	Belvedere	159,535		
Buick Riviera	34,586	Falcon	227,362	Barracuda	61,521		
Cadillac	181,135	Thunderbird	74,972	Dodge Polara	134,771		
Chevrolet	1,674,572	Mustang	559,451	Dodge Coronet	209,393		
Chevy II	130,426	Mercury	181,696	Dodge Dart	206,631		
Corvair	237,056	Mercury Comet	165,052	Chrysler	188,548		
Corvette	23,562	Lincoln	40,180	Imperial	18,399		
Chevelle	343,894			Valiant	159,197		
Oldsmobile	379,934						
Oldsmobile F-85	212,870						
Pontiac	494,917						
Pontiac Tempest	307,083						

1966 Ford Fairlane GTA two-door hardtop **Phil Kunz**

1 9 6 6

This was the year for major styling changes to the mid-size or "intermediate" cars. The Dodge Coronet, Plymouth Belvedere, Ford Fairlane and Mercury Comet got new bodies while the Buick Special, Pontiac Tempest and Olds F-85 all got facelifts. Other models that got the all-new treatment included small (Ford Falcon and Chevy II) and large (Lincoln and Buick Riviera) models.

Government safety equipment regulations started to become more apparent this year, although the big meddling was still a year down the road. For some reason, six-cylinder engines got some major attention, with Olds swapping its small-car V-6 for a straight six, Chevy going to a bigger six and Pontiac releasing a unique overhead-cam six that promised more than it could deliver.

Oldsmobile's Toronado was a real innovation – the first front-wheel-drive American car since the "coffin-nose" Cord of the late 1930s. Though big in size and power, the Toronado was designed as a sporty hardtop with a radical fastback roof line. The public's craving for options continued in 1966. Ford offered such items as a rear seat television (not a big seller), a stereo tape system and a dual-action tailgate for station wagons that opened from the top or side. Chrysler put safer recessed door handles on many models and all cars adopted a double-thick laminated windshield. Cadillac buyers could drive on heated seats and vent windows disappeared from the Riviera. In the Chevy stable, the Caprice became a full-blown Chevy luxury model.

For the growing legion of high-performance buffs, 1966 was the last year to get a Rochester fuel-injected V-8 from "The General." On the other hand, it was the first year for Mopar buffs to order a "Street Hemi" and 3,629 of the 426-cid V-8s were sold. Ford put its "390" into 476,601 cars, its "410" into 44,686 cars, its "427" into 237 cars and its "428" into another 43,055 cars.

Big 3 U.S. Automobile 1966 Model-Year Production

General Motors		Ford		Chrysler		Other Companies	
Buick	304,208	Ford	951,391	Plymouth	290,872	AMC	295,897
Buick Special	209,318	Fairlane	303,935	Belvedere	189,282		
Buick Riviera	45,348	Falcon	161,762	Barracuda	38,029		
Cadillac	196,675	Thunderbird	69,176	Valiant	138,137		
Chevrolet	1,499,876	Mustang	607,568	Dodge Polara	136,674		
Chevy II	172,485	Mercury	165,466	Dodge Coronet	250,842		
Corvair	103,743	Mercury Comet	158,254	Dodge Charger	37,344		
Corvette	27,720	Lincoln	54,755	Dodge Dart	112,290		
Chevelle	412,680			Chrysler	240,382		
Oldsmobile	316,220			Imperial	13,742		
Oldsmobile F-85	229,021						
Toronado	40,693						
Pontiac	472,233						
Pontiac Tempest	359,098						

Most compacts got a major makeover for 1967 and the trend was toward more sportiness and the long-hood/short-deck school of car design. The U.S. Government's heavy hand was felt by the industry, which voluntarily adopted 17 new safety standards issued by the General Services Administration. These had a major influence on car design—and pricing. A government study said that the built-in safety features justified an average price increase of $55.

Model-year 1967 brought a second wave of "pony cars" (Camaro, Cougar and Firebird), a second "luxo" front-driver from GM (Eldorado), a longer AMC Marlin, a re-shaped Plymouth Barracuda and a Thunderbird with an extra set of doors hinged backwards. Ventless side windows were new for the T-Bird and Pontiacs got "disappearing" windshield wipers that hid under a lip at the rear of the hood panel. Thunderbird also changed from unit-body to full-frame construction, while the Imperial went in the other direction.

Under the hood, the number of cars with V-8 engines rose to 84 percent and V-8 installations in the 301- to 350-cid range tripled. Six-cylinder engine usage varied by company: 12 percent at GM, 14 percent at Ford, 25 percent at Chrysler and 56 percent at AMC, which was definitely behind the curve and knew it. Over 30 percent of GM cars had V-8s with more than 400 cubic inches. Chrysler made only 1,258 of the 426-cid "Street Hemi" V-8s, but also built 116,020 of 440 cubic inches. Even rarer was Ford's hot "427" which went into just 369 cars. But Ford also made 29,855 high-performance "428s."

Realizing that it was lagging behind the market trends, AMC introduced 290- and 343-cid V-8s. New at Buick were 401- and 430-cid engines. The Camaro's old "327" base V-8 was replaced with a Chevy-built "350." Chrysler added a "318" and Pontiac brought out a "400."

If many '67s could go better, they also stopped with greater reliability as dual braking systems with a telltale warning light were made mandatory on all U.S. cars. There were more offerings of front disc brakes as optional equipment.

All 1967 cars, except Fords, got an energy-absorbing steering column. For the muscle car lover forced to share use of a car with his better half, Ford created the GTA sport-shift option for cars with Cruise-O-Matic transmission. It allowed the car to be driven as if it had a conventional automatic transmission or as if it had a manual gearbox. Oldsmobile developed a simpler no-spin differential with fewer parts. More upscale cars like the Cadillac Eldorado, Caddy limos and Buick LeSabre, Wildcat, Electra and Riviera models offered automatic air leveling systems.

Big 3 U.S. Automobile 1967 Model-Year Production

General Motors		Ford		Chrysler		Other Companies	
Buick	326,375	Ford	877,127	Plymouth	266,356	AMC	235,522
Buick Special	193,333	Fairlane	238,688	Belvedere	152,497		
Buick Riviera	42,799	Falcon	76,419	Barracuda	62,534		
Cadillac	182,070	Thunderbird	77,956	Valiant	108,969		
Eldorado	17,930	Mustang	472,121	Dodge Polara	55,588		
Camaro	220,906	Mercury	122,894	Dodge Charger	15,788		
Chevrolet	1,141,822	Mercury Comet	81,133	Dodge Coronet	184,162		
Chevy II Nova	117,995	Mercury Cougar	150,893	Dodge Dart	171,413		
Corvair	27,253	Lincoln	45,667	Chrysler	218,716		
Corvette	22,940			Imperial	17,614		
Chevelle	369,133						
Oldsmobile	272,991						
Oldsmobile F-85	251,461						
Toronado	21,790						
Pontiac	434,197						
Pontiac Firebird	82,560						
Pontiac Tempest	301,069						

1 9 6 8

Every couple of years during the 1960s, the United Auto Workers union (UAW) would enter contract negotiations with one of the Big 3 automakers, then use the first settlement to close deals with the others. In 1968, it was Ford's turn to go first and the company wound up not building 500,000 cars and 100,000 trucks due to strikes. General Motors came next and suffered a 100,000-unit production loss due to local strikes, even after the national agreement was signed. By the end of the year, Ford's model-year production was down almost four percent, but GM was up. Chrysler enjoyed a 2.5 percent increase and AMC was up slightly.

Pontiac excited the industry in 1968 with its Endura plastic nose and a new Delcotron that combined the functions of alternator and voltage regulator. Pontiac—like other GM divisions—also went to the use of two wheelbases under its mid-sized cars . . . one for two-door models and a longer one for four-door models. Most other automakers also redid their intermediates. Mercury's new Montego replaced the Comet and Buick's Special became better known as a Skylark.

Luxury cars made headlines. Cadillac got the largest (472 cid) engine in the industry and Lincoln launched a new Continental Mark III model. The Eldorado got the big new V-8 and recessed windshield wipers. Chrysler added a twin-action tailgate to its rather fancy station wagons. The Imperial got a new grille and a new 440-cid V-8. Thunderbird offered its unique four-door in a Town Sedan package and added a new 429-cid engine option.

1968 GTO **Phil Kunz**

High-performance buffs had a field day in 1968 with a brand new GTO earning "Car of the Year" honors from *Motor Trend* magazine. Plymouth hit a home run by spinning off a budget-priced Road Runner model from its Belvedere line. American Motors launched the AMX two-seater, which it promoted as the "first American sports car for under $3,300 since 1957." It offered an optional 390-cid engine. Chevy's Corvette was new and included a T-Top option with a built-in roll bar. A less-than-fastback roofline made the new Dodge Charger a looker.

With all of the improvements and new features—plus added safety standards like shoulder harnesses and key-in-ignition buzzers—it was no wonder that average U.S. car prices jumped over 3.75 percent at the wholesale level.

Big 3 U.S. Automobile 1968 Model-Year Production

General Motors		FORD		Chrysler		Other Companies	
Buick	375,079	Ford	790,670	Plymouth	285,046	AMC	272,726
Buick Special	227,460	Fairlane	372,327	Belvedere	240,940		
Buick Riviera	49,284	Falcon	41,650	Barracuda	45,412		
Cadillac	205,475	Thunderbird	64,931	Valiant	110,795		
Eldorado	17,930	Mustang	317,404	Dodge Polara	115,510		
Camaro	235,151	Mercury	117,491	Dodge Charger	96,108		
Chevrolet	1,236,405	Montego	123,113	Dodge Coronet	222,559		
Chevy II Nova	201,005	Mercury Cougar	113,726	Dodge Dart	191,978		
Corvair	15,399	Lincoln	39,134	Chrysler	264,863		
Corvette	28,573			Imperial	15,361		
Chevelle	422,893						
Oldsmobile	315,995						
Oldsmobile F-85	275,128						
Toronado	26,521						
Pontiac	457,459						
Pontiac Firebird	107,112						
Pontiac Tempest	346,406						

What if Pontiac decided to build a car like this? Pontiac decided.

The 1969 edition of the Pontiac Grand Prix was the best selling version of the decade.

1 9 6 9

Big cars received big redos this year and shared substantial start-of-year price increases with all U.S. models. The high-po models were hotter-selling than ever before. Chevy IIs became Novas, Ford's Fairlane got a Cobra model and both the Cougar and Road Runner lines added ragtops. Pontiac's Grand Prix got its own car line and the longest hood the industry had seen since the days of the Duesenberg. It also introduced a wrapround "cockpit" style dashboard and the in-the-windshield radio antenna we all loved to hate.

Chrysler Corp.'s Plymouth Fury, Dodge Polara, Dodge Monaco and Imperial grew five inches and took off in new "airplane fuselage" styling. AMC's Ambassador was four inches longer, as Kenosha worked hard to shed its economy-car image with added luxury and performance. Mercury replaced the Parklane and Montclair with the luxurious Marquis and Marquis Brougham. Buick shrunk the LeSabre and Wildcat and also made major changes to its Electra "luxomobile."

There were many technical advances. An important one was GM's introduction of Turbo-Hydra-Matic drive. Fords got a more powerful "big six" and a 351-cid V-8 (actually two called "Cleveland" and "Windsor" versions). Chevys got automatic headlight washers, Chrysler and Ford products adopted recessed windshield wipers, GM cars used a ignition-steering column lock and tamper-proof speedometer, while some FoMoCo products (T-bird and Mark III) had anti-skid brakes. Other new industry developments included the 4-piston "floating" disc brake caliper and glass-belted tires. The Buick Riviera added an electric fuel pump to its standard equipment list and numerous '69s had electric rear window defrosters. On January 1, 1969, front head restraints became a mandatory safety feature in all U.S. cars.

Big 3 U.S. Automobile 1969 Model-Year Production

General Motors		Ford		Chrysler		Other Companies	
Buick	423,937	Ford	896,343	Plymouth	259,917	AMC	275,350
Buick Special	188,613	Fairlane/Torino	366,911	Belvedere	246,018		
Buick Riviera	52,872	Falcon	71,156	Barracuda	31,987		
Cadillac	199,904	Maverick	48,618	Valiant	107,208		
Eldorado	23,333	Mustang	299,824	Dodge Polara	70,194		
Camaro	243,085	Thunderbird	49,272	Dodge Charger	89,199		
Chevrolet	1,109,013	Mercury	140,516	Dodge Coronet	203,432		
Chevy II Nova	269,988	Montego/Comet	117,421	Dodge Dart	214,751		
Corvair	6,000	Mercury Cougar	100,069	Chrysler	260,771		
Corvette	38,762	Lincoln	38,290	Imperial	22,077		
Chevelle	439,611	Mark III	23,088				
Oldsmobile	368,870						
Oldsmobile F-85	239,289						
Toronado	28,520						
Pontiac	382,419						
Pontiac Firebird	87,708						
Pontiac Tempest	287,915						
Grand Prix	112,486						

CHAPTER ONE

The 1960s . . . Mid-Size Muscle Cars

1961 Pontiac Ventura **Doug Mitchell**

Some say the 1949 Olds 88 was the first muscle car. Others give that honor to the 1955 Chrysler C-300. Purists of the bucket seat, four-speed and fat tire sect insist that a 1964 Pontiac GTO was the original muscle car. Whatever your view, the GTO has become the "icon" of the genre – the factory hot rod – the mid-size car with the super-sized V-8 stuffed under its hood. And that's the kind of machine that this section of our book is all about.

While it's true that the "classic" muscle car is considered a GTO-like model, it doesn't have to be a Pontiac. AMC, Buick, Chevy, Dodge, Ford, Mercury, Oldsmobile and Plymouth—in alphabetical order—all made their own versions. The term muscle car wasn't heard a lot back when these vehicles were the newest thing since sliced bread. In those days, the enthusiast magazines favored "super car." The term seemed to be derived from Super-Stock drag racing. Early super cars usually could be spotted by their solid color vinyl interiors, hood scoops, consoles, mag wheels and floor shifts. Many had massive engines in small bodies, which made them great for drag racing.

Compact cars and pony cars came with muscle car equipment. There were also some huge cars that proved to be quite fast when big engines were stuffed into them: Thunderbirds, Marlins, Pontiac 2+2s and Chrysler Letter Cars come to mind. These machines were muscular, too, but they weren't the same as classic mid-sized muscle cars like the GTO. It was really the "factory hot rod" concept

that genuine muscle cars represented. They were small-sized standard cars—modern "Deuce Coupes" –with big motors to make them go fast.

Eventually, the super car name started to disappear. The term "muscle car" took its place and stuck like an F60-14 RWL tire on hot asphalt. Nowadays, collectors say "muscle car" as if it rhymed with "Duesenberg." I had a call from North Carolina this morning. "Muscle cars are starting to bring some big prices, don't-cha think?" the man asked. I politely told him to check our website www.krause.com to see the books and magazines we put out for car collectors. If he read them, maybe he'd know that people have been collecting muscle cars at least since I came here in 1978. Inside, I was really thinking, "Where have you been for the last 30 years, man?" This muscle car thing isn't new.

At classic car auctions, some muscle cars are now bringing six-figure prices. Even the "standard" versions are usually good for $15,000 fixed up and at least $30,000 when really restored. Fords were probably the first muscle cars to catch the attention of collectors, but then Chevys came on strong. The "bow tie" boys had the limelight for a good many years. These days it's Mopars that pull down knock-your-socks-off prices and in 2-0-0-5 that even includes AMCs—remember that Chrysler bought the "Kenosha Cadillac Co."

The growth of the mid-size muscle car market niche in the 1960s is hard to trace using statistics from industry trade journals. Muscle cars were usually lumped in with other mid-size cars and you have to remember that the bulk of the sales went to Chevelle 300 taxis and grocery-getter Fairlanes. The car counters at the factory didn't differentiate between a Coronet and a Coronet R/T. Looking at charts that show engine displacements can be helpful, but they don't tell the whole story either. The following charts show the number of over-300-cid engines built from 1963-1969. They include many of the top muscle V-8s (including some extremely rare ones), but they also include big Lincoln and Cadillac engines never used in any muscle car.

GTO logo and stacked headlights **Greg Hertel**

U.S. Production of V-8s Over 300 Cubic Inches

GM		Mopar		FoMoCo		AMC	
CID	Units	CID	Units	CID	Units	CID	Units
1 9 6 3							
326	50,229	318	239,581	352	355,543	327	37,811
327	316,761	383	52,897	390	308,549		
389	454,946	413	43,705	406	4,716		
390	163,174	426	2,130	427	4,978		
394	357,943			430	31,233		
401	305,595						
409	16,902						
421	3,670						
425	3,473						
1 9 6 4							
300	244,172	318	303,497	352	317,092	327	18,647
326	103,894	361	121,166	390	330,934		
327	375,685	383	83,259	427	3,168		
330	208,013	413	59,125	430	36,297		
389	507,194	426	6,359				
394	305,989						
401	152,231						
409	8,684						
421	5,391						
425	49,104						
429	165,959						

1964 Chevrolet Biscayne two-door **Tom Glatch**

1964 Ford Thunderbolt

1965 Chevelle Malibu SS
(Z-16 package) **Phil Kunz**

U.S. Production of V-8s Over 300 Cubic Inches

GM		Mopar		FoMoCo		AMC	
CID	Units	CID	Units	CID	Units	CID	Units

1 9 6 5

GM		Mopar		FoMoCo		AMC	
300	305,167	318	339,642	352	445,512	327	36,527
326	161,486	361	25,007	390	367,322		
327	501,793	383	350,412	427	327		
330	221,511	413	73,916	430	40,180		
389	553,145	426	6,929				
394	305,989						
396	59,650						
400	25,031						
401	218,163						
409	2,828						
421	17,124						
425	342,293						
429	181,435						

1 9 6 6

GM		Mopar		FoMoCo		AMC	
300	100,929	318	420,065	352	238,748	327	45,235
326	171,402	361	32,791	390	476,601		
327	431,694	383	424,772	427	237		
330	219,874	426	3,629	428	43,055		
340	203,742	440	69,952	462	54,755		
389	557,415						
396	179,141						
399.5	22,010						
400	13,816						
409	2,828						
401	147,834						
421	11,764						
425	381,139						
427	15,517						
429	196,675						

1965 GTO **Phil Kunz**

"Make no mistake about it," said *Ward's 1970 Automotive Yearbook.* "The muscle or hot performance cars influenced the engine trend in U.S. cars, particularly in the '69 calendar year and '69 model year when they chewed into 560,000 and nearly 700,000 of industry automobile output, respectively." But *Ward's* also threw out an ominous warning, saying "Commencing in the last half of 1969, however, insurance companies took a tougher stance on writing policies for high performance cars on the claim that they have higher accident loss rates. Washington chimed in, the Transportation Secretary in January 1970 stating publicly that he would seek the power to curb muscle car advertising, if necessary, some of which in fact had become far-fetched."

Other car industry statistics reflecting the growth of interest in muscle cars included numbers showing trends towards the production of more two-door hardtops between 1964 and 1969, the constantly increasing installation rates for options like four-speed manual transmissions and no-spin rear axles, plus production increases for certain types and sizes of tires used mostly on muscle cars. If the insurance companies and the government watchdogs hadn't stepped in, there was no telling how powerful the cars would have become or how big the market would have grown.

The launch of the muscle car in 1964, with the GTO, was followed by the glory years of 1965 and 1966, when automakers tried to out-do each other with their GTO clones. Chevy created awesome mid-sized muscle cars like the SS 396 Chevelle. Dodge kicked off with the hot Coronet. A "Street Hemi" engine could be had. Ford's earliest almost-mid-size muscle was a rarity called the Thunderbolt, a strictly-for-racing early Fairlane. The later Fairlane—a true mid-size car—became FoMoCo's GTO fighter with up to 7 liters of V-8 under its hood. Mercury shoehorned big engines into its Comet and had a very serious factory-backed drag racing team. Plymouth turned to its Belvedere intermediate to create models like the GTX and Satellite powered by big blocks and even Hemis.

The car wars weren't just corporate battles, either. Buick and Oldsmobile— once regarded as hotter rides than a Pontiac—found themselves losing sales to their cousin, which had managed to nail down third place on the sales chart. Both came up with neat answers to the problem. The Skylark-based Buick GS was a glittery muscle car with a few more cubic inches, while the Oldsmobile 4-4-2 (the model name meant different things at different times) was simply one of the best muscle cars to be had anywhere.

In the 1967 to '69 period, two new trends evolved in the muscle market, as engines and options continued to grown "hairier" thanks to intense competition. Some mid-sized super cars like the Endura-nosed GTO and the fastback Ford Torino began to look more like pony cars. Plymouth introduced the bargain-basement Road Runner, which soon inspired the Dodge Super Bee, GTO Judge and Ford Falcon-Torino. Engines continued to grow larger, with many now over 400 cubes, but fuel injection and multi-carb setups disappeared. Ram-air-induction was devised to keep up the power level.

During these years, the car industry experienced its first direct government intervention, with seat belts required in some states by 1961 through 1963 and federal safety mandates kicking in by 1967. The handwriting was on the wall and, by the dawn of the '70s, insiders understood that it was basically over for muscle cars.

Almost in reaction to the clouds darkening over the segment, Detroit used the period from 1970 through 1972 to build some of the all-time ultimate muscle cars.

Of course, they were based on 1960s models—since the '60s rule!

U.S. Production of V-8s Over 300 Cubic Inches

GM		Mopar		FoMoCo		AMC	
CID	Units	CID	Units	CID	Units	CID	Units

1 9 6 7

GM		Mopar		FoMoCo		AMC	
300	94,496	318	352,378	390	661,729	343	34,026
326	200,971	383	310,389	410	36,165		
327	508,675	426	1,258	427	369		
330	245,590	440	116,020	428	29,855		
340	220,705			462	45,667		
350	29,270						
396	130,092						
400	568,359						
425	258,319						
427	14,044						
428	7,476						
430	413,984						

1 9 6 8

GM		Mopar		FoMoCo		AMC	
302	7,200	318	531,300	302	746,500	343	47,100
307	856,000	340	11,600	390	577,200	390	5,500
327	726,000	383	466,500	428	20,600		
350	939,100	426	2,400	429	64,900		
396	131,700	440	159,300	460	27,400		
400	633,400			462	19,500		
427	15,400						
428	6,700						
430	244,600						
455	276,500						
472	230,000						

Note: Rounded figures only for 1968

1 9 6 9

GM		Mopar		FoMoCo		AMC	
302	17,998	318	558,190	302	671,216	343	55,198
307	309,695	340	24,830	351	403,092	390	17,147
327	695,715	383	504,982	390	551,975		
350	1,514,467	426	1,696	428	43,477		
396	170,155	440	154,217	429	199,355		
400	506,859			460	61,378		
427	34,729						
428	123,033						
430	278,943						
455	322,531						
472	223,267						

1964-1969 Pontiac GTO

1969 Judge **Phil Kunz**

The GTO package arrived in mid-1964. It included a big 389 V-8 and some special appearance items in place of regular LeMans trim. The GTO version of the 389 had big valves, a hot cam, a heavy-duty cooling system, starter and battery and low-restriction dual exhausts. The base four-barrel version produced 325 hp at 4,800 rpm. Tri-Power gave you 348 hp at 4900 rpm.

With the GTO option, a Tempest coupe was $2,852 and 7,384 GTO coupes were made. The two-door hardtop was the most popular GTO. It cost a bit over $100 more than the coupe and Pontiac built 18,422 of these. The convertible, priced at $3,081, had a 6,644-unit production run.

By 1965, the GTO was a rage. Technical improvements included a new camshaft, better heads, a revised intake manifold design and chassis upgrades. A four-barrel 389 cid V-8 with 335 hp at 5000 rpm was standard. A Tri-Power 389-cid V-8 with 10.75:1 compression and 360 hp at 5200 rpm was $116 extra. Late in the year a 389-cid Ram Air engine with Tri-Power arrived. Advertised with 360 hp, it was put in only about 200 GTOs.

The 1966 GTO wasn't an optioned LeMans. It had its own series. A wire mesh grille with rectangular parking lamps was used. A GTO nameplate was on the left side. The upper belt line contour was pinstriped and horizontal twin-slot tail lamps were new. Model-year deliveries were 10,363 coupes, 73,785 hardtops and 12,798 ragtops. Standard equipment included walnut grain dash panel inserts, dual exhausts, heavy-duty shocks, springs and stabilizer bar, 7.75 x 14 redline or whitewall tires and a 335-hp four-barrel V-8. A 360-hp V-8 was optional.

The 1967 GTO looked like the '66. The lower body sides had bright, wide underscores. This year the GTO's popularity dropped 15 percent due to increased competition from new muscle cars. Total production was 81,722 GTOs. Four versions of a new 400-cid V-8 were offered in GTOs. Three had a 10.75:1 compression and a Rochester four-barrel. A 335-hp version was standard. A 360-hp HO V-8 was the first-level option. A more powerful option was the Ram Air 400 V-8, which also had a 360-hp

1964 GTO **Phil Kunz**

rating. A 255-hp version of the 400 with 8.6:1 compression and a two-barrel was an economy option.

The 1968 GTO got the famous "Endura" rubber front bumper, hidden headlights and a twin-air-scoop hood. In one ad, general manager John Delorean sledge hammered an Endura nose and nothing happened, but the feature scared some folks, so a regular bumper was optional. A coupe was no longer offered. Pontiac built 77,704 hardtops and 9,980 convertibles. The base V-8 was a 350-hp 400. The HO version produced 360 hp at 5100 rpm and the Ram Air version 360 hp at 5400 rpm. Late in the year, a new 366-hp Ram Air II option with round-port cylinder heads was released to replace the Ram Air 400.

The 1968 GTO was *Motor Trend's* "Car of the Year." At *Car Life* it was a "10 Best" pick. "The GTO has become a classic in its own time," said the magazine.

In 1969, a special "The Judge" option included a standard Ram Air V-8. The Judge's rival was Plymouth's Road Runner, a bare-bones model with serious standard hardware. The Judge was a bundle of real performance goodies at a good package price. Unfortunately, after six straight years of increasing, Pontiac sales fell off in 1969. It wasn't Pontiac's fault that the insurance companies and the feds were ganging up on the muscle car pack. However, it had been great while it lasted and the GTO—The Great One—was probably the greatest of them all!

1966 GTO **David Lyon**

1969 GTO **Phil Kunz**

1965 GTO convertible **David Lyon**

1960s "solid gold"

1965 Pontiac GTO convertible

6	5	4	3	2	1
$1,480	$4,440	$7,400	$16,650	$25,900	$37,000

Estimated values in today's marketplace taken from the 2006 Collector Car Price Guide.

1969 Chevelle SS 396 two door hardtop **Phil Kunz**

1965-1969 Chevelle SS 396 and SS 427

The first "SS 396" snuck to market like the GTO. Everyone thought the Chevelle had been overlooked in Chevy's big-block "Mystery" V-8 program. They were wrong. Chevy made the 375-hp engine available in a new Malibu SS 396 (RPO Z16). The hot coupe had a convertible frame, rear suspension reinforcements and two additional body mounts. Its big 11-inch-drum power brakes came from full-size Chevys. Stiff springs and shocks, shot-peened ball-joint studs and Arma-steel hubs with special six-inch wheels were included.

The 396-cid V-8 required special left- and right-side exhaust manifolds to fit on the car. The engine was linked to a four-speed Muncie gearbox with a 2.56:1 first gear. The clutch conformed to big-car specs, too. Many features were unique to the Z16 like "396 Turbo-jet" front fender emblems, a special taillight board with an SS emblem and a unique ribbed molding with black paint. All Z16s had a 160-mph speedo, a four-speaker AM-FM Multiplex stereo, an in-dash tach and a dash-mounted clock. Only 201 cars were built.

1967 Chevelle SS 396 two-door hardtop

The 1966 SS 396 was a separate Chevelle model distinct from the Malibu, 300 Deluxe and 300 models. It had a new cigar-shaped body with "lean-forward" front fenders. The SS 396 hardtop was $2,276 and the convertible was $2,984. The two body styles accounted for 72,272 assemblies. The SS kit included twin simulated hood air intakes, ribbed color-accented sill and rear fender lower moldings, a blackout grille, black rear cove accents and "Super Sport" rear fender lettering. Specific wheel covers and red stripe tires were included. An all-vinyl bench seat interior was standard. More than one buff book compared the SS 396 to a 1955 Chevy hot rod.

The standard 396 (L35) engine produced 325 hp at 4800 rpm. Next came the L34 with its forged alloy crank, dual exhausts, high-lift cam and chrome rings. Can you say 360 hp at 5200 rpm? The 360-hp SS 396 hardtop did 0 to 60 mph in 7.9 seconds and the quarter in 15.5. Still more powerful was the L78 engine, a rare midyear release. It had 11.0:1 compression, fatter tailpipes, a hotter solid-lifter cam and go-fast goodies that jacked its output to 375 hp at 5600 rpm. L78 Chevelles did 0 to 60 mph in about 6.5 seconds. Wow!

1966 Chevelle SS 396 convertible **Phil Kunz**

Chevrolet's "GTO" had only a modest facelift for 1967. The grille had more prominent horizontal bars. This year 63,006 hardtops and convertibles were put together. Standard SS 396 content included fake hood air intakes, ribbed body moldings, a black-out grille and rear cove, "Super Sport" rear fender script, SS wheel covers, red-stripe tires and an all-vinyl bench seat interior.

The 325-hp L35 was carried over as the base 396 V-8. The L34 version was lowered to 350 hp. The 375-hp L78 was not listed on Chevy specifications sheets, but it was possible to purchase the components needed to "build" this motor right at your Chevy dealer's parts counter for about $475. Tranny options included heavy-duty three-speed manual, four-speed manual and Powerglide automatic (or later in the year, Turbo-Hydra-Matic). There was a wide choice of axle ratios from 3.07:1 to 4.88:1, depending on engine and transmission setup. The 375-hp hardtop did 0 to 60 in 6.5 seconds and the quarter mile in 14.9.

Chevy's said the Chevelle was "Brilliantly original for 1968!" It had a "wrap-over" front end, long hood-short deck styling and sportier-looks. The high-po SS 396 was in its own series with a $2,899 hardtop and a $3,102 convertible. They had matte black finish around the full lower body perimeter (except when the cars were dark colored). SS features included F70 x 14 wide-oval red-stripe tires, body stripes, a twin-domed hood with simulated air intakes, "SS" badges, vinyl upholstery and a heavy-duty three-speed transmission with floor shift.

The 325-hp V-8 was standard and 350 hp was $105 extra. At midyear, to keep up with new competition,

1961 Chevrolet Impala SS two-door hardtop   **Doug Mitchell**

Chevy re-released the 375-hp L78 option. A wide range of transmission and rear axle options was again available. Standard were finned front brake drums and new bonded brake linings. Some 57,600 SS 396s were made including 4,751 L78s and 4,082 L34s.

Chevy made no basic changes in its mid-size muscle car in 1969. There was no separate SS 396. The Super Sport equipment became the Z25 option and was ordered by 86,307 buyers. The $440 package had mostly the same content as before. Once again three regular production engine options were available with 350 or 375 hp. A new L78/L89 was jokingly advertised at 375 hp, but its actual output was much higher, thanks to special hardware like a pair of high-performance aluminum cylinder heads. The 1969 SS 396 with 375 hp did 0 to 60 mph in 7.6 seconds and the quarter mile in 15.4 seconds.

An extremely rare 1969 engine was a 427-cid V-8 available, in very limited numbers, on a special Central Office Production Order (COPO) basis. These engines came from GM's Tonawanda, New York, factory. Only 358 were assembled and most or all of them went to dealer Don Yenko, who custom installed them in cars at Yenko Sports Cars in Canonsburg, Pennsylvania.

1969 COPO Chevelle with the rare 427 engine option   **Tom Glatch**

1960s "solid gold"

1965 Chevelle SS 396 two-door hardtop

6	5	4	3	2	1
$1,320	$3,960	$6,600	$14,850	$23,100	$33,000

Estimated values in today's marketplace taken from the 2006 Collector Car Price Guide.

1968-1969 Plymouth Road Runner

You have to understand the history of Plymouth. It started as a low-bucks car. My father's first car was a Plymouth of the 1930s. My girlfriend's father had a Plymouth for his first car, too. So it was completely natural for Plymouth to bring out the world's first bargain-basement muscle car. In fact, you have to wonder why they waited until 1968 to dream up such a great idea.

The idea of putting a huge, brutal engine in the cheapest, lightest coupe was not exactly switching on a new light bulb, but with the Road Runner, Plymouth did all the work. The customer didn't have to check option boxes to get a big-block. It was standard. And the four-speed transmission was standard. Plastering the car with the famed Warner Brothers "Road Runner" got attention on the streets, where the best muscle car salesmen worked. If you got beat by this Road Runner, you wanted one.

A "stripper" Belvedere coupe was the basis for the Road Runner. And it came with a park bench seat, Rubbermaid floor mats, the big mill, the floor shift, a H.D. suspension, big drum brakes and Red Stripe tires. It came

1969 Road Runner 426 Hemi   **Doug Mitchel**

in a coupe for $2,896 and the hardtop was $3,034. If you wanted carpets and chrome, then you paid extra. In other words, the important stuff was included and the tinsel wasn't. You had to cough up $714 bucks extra for a Street Hemi. Plymouth built 15,359 hardtops and 29,240 coupes and stuck the Hemi in 1,019 cars.

Also offered were 350- and 375-hp versions of the 440. Performance stats for the base 383 Road Runner were 7.3 seconds 0-to-60 and 15.37 seconds for the quarter mile. Out of the way, prairie puppy!

1969 Road Runner 383 two-door   **Phil Kunz**

1968 Plymouth Road Runner 383 two-door hardtop **Jerry Heasley**

1968 Road Runner 426 two-door **Phil Kunz**

I think there's a rule in Detroit that if the 1968 grille had horizontal bars, the 1969 grille must have vertical bars. Same for those square taillights used last year – make them round. So minor grille changes and rear styling updates characterized the second Road Runner coupe and hardtop and new-for-'69 convertible. Standard H.D. features included suspension, brakes and shocks. "Road Runner" was on the dash, deck and doors. Top-opening hood scoops, chrome engine parts, an un-silenced air cleaner, red or white streak tires, a four-speed transmission with a Hurst gear shifter, a pseudo walnut shift knob, back-up lights and (for some reason) a Deluxe steering wheel were included.

The standard Road Runner V-8 was the 383 topped with a Carter AVS four-barrel carburetor. It had a 10.0:1 compression ratio and produced 335 hp at 4600 rpm. Options included the 440-cid V-8 and the 426-cid Street Hemi. *Car and Driver* bummed a Hemi Road Runner coupe for its January 1969 comparison test of six "econo-racers." With extras, the car cost $4,362.

The Street Hemi had a slightly larger 3.75-inch stroke, but the hemi heads, a 10.25:1 compression ratio and dual 4-barrel Carter carbs boosted its output considerably. The Road Runner may have been inspired by the Warner Brothers cartoon, but its performance was no laughing matter to GM and Mopar buffs. The Hemi Road Runner ran from 0 to 60 mph in just 5.2 seconds. You could go from one end of a drag strip to another in 13.54 seconds and your speedometer needle would be tapping 106 mph going through the traps.

Road Runner logo **Greg Hertel**

1960s "solid gold"

1968 Plymouth Road Runner two-door hardtop

6	5	4	3	2	I
$1,400	$4,200	$7,000	$15,750	$24,500	$35,000

Estimated values in today's marketplace taken from the 2006 Collector Car Price Guide.

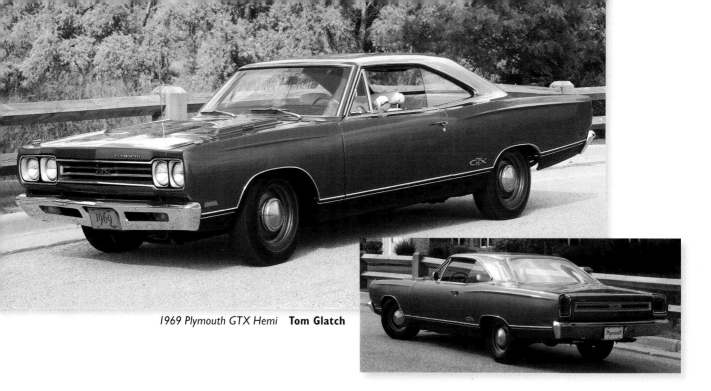

1969 Plymouth GTX Hemi **Tom Glatch**

1967-1969 Plymouth GTX

The big-cubic-inch mid-size super car was a core holding in every automaker's muscle portfolio in the 1960s. Plymouth started early with lightweight Super Stockers based on the low-end Belvedere. Big Wedge V-8s came first, then the Race Hemis and Street Hemis. Plymouth already made cars that were far faster than the GTO, but only in limited numbers. By the time the company was ready to attack the mass market, the muscle car had moved upscale, so Plymouth dressed up the Belvedere to create the GTX.

Vital to creation of the first GTX was the 1966 introduction of the Street Hemi and the release of the "Super Commando" 440-cid Wedge engine in 1967. Combining these with the Belvedere's 116-inch wheelbase,

top-of-the-line bucket seats, fake scoops, stripes and tasteful chrome accents made a fast and fancy muscle machine that was right in tune with the times.

You could get the GTX goodies in a hardtop for $3,178 or in a ragtop for $240 additional. About 12,500 GTXs were made and only 720 were Hemis. Of those, 312 had four-speeds and 408 had TorqueFlite. Rare Hemi ragtops left the factory about 17 times so don't expect to see one at the grocery store this weekend. The Hemi GTX ran a tad slower than its lighter Road Runner counterpart: 0 to 60 in 6.6 seconds and a 15.2-second quarter mile at 97 mph.

Plymouth built 17,914 GTX hardtops and 2,026 GTX convertibles in 1968—more than the first year, but

Popular Plymouths like the 1967 Satellite 426 convertible convinced executives to create the GTX series. **Elton McFall**

1968 Plymouth Belvedere GTX 426   **Phil Kunz**

1969 Plymouth Belvedere GTX 440 convertible   **Phil Kunz**

1967 Plymouth GTX

nothing close to the 44,599 Road Runners made. Once again the Super Commando 440 V-8 was standard. *Car Life* road tested a 375-hp 440-powered GTX with automatic transmission and reported a top speed of about 121 mph. "Exciting, enjoyable, extremely capable . . . to those who like super cars, they just may be the epitome."

Hemi GTXs were rare again, with only 410 hardtops and about 36 convertibles built.

"The Hemi GTX will appeal to the acceleration enthusiast who wants the ultimate – the fastest standard car on the market," added *Car Life*.

The 1969 GTX received the mandatory restylings at the front and rear. New features included side marker lights and slightly revised grille and taillight treatments. A wider choice of rear axles was offered. A Hurst shifter could be ordered. Also new was an "Air Grabber" hood scoop that opened and closed through the use of a dashboard shut off. The Street Hemi V-8 was a $701 option. This hairy V-8 was ordered for just 198 hardtops and only 11 ragtops.

1967 Plymouth GTX   **Phil Kunz**

1967 Plymouth GTX 440   **Tom Glatch**

GTX sales continued to slip. Only around 15,000 of the cars were built. In addition to previous power train offerings, at midyear Plymouth stuck three two-barrel carbs on the 440 to make the "440+6" option. This "Six Pack" cost $119 and gave 375 hp, good for a 13.70-second quarter mile at 102.8 mph.

"One primary purpose of a super car is to get from here to there, from this light to the next, in the shortest elapsed time," said *Motor Trend*'s Bill Sanders. "To this end, the Plymouth GTX is the flat out, best qualifier of all." While that was true, its sales didn't qualify the GTX for a long life. It clung to survival in 1971 and 1972, but ran out of luck past that point.

The 1965 Satellite 426 predicted the GTX series.   **Phil Kunz**

1960s "solid gold"

1968 Plymouth GTX convertible

6	5	4	3	2	1
$1,680	$5,040	$8,400	$18,900	$29,400	$42,000

Estimated values in today's marketplace taken from the 2006 Collector Car Price Guide.

1965-1969 Dodge Coronet, Charger and Super Bee

1969 Dodge Coronet Super Bee   **Jerry Heasley**

The Coronet was one of the Dodge "Rebellion" muscle cars. This squarish intermediate had the classic "factory hot rod" formula. When it was introduced in 1965, ads teased "Why not drop a Hemi in the new Coronet 500?" but most hot Coronets on the streets ran with big "wedge" V-8s. The Race Hemi was a possibility, but not best for Boulevard-prowling muscle cars.

The restyled 1966 Coronet had crisp, well-defined character lines. The upscale 500 had sporty bucket seats with vinyl or vinyl-and-fabric upholstery. The 426-cid 425-hp dual-quad Street Hemi was offered. Displacement and power-wise, it matched the race Hemi, but it used hydraulic lifters and a 10.5:1 compression ratio. It was the most powerful production engine of its day.

The Charger was Dodge's answer to the fastback craze – a Coronet from the waist down. A big, wide body gave it a "flat" look far different from a Mustang 2+2.

1966 Dodge Charger   **Phil Kunz**

Dodge called its Charger a "Sports Sedan." It was aimed at young-at-heart dads able to sell their better half on buying it as a "station wagon." V-8s included a base 318-cid 230-hp job or the one-step-up 361-cid 265-hp option (both two-barrels). Once you got to the 383 you were talking "muscle." A nicely outfitted 383 Charger with automatic went out the door a tad over $3,100. Production of 1966 Chargers hit 37,300, including just 468 Hemis.

Many "street" muscle cars were weekend dragsters. Starting in 1967, Dodge added a Coronet R/T to emphasize this street-and-strip nature. *Motor Trend* called the R/T "a Dodge with a set of mag wheels, wide oval tires and a bumblebee stripe on its rear end." A 375-hp 440 Magnum V-8 was standard.

Dodge wanted the 1967 Charger to reflect the company's racing image. Standard was a 318-cid 230-hp V-8 good for 0 to 60 mph in 10.9 seconds. Next came a 383-cid 326-hp big-block that took the Charger from 0 to 60 mph in 8.9 seconds and down the quarter mile in 16.5

1969 Dodge Charger R/T   **Phil Kunz**

seconds at 86.4 mph. There was also the 440-cid 375-hp V-8 good for 0 to 60 in 8 seconds and a 15.5-second quarter mile at 93 mph. Top dog was the 426-cid 425-hp Hemi. It went 0 to 60 mph in 7.6 seconds and did the quarter in 14.4 seconds at 100 mph!

The '67 Chargers were much rarer than 1966 versions. Only 15,788 were built. This included 118 with a Hemi, of which half were four-speeds. If you're considering buying a 1967 Hemi Charger today, you might appreciate knowing that it gets 11.7 mpg in city driving and about 14.4 mpg on the open highway. Don't tell that to the people who set CAFE standards. One of them might have a heart attack!

The Coronet was reinvented in 1968. Two R/Ts were available, a $3,353 hardtop and a $3,613 convertible. R/T equipment included bucket seats, dual exhausts, stiff suspension, heavy-duty brakes and more. TorqueFlite was standard. Bumblebee stripes or side stripes were provided. Coronet R/Ts used the Coronet 500 interior and a "power bulge" hood with simulated air vents.

1969 Dodge Daytona
Hemi 426 **Tom Glatch**

1969 Dodge Coronet R/T

Some days you win

Some days you lose

The fortunes on the straight and narrow warpath change as quickly as the gears in the go-box! Today you tear 'em up. Tomorrow is another day. Your machine has got to be mean . . . you've got to be good . . . and you've got to come out of the hole with more togetherness than Amos and Andy! That's the drama of the drag strip, man and machine.

That's why more than 100,000 buffs bulged the track at Indy for the NHRA's big showdown—the world championships.

And what a showdown! On Saturday, Jim Thornton in a '63 Dodge downed his Ramcharger teammate, Herman Mozer, on his

way to royalty in the Super Stock Automatic Class. Next day, running for the meet's most coveted honor—Top Stock Eliminator —Mozer turned the tables and gave Thornton the thumb. But the event was far from over. Mozer still had to face the present "Mr. Eliminator," Al Eckstrand in Lawman, another specially equipped '63 Dodge. And another winner is defeated. Mozer edged him by 1/100th of a second with an e.t. of 12.22.

Some days you win. Some days you lose. That's what keeps the quarter-mile jaunt so interesting. But have you noticed? When a Dodge loses these days . . . it's to another Dodge.

Hot Dodge

DODGE DIVISION ✦ CHRYSLER MOTORS CORPORATION

The 1963 Dodge Ramcharger drag racing teams set the table for the muscle-era Dodges.

The standard 440-cid Magnum V-8 was the same as the 1967 version. Horsepower (375 at 4600 rpm) remained unchanged. High-performance tires and bucket seats were standard. Options included a limited-slip differential, custom wheels, front disc brakes and a console. The $605 optional Street Hemi was ordered for 94 Coronet R/Ts with four-speeds and 136 with TorqueFlite. Hemi cars came with a special heavy-duty suspension, but no A/C.

New for 1968 was a bargain-basement Super Bee based on the Coronet 440 coupe. It included the 383-cid 335-hp V-8, a heavy-duty four-speed with a Hurst "Competition-Plus" shifter, dual exhausts, F40 x 14 tires and a heavy-duty suspension at a low package price. You couldn't get a vinyl top, but $712 got you a Hemi. Only 166 Hemi Super Bees were made. The Super Bee—with carpets, pleated vinyl seats and door panels and a Charger dash—was fancier than a Road Runner. The wheel lips and rear panel had bright accents.

1967 Dodge Coronet two-door hardtop **Phil Kunz**

The 1968 Chargers gave up the wide "jumping-ramp" roof and adopted the late-1960s "Coke bottle" shape to a smoother, rounded fastback body. The R/T muscle version included an integral rear deck lid spoiler and competition-type gas filler. Chargers retained a 117-inch wheelbase, but the rear track was widened nearly an inch. The $3,480 R/T (TorqueFlite was standard) could move from 0 to 60 mph in 6.5 seconds and down a drag strip in 15 seconds at 93 mph. This was the only '68 Charger that got the Hemi. The engine option cost $605 and only 475 such cars were put together.

In 1969, the Coronet R/T soldiered on as the Coronet series muscle car. Content included the Magnum

1968 Dodge Coronet R/T two-door hardtop

440-cid V-8, TorqueFlite and bumblebee stripes. Simulated air scoops located on the rear fenders, just ahead of the rear wheels, were optional. A "six-pack" carburetor setup was the big news for the '69 Coronet R/T. The six-pack R/T did a 105.14-mph 13.65-second quarter-mile run. Its 0-to-60 time was 6.6 seconds. Also available was a Ramcharger fresh-air induction system (standard on Hemis) with twin air scoops that fed cold air into a fiberglass plenum bolted under the hood. Model-year production totaled 7,238 hardtops and convertibles combined. Hemis went in 97 two-door hardtops (58 with a four-speed) and 10 ragtops (four with a four-speed).

1969 Dodge Coronet Super Bee 426   **Phil Kunz**

A two-door hardtop with a $3,138 base price joined the Coronet Super Bee line in 1969. The Sport Coupe returned at $3,076. There were few changes in appearance or standard equipment. The new 390-hp "six-pack" performance option was available. It included a black fiberglass hood that locked in place with four chrome pins and was entirely removeable for engine access. Also available was the new Ramcharger cold-air induction system. A total of 27,800 Super Bees were built. This included 166 Hemi cars, 92 of them with four-speeds.

The 1969 Charger didn't change much. As *Motor Trend* magazine put it, "That brute Charger styling, that symbol of masculine virility, was still intact." The 1969 grille was divided into two sections and the taillights were modified a bit. However, the fastback Dodge was basically the same good-looking beast as before on the outside. The inside also had only a few changes like a large-faced tach and gauges done in white on black to make them stand out more.

The R/T was the high-performance version of the Charger. A new Charger 500 was issued as a special limited-production model. It was based on a prototype race car. Dodge said it was offered specifically for high-performance racing tracks and available only to qualified race drivers. Muscle car lovers flocked to Dodge dealerships trying to buy one. Chances are good they at least drove away in another Charger or a jazzy Coronet. The Charger 500's body modifications were the workmanship of Creative Industries, a Detroit aftermarket firm. A minimum of 500 such cars had to be sold to the public to authorize the changes and make the Charger legal for racing under NASCAR rules. The Charger 500 model designation was based on that number. Officially, 32 Hemi-powered Charger 500s were built, though experts have tracked down serial numbers for 35 such vehicles.

One of Chrysler's famous "winged warriors" was the Dodge Charger Daytona. Creative Industries also received the contract to build 500 Daytonas to legalize the 200-mph body modifications for stock car competition. The winged cars won so many races that NASCAR outlawed the Hemi and wedge V-8s. Officially, 433 cars with base 375-hp 440 Magnum V-8s were built for the streets and 70 were turned out with Hemi V-8s under their snout. One Daytona with 5,000 original miles has been documented as a car with a dealer-installed 440 Six-Pack V-8, although Dodge did not offer this engine as a *factory* option.

1960s "solid gold"

1966 Dodge Charger two-door hardtop

6	5	4	3	2	1
$1,040	$3,120	$5,200	$11,700	$18,200	$26,000

Chargers equipped with the 426 Hemi have an inestimable value.

1968 Dodge Coronet Super Bee coupe

6	5	4	3	2	1
$1,480	$4,440	$7,400	$16,650	$25,900	$37,000

Estimated values in today's marketplace taken from the 2006 Collector Car Price Guide.

1969 Dodge Charger Daytona 500

1965 Buick Gran Sport two-door hardtop **Phil Kunz**

1965-1969 Buick Gran Sport

The mid-size Buick was the Skylark. The hi-po Skylark was the Gran Sport, GS for short. The GS was Buick's GTO. Actually, it was better than the GTO since all three Skylarks—the coupe ($2,895), hardtop ($2,945) and ragtop ($3,095)—were built on the heavy convertible frame. With a big 4-barrel V-8 the GS package was $253 with a 3-speed, $420 with a 4-speed and $457 with Super Turbine 300 automatic. H.D. shocks and springs and a stiffer front anti-roll bar were included. "Like a howitzer with windshield wipers," said Buick. "116 mph," said *Motor Trend*. The magazine also noted that a race-prepped 1965 clocked a 13.42-second 104.46-mph quarter mile run at the Winternational Drags.

With a 115-inch wheelbase and 209-inch length, the GS models weighed in between 3,428 and 3,532 pounds. The 400-cid "nailhead" V-8 pounded out 325 hp. That equated to 0 to 60 mph in 7.8 seconds and the quarter mile in 16.6 seconds at 86 mph. Buick "blamed" its techies for the GS. "There is mounting evidence that our engineers have turned into a bunch of performance enthusiasts," said Buick. "First they stuff the Wildcat full of engine. Then the Riviera Gran Sport. And now this, the Skylark GS, which is almost like having your own, personal-type nuclear deterrent." Or GTO deterrent, maybe!

1965 Buick Gran Sport coupe

Now in its own series, the 1966 GS had the plushy Skylark goodies, plus bright simulated hood scoops, side stripes, a blacked-out grille and rear panel, GS badges, heavy-duty underpinnings, all-vinyl notchback bench seats, carpeting, full wheel covers and 7.75 x 14 whitewall or redline tires, but no hood ornament.

The same Wildcat 401 V-8 was used. To keep the GM brass from having a panic attack, the engine was called the "400." That form of corporate stress management made the motor "legal" in a mid-size car.

Don't you just love it when the car mags compete? *Car and Driver* reported a 14.92-second quarter mile at 95.13 mph for a 1966 GS. Naturally, *Motor Trend's* test driver had to outdo that with 0 to 60 mph in 5.7 seconds and the quarter mile in 14 seconds at 101 mph! Sports car racer Masten Gregory said of the GS, "I didn't like the car at first, because I thought it was too soft, but as I got used to it, I started liking it quite a bit." And for the model's second year, Buick built 1,835 GS coupes, 9,934 hardtops and 2,047 ragtops.

1965 Buick Gran Sport convertible

A brand new 400-cid V-8 replaced the nailhead in '67 and the GS became the GS 400 (there was a less muscular GS 340, too). The new hydraulic-lifter engine was more modern and smoother and tolerated higher rpms. It had 10.25:1 compression and a big four-barrel carb. Hooked behind it you could get a three-speed or a four-speed or a new three-speed automatic that could be shifted manually. Options included a tach and a 3.90:1 posi rear.

This year the GS 400s were in their own series. Hardtop, post-coupe and ragtop versions were offered. *Motor Trend* said that the GS 400 had "the best road behavior of any car we've driven in quite a while." Power front disk brakes were a new $147 handling option. Production included 1,014 post-coupes, 10,659 hardtops and 2,140 convertibles. Buick advertised the GS 400 as "The car that enthusiasts are enthusiastic about."

Completely restyled in '68 was a Skylark GS 400 with even more of an aircraft fuselage look and S-shaped body side feature lines. It had a large scoop at the rear of the hood and chrome. The 340-hp 400 V-8 was carried over. *Hot Rod's* Eric Dahlquist tested a hardtop with a homemade cold-air package to 14.78 seconds at 94 mph in the quarter. Dahlquist noted that factory cold-air packages were due January 1, 1968. Stage 1 and Stage 2 packages were offered, along with forged aluminum pistons, a special intake manifold gasket that blocked the heat riser; oversize rods, fully-grooved main bearings, six percent richer carburetor metering rods, special spark plugs and headers.

Even with all the drastic updates, total GS production was in the same range as in 1967 with 10,743 hardtops and 2,454 convertibles built (the coupe was no more). *Motor Trend* said the '68 GS 400 had "surprisingly good" performance and was "very tight and hard to excel." The magazine liked the construction, comfort and general quality of the car.

In 1969, technical improvements to the GS 400 were in the spotlight. A new hood scoop actually sucked in cold air. The Stage 1 and Stage 2 engine options offered drag strip-style performance for serious enthusiasts. Buick sold you the Stage 1 kit installed. It incorporated a high-lift cam, tubular push rods, H.D. valve springs and other goodies. The tranny got a 5200-rpm governor to protect against over-revving the engine. Stage 2 hardware was a D-I-Y add-on that you ordered from your Buick dealer's parts department. It included an even wilder cam and was *not* recommended for street use on cars with mufflers.

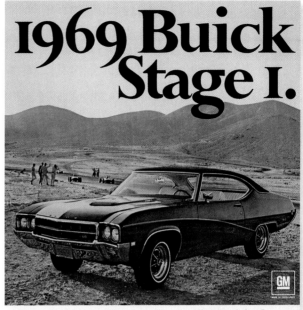

Some overlooked the 1969 Buick Gran Sport Stage I—but not its happy drivers!

Car Life found the GS 400 to be the fastest muscle car it tested in 1969. *Motor Trend's* 400 ran from 0 to 60 mph in 7.7 seconds and did the quarter mile in 15.9 seconds at 89 mph.

1968 Buick Gran Sport convertible   **Tom Glatch**

1960s "solid gold"

1968 Buick Gran Sport GS 400 two-door hardtop

6	5	4	3	2	1
$ 840	$2,520	$4,200	$9,450	$14,700	$21,000

Note: Add 30 percent for the Stage 1 option.

Estimated values in today's marketplace taken from the 2006 Collector Car Price Guide.

The 1968 Hurst/Olds coupe was a special Cutlass-based car. **Tom Glatch**

1966-1969 Oldsmobile Cutlass 4-4-2

The Oldsmobile *Product Selling Information for Salesmen* guide explained the 4-4-2 like this, "police needed it—Olds built it—pursuit proved it." The name originally meant four-barrel carburetor, four on the floor and dual exhausts. Later the meaning became 400 cubic inch, four barrel dual exhausts.

The 4-4-2 had a base price of $2,784. With a 115-inch wheelbase, it stretched 204.3 inches long. "What Olds engineers have done, in the final analysis, is produce a car which at long last lives up to the claims of the company's advertising copywriters and top-level spokesmen," said *Car Life.* "The 4-4-2 is indeed 'where the action is.' No better Oldsmobile has rolled off the Lansing assembly line in many a year and though it isn't quite the sports car that corporate brass likes to think, it doesn't miss by much."

The Cutlass line was mildly face lifted for 1965 and the 4-4-2 performance and handling package gained popularity. The hi-po kit was available on the standard F-85 coupe and hardtop, or the Cutlass coupe, hardtop and convertible. Prices for the five models ranged from $2,695 to $3,140. A new 400-cid V-8 added 35 hp." A total of 25,003 cars got the 4-4-2 package this year.

The 1966 Cutlass F-85 was totally restyled. There was a pronounced "hump" over the rear windows and large C-pillars extending beyond the backlight.

The 4-4-2 again included the 400-cid V-8, tweaked to 350 hp. This setup was good for a 14.8-second quarter mile at 97 mph.

Late in the year, the adrenalin was pumped to 360 hp with TriPower. New W-30 air-induction was offered, plus five gearboxes and eight axle ratios. From the standpoints of both performance and rarity, the 1966 Olds Cutlass 4-4-2 equipped with the 360-hp factory Tri-Power installation is the most desirable example of these production years to a real muscle car enthusiast.

The 1967 4-4-2 option was available for Cutlass Supreme two-doors. It included the 350-hp 400 V-8, H.D. suspension, F70 x 14 Red Line tires, bucket seats and 4-4-2 badges. Another $184 added a four-speed gearbox. For those who preferred something simpler to drive, 4-4-2s could be had with Turbo Hydra-Matic for $236. Bucket seats and a console were available.

1965 Oldsmobile Cutlass 4-4-2 two-door hardtop **Doug Mitchel**

The Cutlass-based 1969 Hurst/Olds coupe is a muscle era classic. **Phil Kunz**

got a Hurst shifter. Automatics had 3-on-the-tree, but a console shifter was optional. W-30s had special hood stripes and front fender decals. Strato bucket seats, red-stripe Wide-Oval tires, a juicy battery, dual exhausts and a beefy suspension were included. An anti-spin rear axle was mandatory.

Output by body style included 2,475 coupes, 19,587 hardtops and 4,295 ragtops. Only 1,389 cars had W-30 Force-Air. New was a calmer W-31 Force-Air setup for F-85s with THM. This "for-the-street" extra was aimed at the youth niche where heavy breathing and heavy spending didn't co-mingle. At $310, the package was costlier than the W-30 at $264. However, the car-and-equipment tab was lower. So was production. One percent of all Olds were W-31s. Oldsmobile advertised that the 4-4-2 was, "Built like a 1-3/4-ton watch."

The 350 hp V-8 was standard. The hood louvers over the air cleaner were functional, but had no ram-air effect. Using factory ducting in the front of the car, the W-30 option rammed in enough cold air to produce 360 hp. An Olds ad summed up the 1967 Cutlass Supreme 4-4-2 by stating: "Sedate it ain't!"

The 1968 4-4-2 was a model—not an option. It had more curves on its long hood, a short rear deck, razor-edge fenders, a swoopy rear, big 4-4-2 emblems and dual through-the-bumper exhausts. A new 400-cid V-8 had a 3.87 x 4.25-inch bore and stroke versus 4 x 3.975-inch in 1967. Of three four-barrel versions of this 10.5:1 compression V-8, the hottest had the W-30 Force Air package. A 290-hp two-barrel "Turnpike Cruiser" economy V-8 was optional.

Buyers who ordered the Force Air induction system got large 15 x 2-inch air scoops below the front bumper, a special camshaft for a higher torque peak, modified intake and exhaust ports, a free-flowing exhaust system and low-friction components. Another performance extra was a "Rocket Rally Pac."

Production of the 1968 Cutlass 4-4-2 came to 4,282 Sports Coupes, 5,142 convertibles and 24,183 Holiday hardtops for a total of 33,607 units, compared to 24,829 the previous year. *Car Life* said that the 4-4-2 was "A true high-performance car and the best handling of today's super cars"

"Dr. Olds" pitched the '69 Olds 4-4-2's bolder split grille, fat hood stripes and new name badges. The wimpy "Turnpike Cruiser" option was dropped, but other engine-transmission combos were unchanged. Stick shift cars

1968 Oldsmobile 4-4-2 two-door hardtop **Phil Kunz**

1968 Oldsmobile Cutlass W-30 coupe **Tom Glatch**

1960s "solid gold"

1966 Olds Cutlass 4-4-2 convertible

6	5	4	3	2	1
$1,120	$3,360	$5,600	$12,600	$19,600	$28,000

Note: Add 30 percent for triple two-barrel carbs and add 90 percent for the W-30 option.

Estimated values in today's marketplace taken from the 2006 Collector Car Price Guide.

1966-1969 AMC Rebel

1967 AMC Rebel SST convertible

for a muscle car, you wanted the hotter one. This version substituted a 10.2:1 compression ratio for the regular 9.0:1 and upgraded to a Carter AFB four-barrel (from a Holley two-barrel). It served up 280 hp at 4800 rpm and 365 ft.-lbs. of torque at 3,000 rpm. A dual exhaust system was optional. With the 343, a buyer could turn the AMC Rebel into a decent budget-priced muscle car.

A road test by Steve Kelly in the February 1967 issue of *Motor Trend* concluded that the Rebel SST was "not the performer its competitors are, but minor changes could bring it closer." Kelly's story compared the 343/280 SST to an Ambassador DPL sharing the same body and engine. The SST had the optional Shift Command console selector that allowed better up and down shift control. It also had Goodyear wide-tread tires for better grip and a heavy-duty suspension.

The main problems with the car were a high axle ratio and the lack of a strong valve train. It went from 0-to-60 mph in 9 seconds and did the quarter mile in 16.9 seconds at 83 mph. "Wheel-spinning take-offs, low acceleration times and rpms over 5,000 are out of the question," Kelly wrote.

The 1968 Rebel was modestly restyled. The triple-segment taillights were new. The SST came only with V-8 power and had the only ragtop in the lineup. This last-ever AMC convertible sold for $2,995 and only 823 were built. With 9,876 assemblies, the hardtop was more prevalent. The 200-hp two-barrel Typhoon 290 V-8 was standard equipment, but the 343-cid 280-hp option was carried over for those wishing to go fast.

In an effort to rejuvenate Rambler sales, AMC executives upgraded their product line for 1966. A top-of-the-line Rebel Rogue was added to the mid-size Classic series. More sporty equipment was made available, including vinyl roofs and four-speed manual gearboxes. To promote its new image, AMC hired a new ad agency, Benton and Bowles, Inc.

Base priced at $2,523, the Rebel was a top-of-the-line two-door hardtop on the 112-inch. A six was standard, but for just $65 extra you could get a 327-cid that delivered 270 hp. Options like that were pointing AMC in the muscle car direction. Only 7,512 Rebels were made in 1966. A fraction had the 270-hp V-8.

For 1967, Rebel nameplates adorned the mid-size AMC cars that were formerly known as Classics. In addition to being renamed, they were totally redesigned on a larger 114-inch wheelbase. There were three car lines: Rebel 550, Rebel 770 and Rebel SST. Muscular versions of the Rebel were based on the SST, which featured simulated air intakes just ahead of the rear wheels. The series offered a $2,604 two-door hardtop and a $2,872 convertible. Production came to 16,973 total cars and included just 1,686 ragtops. Another new ad agency, Wells, Rich, Green, Inc., created humorous ads that successfully pointed out the features and benefits of AMC cars.

A six was standard again in 1967 and pair of 290-cid V-8s was optional. A new 343-cid V-8 replaced the 327. This motor came in two formats and if you yearned

1967 AMC Rebel SST two-door hardtop

In its chase for muscle car buyers, AMC teamed with piston ring maker Grant Industries to build a red, white and blue '68 Rebel SST race car that made a 37-city cross-country promotional tour. The car was engineered for all-out competition and driven by Hayden Proffitt. It had an AMC V-8 set up to run in the sophisticated X/S (experimental stock) class on a nitro-alcohol mixture. It put out 1200 hp at 9000 rpm and set a speed record at Green Valley Raceway in Texas and the lowest E.T. mark at Greater Evansville Speedway near Evansville, Indiana.

Between race weekends, the car was displayed at AMC dealerships to give the public a close-up look and to allow enthusiasts to meet the crew. Proffitt said his 1968 SST would "run up an even greater score" than a '67 Rebel he drove a year earlier. The 1968 hit 181.25 mph in 8.41 seconds in the quarter mile at Green Valley Raceway in Texas. The car held the national record for 1/8-mile courses and set six new quarter-mile marks. It was featured in writeups and ads and showed up in the February 1967 issue of *Hot Rod* magazine.

While the 1968 Grant Race Car would more or less serve as the inspiration for the hot 1970 Rebel Machine, model-year 1969 seemed to aim the Rebel SST in more of a "family car" direction. A four-door sedan and a station wagon were two new body styles added to the line. The two-door hardtop made the cut and returned once again to give muscle car enthusiasts an AMC platform they could use to option out a street performer or weekend drag racer. On this model only, there were simulated louvers forward of the rear wheel openings. (Wagons and sedans had traditional stainless steel trim.)

In 1966, AMC began to change its image with its exciting and muscular Rebel series.

Three of the five AMC V-8s offered this year were available in the Rebel SST hardtop. They were the base two-barrel 200-hp version of the 290, the two-barrel 235-hp version of the 343 and the four-barrel version of the 343 with 280 hp. The Rebel did not offer the new 390-cid V-8.

1968 AMC Rebel SST two-door hardtop

1960s "solid gold"

1968 AMC Rebel SST two-door hardtop

6	5	4	3	2	1
$420	$1,260	$2,100	$4,730	$7,350	$10,500

Estimated values in today's marketplace taken from the 2006 Collector Car Price Guide.

1964 Ford Thunderbolt

Ford used the slogan "total performance" to put a positive spin on racetrack competition. The idea was things learned through racing, not only speed, made the total car a better performing machine, whether it was braking performance, handling performance, etc.

To go with the total performance approach was a new-sized Fairlane with engine options based on the 289-cid V-8. The original version of this engine was the 221-cid V-8, which grew to 260 cid and then to 289 cid. Originally, the 289 V-8 was designed for use in the mid-sized Fairlane and was an option for Falcons and Comets. However, it was most famous as a Mustang power plant. The Mustang was marketed with the support of a "Cobra" parts program that could take the hot "K" code 271-hp of the 289 and make it even hotter.

In May 1964, *Car Life* magazine's Allen Hunt wrote, "Obviously it's a racing car . . . and one calculated to get Ford right back in the front row on the drag strips this summer." Hunt was talking about a special version of Ford's Fairlane, a mid-size model. A very limited number of totally awesome 427-powered Fairlane "Thunderbolts" were built. The reason was Ford's "Total Performance" program.

Back in the 1950s, Ford had been heavily involved in racing and found that it helped sell new cars. Then, in 1957, the Automobile Manufacturers Association adopted a policy banning the use of horsepower figures or racing results in car advertising. After that ban, all racing activities had to be either curtailed or carried on via secret, under-the-counter methods.

Nationally televised coverage of motor sports, beginning with the inaugural Daytona 500 in 1959, was a magnet that started to draw automakers back into racing. Ford and Pontiac had particularly strong under-the-counter efforts going and found that their racing involvement helped sell cars. Despite Pontiac's performance image, GM issued an edict in the fall of 1963, giving its divisions a few weeks to end all factory associations with race teams.

GM's racing ban opened the gates for Ford (and Chrysler) to fill the racing void, so they did.

In 1964, the "C" code version of the Challenger 289 had a 9.0:1 compression ratio and a two-barrel carb. It generated a non-muscular 195 hp at 4400 rpm. There was an "A" code edition with a four-barrel carburetor and a 9.8:1 compression ratio, which generated 225 hp—acceptable for keeping up with traffic on the freeway. But for muscle car fans, the only way to order it was as a "K" code or "Hi-Po" version. This meant that you got a 10.5:1 compression ratio and 271 horses at 6000 rpm with a single Holley four-barrel carb.

Thunderbolts had fiberglass fenders. They also came with teardrop-shaped hood blisters, Plexiglas windows, lightweight bucket seats, a cold-air induction system, an 8,000-rpm Rotunda tachometer, a modified front suspension (to accommodate the 427-cid V-8), a

1964 Ford Thunderbolt

What kind of a crazy laboratory is this?

This isn't much like the usual slick image of white-coated technicians, million-dollar test rigs and landscaped acres of proving ground. But these modified cars *are* a laboratory, the most effective laboratory for creating and testing *total performance* that an automaker ever put together.

Its foundation is Ford's conviction that open competition is an excellent way to develop great cars. Look at the six vehicles above and you'll know that Ford means all kinds of cars, in all kinds of competition.

This is a laboratory full of soaring triumphs and bitter setbacks, of endless overtime and eternal urgency, of raw excitement and unholy pressure. It devours ideas and spits out answers—answers *right now!*

The Monte Carlo and Shell "4000" rallies helped give Falcon V-8's sharper steering, tougher front suspension. The Indianapolis "500" proved the tremendous potential of the Fairlane V-8 design and sparked immediate development of overhead cams and fuel injection. From stock car competition the big Fords have extracted a new freedom from air drag and a fabulous level of engine performance and durability. Ford-powered Cobras, America's production sports car champions, cast new light on cams and carburetion. The newest contenders in the special world of drag racing, the Fairlane "427's," right now are uncorking answers on high-performance transmissions, acceleration, weight transfer and traction. We've got another research vehicle about ready to fly, the Ford GT. This 200-mile-per-hour projectile will probe into the problems of driver environment, of ducted ventilation and of high-speed stability. We'll take our lumps, learning. But when we're through we'll have more data—and more fine machinery—than anybody else.

That's what's great about this crazy laboratory; it's the thing that puts the *total* in the total performance cars you drive. What's crazy about that?

TRY *TOTAL PERFORMANCE*
FOR A CHANGE!

FORD

Falcon · Fairlane · Ford · Thunderbird

PRODUCTS OF *Ford* MOTOR COMPANY

*Ford Motor Company included the Ford Thunderbolt
(top left) in its 1964 advertising.*

long list of equipment deletions and many special competition equipment features. The 425-hp big-block V-8 actually cranked out more like 500 hp. It was linked to a beefed-up Lincoln automatic transmission or a Borg-Warner T-10 four-speed manual transmission.

The 1964 Fairlane Special Performance drag vehicles soon adopted the Thunderbolt name and also became known as "T-Bolts." Demand was strong enough to prompt the ordering of a second batch of 54 all-white cars. Racing driver Gas Ronda dominated NHRA's 1964 World Championship with 190 points by running his T-Bolt through the quarter mile in 11.6 seconds at 124 mph.

Ford records show that the first 11 cars left the factory painted maroon and 10 of them had four-speed transmissions. The 100 additional cars produced were painted white when they were built and 89 of them had four-speed gearboxes. At least one 1965 Thunderbolt-style car was raced by Darrell Droke. However, the new Mustang soon took over as Ford's best offering for drag-car enthusiasts and the short life of T-Bolts halted at that point.

1964 Ford Thunderbolt in drag racing action

1960s "solid gold"

1964 Ford Thunderbolt two-door sedan

Note: The 2006 Collector Car Price Guide by K P Books lists the T-Bolt's value as inestimable. In 1995 and 1999, Barrett-Jackson reported auction sales in the $50,000-plus range. In 2004, R-M Auctions reported a 1964 Ford Thunderbolt was sold at auction in Monterey, California, for $110,000.

1966-1969 Ford Fairlane and Torino

1969 Ford Fairlane CJ 428 two-door hardtop   **Phil Kunz**

A recessed grille, twin hood ornaments with built-in turn signal indicators, optional power disc-drum brakes and wide-oval tires were features of the 1967 Fairlane. There were 13 models in nine series. The Fairlane, Fairlane 500, 500XL and station wagon models were available in six-cylinder and V-8 series. The GT hardtop and convertible came only with a V-8. The GTA was an option. Engines ranged from a 120-hp in-line six to the 427-cid 425-hp V-8.

Racing-type 427s offered an "8-barrel" intake system with some 30 extra ponies. A tunnel-port version of the 427 could be had as an over-the-counter kit. It had a tunnel-port intake on special heads and a special intake manifold. In NASCAR, the 427 Fairlanes swept early 1967 races. Then Chrysler complained. The rules were then changed to handicap the Fords. NHRA placed the Fairlane

The 1966 Ford Fairlane was totally redesigned. The outside size didn't change much, but there was more room under the hood. This allowed the use of big-block V-8s in the mid-size models for the first time. A 390-cid 315-hp V-8 was standard in the GT. A 335-hp 390 with chrome accents, a high-lift cam, a bigger carb and the two-way Sport Shift automatic tranny was *standard* in the GTA. A limited number of these cars had super-sized "side-oiler" 427 wedge V-8s. These cars—some raced in NASCAR—had a big honking hood scoop to snort in cold air. Some 60 Fairlane 427s were built. They're rare. Don't sell yours!

GTs were dressed up Fairlane 500/XLs. The package included badges, special hood, striping, engine dress-up parts, a H.D. suspension, front discs, bucket seats, a center console and a sport steering wheel. Ford built 33,015 two-door hardtops and 4,327 convertibles. Even the base 315-hp V-8 featured a hot cam, special manifolds and a single four-barrel carburetor. The '66 GTA ("A" = automatic) 335-hp hardtop moved just 10.5 pounds per horsepower. It could do 0 to 60 mph in under 7 seconds and the quarter mile in just over 15.

1969 Torino CJ 428 fastback   **Phil Kunz**

427s in SS/B class to keep them from dominating drag racing. A 427 Fairlane did 0-to-60 in 6.5 seconds and the quarter in 14.66 seconds at 99.88 mph.

Ford advertised, "The 427 Fairlane is also available without numbers." The 1967 edition of *Car Fax* shows the 427-cid "sideoiler" optional in non-GT Fairlane Club Coupes and Sport Coupes. A notation indicates prices for the two 427 Fairlane options were not available in late 1966, but the 410-hp 427 in a Galaxie without the 7-Liter package was $975, which is likely in the same ballpark as the 427 Fairlane option. The 410-hp version with one four-barrel carb was first choice. A hairier 425-hp version with twin Holley four-barrels was extra. Both included transistorized ignition, a H.D. battery, a H.D. suspension, an extra-cooling package and a four-speed gearbox. Also mandatory on Fairlane 427s ($47 extra) was a set of 8.15 x 15 four-ply-rated black nylon tires.

1967 Ford Fairlane 500 two-door hardtop   **Phil Kunz**

Cobra strikes again!

Torino Cobra wins Daytona 500

Three races—three wins. Right on top of a 1-2-3 finish in the Riverside 500 and victory in the ARCA 300, Ford's Torino Cobras take three of the top four places in the Daytona 500, with Lee Roy Yarbrough piloting the winning car. All of the 50 cars that started were specially modified for racing. Only 28 finished. Proof that Torino Cobra can take it.

You get a lot of this same kind of winner-take-all action in the Cobras at your Ford Dealer's Performance Corner. Cobra comes with a standard 4-barrel

428 CID V-8, rated at 335 horsepower. There's a Cobra Jet Ram-Air version available. Transmission is a trigger-quick, fully synchronized 4-speed box. There's a chassis to match, with competition suspension, staggered rear shocks, 6-inch wheel rims, belted wide-tread F70 x 14 white sidewall tires, hood lock pins—the works. Two-Door Sports-Roof or Hardtop models. Try some Cobra action for yourself at your Ford Dealer's Performance Corner. See why Going Ford is the Going Thing!

Ford has a Corner on Performance

February 1—Riverside 500. Torino Cobras sweep 1st, 2nd and 3rd—Richard Petty sets new record in his first race in a Ford.

February 16—ARCA 300. Torino Cobra wins with ARCA champion Benny Parsons at the wheel.

February 23—Daytona 500. Torino Cobras win, taking three of the first four places. Lee Roy Yarbrough drove the winner.

All cars entered were specially modified for racing.

COBRA *Ford*

"Cobra Strikes Again" was the way Ford proclaimed its Torino racing success in 1969.

The Fairlane grew in 1968. It retained a 116-inch wheelbase, but grew to 201 inches long. Some felt it looked like a big car, although the Fords were a foot longer. In addition to the Fairlanes, 500s and GTs, there was a new top-trim-level Torino. The fastback that muscle car fans favored came only as a 500 or GT. The GT version was the dragster, but with a base 302 or optional 390.

At the start of the year, you could order the 427-cid V-8 in a de-tuned 390-hp state. It was a $623 option for Fairlane two-door hardtops. You could not get it with Select Aire air conditioning, power steering, a 55-amp generator, an H.D. suspension or optional tires because it made no sense or the options were already required. The 427 was replaced with two awesome versions of an all-new 428 Cobra-Jet V-8. As *Car Life* put it, "The Cobra may not eat all birds for breakfast, but when it does, it doesn't chew them with its mouth full."

The 428-CJ was a totally different engine than the 427. The base version, code "Q," came with 10.7:1 compression heads and a single Holley four-barrel carburetor. It was advertised at 335 hp at 5600 rpm. The Super Cobra-Jet (SCJ) version, code "R," had a 10.5:1 compression ratio, a single four-barrel with ram-air induction and a rating of 360 hp at 5400 rpm.

The Cobra-Jet V-8 was basically a 1966 Ford "FE" big block fitted with 427 heads. The factory understated the power of the Cobra-Jet V-8 in the mid-sized cars to give them an advantage in drag racing. It turned out that the CJ-428 produced nearly 410 hp in the 1968 Fairlane and Torino. No wonder they went from 0 to 60 mph in just over 6 seconds and did the quarter in 14.5 seconds!

In December 1967 *Motor Trend* tested a 1968 Torino GT SportsRoof and liked most things about it, except rear vision with the fastback. Other minor criticisms were made, but the overall impression was positive. "The new breed of super car from Ford is a full step ahead of its '67 counterpart," the magazine concluded. The test car had the 390-cid four-barrel V-8 with 335 hp at 4800 rpm and 427 ft. lbs. of torque at 3200 rpm. It had a 10.5:1 compression ratio, a three-speed manual transmission and a 3.25:1 rear

The streamlined 1961 Ford Starliner predicted the Torino fastback of the late '60s and brought Ford success in both cases, on the street and the racetrack. **Phil Kunz**

1969 Torino Talladega   **Phil Kunz**

axle. *Motor Trend* reported 7.2 seconds for 0 to 60 mph and 15.1 seconds at 91 mph for the quarter mile.

The 16 mid-sized Fords for 1969 included the Fairlane, Fairlane 500, Torino, Torino GT and a new high-performance Cobra. Aimed at muscle car fans, the Torino Cobra series included just two body types: Formal Hardtop and SportsRoof. Both emphasized go power. Standard equipment included a 428-cid 335-hp Cobra Jet V-8, a four-speed manual transmission, a competition suspension, Wide-Oval tires and six-inch-wide wheels with hubcaps.

The base Cobra V-8 featured a 10.6:1 compression ratio and 335 hp at 5200 rpm and 440 foot-pounds of torque at 2600 rpm. You could get an optional 351-cid 290-hp V-8 if you wanted to save on gas. Also optional was the 428 "Ram Air" V-8, which carried the same 335-hp rating, but achieved it at a higher 5600 rpm peak. Its torque output was 445 foot-pounds at 3400 rpm and it had a 10.7:1 compression ratio. The Ram Air engine featured a functional hood scoop to "ram" cold air into Holley 4-barrel. This set up was $133 extra.

SelectShift automatic was optional for $37 and it came with a floor shift and optional center console. The 3.25:1 rear axle was standard and optional axle ratios included 3.45:1, 3.91:1 and 4.30:1. Power disc brakes were also available for $64.77. A Traction-Lock differential was

$63.51 extra and getting a factory tachometer added $47.92 to the price tag. The Ram Air 428 was tested at 6.3 seconds 0-to-60 and 14.5 seconds at 100 mph for the quarter.

One other muscular version of the '69 Fairlane/Torino was the Talladega, a fastback sired by the Ford's need to "legalize" features for racing use by building a specific number of production cars with the same feature. Named after an Alabama town where a new 2.66-mile super-speedway opened, the Torino Talladega had an extended nose and a flush grille. A revised rear bumper was used up front and the rocker panels were reworked. The car was six inches longer and one inch lower than a stock Torino fastback. Street power came from a 335-hp CJ-428 available only with Cruise-O-Matic.

NASCAR versions ran the 427 V-8. Beginning in March, they got the new "semi-hemi" 429. The 429 *was not* put in showroom cars. The Boss 429 Mustang satisfied the 429's race-sanctioning requirements. David Pearson won his second straight championship driving one of the fastbacks for Holman & Moody. Counting prototypes, Talladega production hit 754. They came in Wimbleton White, Royal Maroon or Presidential Blue with Black bench seats.

1960s "solid gold"

1966 Fairlane 500 GT two-door hardtop

6	5	4	3	2	1
$ 720	$2,160	$3,600	$8,100	$12,600	$18,000

1969 Torino Cobra two-door fastback

6	5	4	3	2	1
$ 920	$2,760	$4,600	$10,350	$16,100	$23,000

Estimated values in today's marketplace taken from the 2006 Collector Car Price Guide.

The 1960s . . . The Pony Cars

The Mustang was the outstanding sales success of the 1960s. In addition to becoming the best-selling new car in history, the Mustang sired a long list of clones by all the major automakers. They became known as "pony cars." The term used for all of these cars was based on the Mustang logo—a galloping horse. The concept behind the Mustang could be traced

1964-1/2 Mustang convertible **Brad Bowling**

back to the sports car craze that swept America right after World War II, starting with the MG TC and the Jaguar XK-120. But the Mustang was not a true sports car – or even a *sporty* two-seater. Ford had learned a lesson with the two-seat Thunderbird of 1955-1957. While the early T-Birds quickly became classics, they proved that the market for two-passenger cars in America was not a very big one.

This was a real problem, because cars like the T-Bird (and the Corvette) were quite expensive to make. Both cars were unique machines that shared few parts with other models. Neither model generated enough sales to make its existence as a two-seat car profitable. Ford increased T-Bird sales and profits by turning it into a four-passenger "sports-personal" car, while GM used the Corvette as an image car to sell other models and ultimately turned it into a luxury sports car with a price tag high enough to justify its continuation.

Lee Iacocca lived through the launch of the T-Bird in 1955. He had also watched its successful transformation into a four-seat car. Iacocca had started working at Ford in the 1950s. When he used a "$56 per month for a '56 Ford" promotion to sell lots of cars, he caught the attention of his boss, Robert S. McNamara. According to Iacocca, his campaign helped sell 70,000 extra cars. Be that true or not, it served as a springboard for him to become National Truck Marketing Manager and ultimately move up to Vice President and General Manager of Ford in 1962. He became a member of the Fairlane Group, a team of 10 Ford executives who met at the Fairlane Inn each week to plan the future.

During one brainstorming session, Iacocca and friends dreamed up a prototype sports-racing car that they then had built as an ultra-lightweight experimental car. Designed by Eugene Bordinat, this Mustang I caused a sensation wherever it was seen. It was far different than a production Mustang, but showed there was still interest at Ford in two-seat sports cars. This interest was also reflected in the two-seat Falcon XT-Bird, a concept car created by Budd, the company that had built two-seat Thunderbird bodies. Budd offered to supply modified T-Bird bodies that fit the Falcon chassis and built them for a very low price. The Fairlane Group turned down the two-seat Falcon XT-Bird. It did not fit a buyer's profile they had created. It was not *the* car, but it was close.

With compact car sales trending towards sportier models, the Fairlane Group was sure there would be demand for a sports-type car, but based on the T-Bird experience, the Ford execs felt that a sporty car had to have a rear seat to sell. Chevrolet's Corvair Monza Spyder was having some luck selling into the enthusiast's market, but its unusual styling and radical engineering had limited its potential. As the Fairlane Group saw it, there was a market for a car that could combine the Spyder's sportiness with Falcon-like pricing and practicality. They were right, but they did not know that this market niche was really a crater.

The so-called "Mustang Generation" was huge. Between its April 17, 1964 introduction at Ford's "Wonder Rotunda" at the New York World's Fair and April 17, 1965, a total of 420,000 Mustangs were sold. A day before the

The Mustang evolved from a show car to become a 1960s icon and the basis for the "pony car" name.

and the Dodge Challenger became yesterday's news by its 1970 arrival.

The Mustang and the competitors that followed it were considered "prestige cars" in the 1960s. This industry classification was not easy to define, because it wasn't determined by brand, size, price or other such concrete factors. *Ward's Automotive Yearbook* said "Prestige is defined as the power to command admiration." A prestige car could be a Cadillac, a Buick Riviera, a GTO or a Mustang. However, sports-type cars like the Mustang appealed to a different group of people than luxury cars or personal-luxury cars.

Ward's said that this difference in sporty-car appeal was: "Partly because they don't cost as much." Ford's surveys showed the 1964 Mustang buyers had a median income of $9,370 and a median age of 31. The average purchase price was $2,812 ($2,441 base price and $371 worth of extras). More than 80 percent of Mustang buyers said that the car's appearance was the single most important factor influencing their buying decision. So the Mustang was more than just a niche-market car—it was a great design that sold for a great price. The "throwback" 2005 Mustang, which follows more or less the same formula, seems to be doing better than the "retro" 2000 T-Bird, which looked great, but had two seats and a much higher price. Is history repeating itself at Ford?

Part of the reason the 1960s Mustang sold so well was that Ford's pricing ladder was different than that of the other Big 3 automakers. For example, in 1966, Ford sold more than half of its cars for under $2,500. GM and Chrysler sold over half of their cars in the $2,501 to $3,500 bracket. With the Mustang, Ford had a styling sensation, as well as a lower price. (AMC sold 86 percent of its 1966 models in the under-$2,500 range, but it did not have a large enough dealer base to be truly competitive).

In 1967, the term prestige car used in industry trade journals was replaced with "specialty car," but the meaning was unchanged. Such cars had sales of about 420,000 units in 1964, 764,419 units in 1965 and 870,695 units in 1966. In August of 1966, *Ward's Automotive Reports* predicted that a record one million specialty cars would be turned out in the 1967 model year.

The continuing rise in popularity of the specialty car could be attributed to an affluent economy and to what one Ford Vice President called "a renewed interest in driving for fun." The average driver was spending more time behind the wheel and felt that it was important to own a car that was comfortable, enjoyable and had the right "image." The

car bowed, Mustang commercials were seen by 29 million TV viewers. Strong advertising and quick road tests of the car in magazines helped generate additional interest. Production quickly fell behind demand. One source said there were 15 buyers for each Mustang built. Originally, all Mustangs were made at Ford's home factory in Dearborn, Michigan, but demand was so great that a second factory in San Jose, California, was used for Mustang production starting in July. Later, the Falcon assembly line at the Metuchen, New Jersey, assembly plant had to be relocated so Mustangs could be built there, too.

With the Mustang leading the way, Ford recorded one of the best years in its history in 1964. On November 30, it sold its two-millionth vehicle of the year. It was the first time that level had been hit. Ford had not only tapped an immense, unfulfilled market demand—it had nearly the only product available in that market segment. Plymouth's new Barracuda was a competitor of sorts, but did not generate anywhere near the amount of sales that the Mustang did. GM would not have a pony car ready until 1967 and AMC enthusiasts had to wait until 1968. Mercury's Cougar–once called "a Mustang with class"–arrived in 1967

Percentage of 1966 cars sold in various price ranges

Price Range	GM	Ford	Chrysler	AMC
$2500 or less	31.03 %	50.05 %	43.68 %	86.08 %
$2501 to $3500	57.68 %	44.85 %	50.89 %	13.92 %
$3501 and up	11.29 %	05.10 %	05.43 %	--

car had to represent the owner's financial status and any personal interests he had.

Said one Ford executive, "Car buying tastes have changed so completely toward the specialty car that it can literally be called a revolution."

In 1966, one Chrysler executive stated that the success or failure of an automobile company would depend on the popularity of its specialty car offerings.

"American sports cars are weapons for the American marketing battle of the future," he said. The exec felt that it would be essential for car companies to capture the loyalty of the young, who were entering the car market for the first time.

A study conducted by the National Automobile Dealers Association sampled high school seniors and found that 25 percent of the males and 11 percent of the females already owned their own cars. In addition, 27 percent planned to buy a car within the next six months. To a large degree, these were the buyers who took early Mustangs home. The car's styling, features and price tag were aimed directly at the so-called youth market.

Specialty car fans typically had more money and more education than the average auto buyer. One study showed that the average buyer of a Mercury Cougar had some college and earned $10,000 annually. Over 60 percent of Camaro buyers had attended college and their median income was $10,400.

Such demographics led to certain buying habits. Specialty car buyers purchased more optional equipment and tended to move up the pricing ladder as they aged. The latter factor is one reason why pony cars grew larger, more luxurious and pricier in the late-1960s and early 1970s.

The '64 Mustang, with its $2,368 price tag, got the enthusiast hooked. Then it was Ford's turn and the corporation made more money when the enthusiast came back for another Mustang in 1968. Those repeat buyers wanted options. They often added a V-8, a vinyl top, an AM/FM radio, mag-style wheels, white-letter tires and many other choices as options.

As new pony cars came on stream, the Mustang's market penetration took a hit, as might be expected. As a group, the Mustang, Corvair and Barracuda took 8.9 percent in 1964, 7.88 percent in 1965 and 6.17 percent in 1966. In calendar year 1966, the Camaro and Cougar bit off a 0.74 percent share. In 1967, the Camaro, Firebird, Cougar and Javelin together took 5.67 percent.

While the new pony cars put the hurt on the original, they also expanded the overall market niche from 11.2 percent in 1966 to 14.6 percent in 1967. Total specialty car registrations rose 17.6 percent in 1967 and that followed an even stronger 18.6 percent rise the year before.

Another sign of the specialty cars' strength was the fact that 13 of the 27 all-new car lines introduced between 1960 and 1967 were specialty models and the bulk of those were pony cars. Of 16 introduced between 1963 and 1967, 13 were in the specialty class and well over half were the Mustang and its clones.

The pony car appeal stretched to more than just high school students. In many major cities, Hertz-Rent-A-Car offered business travelers the opportunity to rent a Shelby GT-350 Mustang. The special GT-350H (H for Hertz) models used in this program are especially collectible today.

Like the compact car market segment, the pony car niche had a growth period, a peak and a decline. In terms of new-car registrations, which are counted by calendar year, there was a steady increase in sales from 1964 to 1967 and a steady decline from that point until 1969. The Dodge Challenger gets factored in these figures – at least cars sold in the fall of 1969 when the new pony car was first introduced.

Notice that Mustang sales follow the same pattern, but peak earlier in 1966. Even after heavy competition came on stream, the Mustang held its own and remained the top-selling pony car.

Pony Car Registrations By Calendar Year 1964 to 1969

Model	1964	1965	1966	1967	1968	1969
Barracuda	--	14,104	28,310	62,485	37,445	32,080
Mustang	248,916	518,252	540,802	379,513	308,190	262,424
Camaro	--	--	41,100	204,862	209,822	172,459
Firebird	--	--	--	94,730	92,498	58,859
Cougar	--	--	20,769	119,875	109,380	86,086
Javelin/Marlin	--	--	--	10,460	40,100	34,096
AMX	--	--	--	--	6,480	6,346
Shelby	--	303	1,872	2,864	2,674	--
Challenger	--	--	--	--	--	19,400
Total	248,916	532,669	632,853	874,789	806,589	671,750

In terms of model-year production, there was also a steady increase in the number of pony cars built from 1964 to 1967, as well as a steady decline from that point until 1969. The prediction of a million-unit year made by *Ward's* never came true, but the numbers got very close to that level by the close of 1967. Notice that Mustang production does *not* follow the same pattern. It peaks in 1966, the same year Barracuda builds dropped off. Of course, the Mustang was the most-produced pony car in all years from 1964 to 1969. However, the combined one-two punch of the Camaro and Firebird stole away nearly half of the Mustang's market between 1967 and 1969. For those three years combined, Ford built 1,089,349 Mustangs to GM's 976,522 F-Cars.

Ford's mid-year sensation, the Mustang convertible, was the 1964 Indianapolis 500 Pace Car.

By 1968, it was clear that the Mustang had opened the door to an astronomical level of consumer interest. With other types of specialty cars like the Charger, Grand Prix, Toronado and Eldorado counted, it could be calculated that up to 19 models had evolved to fill the "Mustang Generation's" quest for distinctive transportation. Another trend of the year was a decline in sales of lower-priced pony cars as the higher-priced Camaro, Firebird, Cougar and Javelin quartet sunk their teeth into the demand curve. Together the four models grabbed off 39.4 percent of specialty car sales, passing Barracuda, Mustang and Corvair combined by 46.6 percent.

The Javelin was the real attention-getter among the '68 crop of models, since it gave American Motors a new image and made it clear that AMC was ready to chase the youth market, after resisting the trend for some years. To enhance the image even more, the AMX two-seater was created. While AMC compared it to a Corvette, it was

part pony car, having evolved from the Javelin. In fact, in the '70s, the AMX morphed into the four-seat Javelin-AMX and then became (even later) a trim package for the AMC Hornet coupe.

As the original pony car, the Mustang became the icon for a whole class of cars and none (with the possible exception of the AMX) strayed far from the Mustang mold. For the 1960s, the Mustang mold started with a 108-inch wheelbase platform carrying a front sub-frame and a unitized two-door body structure (either notchback coupe, fastback coupe or convertible). The car was laid out in the conventional manner with the engine in front, the transmission in the middle and the axle at the rear. Independent suspension (with torsion bars on Mopar models) was used up front and a leaf-spring suspension was fitted at the rear. The interior usually (but not always) featured bucket seats, a floor-mounted gear shifter and a center console or consolette.

Styling followed the long-hood/short-deck configuration that buyers equated with a sports-car look. Another trait was the Coke-bottle shape, which meant that the rear quarters flared out a bit. The "sculptured look" was in for pony cars, probably because the genre actually evolved from the heavily-sculptured Corvair Spyder. A rear seat was provided (except in the two-seat AMX), but

Pony Car Model-Year Production 1964-1969

Model	1964	1965	1966	1967	1968	1969
Barracuda	24,552	65,995	38,028	62,534	45,412	31,987
Mustang	121,538	559,451	607,568	472,121	317,404	299,824
Camaro	--	--	--	220,906	235,151	243,085
Firebird	--	--	--	82,560	107,112	87,708
Cougar	--	--	--	150,893	113,726	100,069
Javelin	--	--	--	--	55,124	40,675
AMX	--	--	--	--	6,725	8,293
Shelby	--	--	--	3,225	2,793	3,150
Total	**146,090**	**625,446**	**645,596**	**992,239**	**883,447**	**814,791**

was always most suitable for kids or just storage space. Mag-style wheels, white-letter tires, scoops, louvers and colorful badges were popular options and decorations. "GT" equipment like grille lights, chrome engine parts and hang-on gauges were very popular. Most young buyers considered an AM/FM radio with a "reverb" to be mandatory hardware for cruising.

Vinyl upholstery was popular and common colors were Black, White, Red or Tan. No pony car buyer would have dreamed of owning a car with neutral gray crushed velvet cloth seats. Wood accents for the dash and steering wheel were often supplied by either the factory or ordered from the *J.C. Whitney Catalog*. Racing stripes were a popular option. On coupes, a vinyl top was a crowning touch preferred by many owners. Until 1967 or 1968, chrome-plated trim was perfectly acceptable. Later, Flat Black finish on trim parts took over and bumpers often came with a coating of body-colored rubber. Hood-mounted tachometers, rear window slats (on fastbacks) and racing-style outside rearview mirrors came into vogue in the later 1960s.

As the pony car became a staple product for many automakers, it also lost some of its "youthful innocence." Convenience equipment like air conditioning, power windows, power seats and power antennas began showing up on more and more ponies. Those neat drilled-for-racing window cranks used on early Mustangs were often replaced with chrome switches that operated power window lifts. Such extras made the pony cars costlier and heavier. Little by little, the V-8 engine took over, again raising the typical

window sticker by $100 or more. Models that had once provided basic transportation with a sporty flair were turning into luxury-sports models with plenty of brawn.

About the same time the Mustang kicked off the pony car market in mid-1964, the Pontiac Tempest GTO started the muscle car movement. At first, the two types of cars went their separate ways and the ponies usually had six-cylinder engines or small-block V-8s. The V-8s could be made zippier with options like four-barrel carburetors, but there were no real "rocket ship" motors. Of course, things didn't stay that way. By the time the Gen II pony cars arrived in 1967, they had engine bays large enough to accommodate big-block V-8 power plants. At first, the factory equipment lists remained conservative, but it wasn't long before specialty dealers like Chevrolet's Don Yenko and Mopar's Mr. Norm were shoehorning the biggest engines into these little cars. Carroll Shelby, who had supplied Cobra kits for early Mustangs, began making turnkey Shelby-Mustangs with hopped-up 289s in 1965. By 1968, a 427 V-8 was optional.

With heat below their hoods, the ponies could turn in awesome performance numbers. A factory-issued Camaro SS 396 hardtop turned 15-second quarter miles. A straight-from-Dearborn Mustang with the 428 Super Cobra Jet V-8 could run the same distance in 13.9 seconds at 102 mph. Mopar built some Hemi-powered Barracudas for exhibition racing, but room under the hood for the monster motor was tight, until the fall of 1969, when a redesign made the 1970 Hemi 'Cuda a reality. It was a 14-second car.

1968 Shelby Mustang GT-500 **Brad Bowling**

1965-1969 Ford Mustang

1965 Mustang two-door hardtop   **David Lyon**

Lee Iacocca was a born "car guy." Trained as an auto engineer, he had better luck selling the cars and while he sold them he dreamed up ideas for better ones. You might say he was the original "better idea" guy at Ford. When he ran out of two-seat T-Birds to sell, Iacocca's customers begged him to tell Ford to build such a car again. As Lee moved up through the ranks at FoMoCo, he didn't forget what he'd learned out in the boondocks. He kept a little black book filled with notes about a car that could capture the T-Bird spirit, but sell even better than the original. The "Lee Bird" had to be cheap to make. It had to have the look – if not the guts – of a sports car. Four-passenger seating was a *must*.   The T-Bird sold much better as a four-passenger car. The car didn't have to win drag races, but it had to feel light and be snappy and nimble to drive.

An exciting car—a fun-to-be-in car. But it had to be *very* affordable – priced below $2,500 in Iacocca's book. How many copies of such a car could he sell? Iacocca guessed 100,000 per year would be possible.

Eventually Ford whipped up a prototype sports car with a German V-4 that resembled an Americanized Lotus. It was an open two-seater that looked exciting, but it wasn't the answer. "How could we sell a lot of those?" Iacocca once asked his Ford friends when he saw the Mustang I on exhibit at a new-car show. "It's too far out there for most people to actually buy one." The designers went back to the drawing board and started to focus on a more practical approach – a small car, built on a standard platform, using existing engines, having four seats and offering "looks that could kill." And all for $2,368 and up!

Fanfare surrounded the Mustang's introduction at the Wonder Rotunda in April 1964 and a big, perfectly-timed advertising and promotional campaign backed up the launch of the new car. In May, a Mustang convertible served as the Indy 500 Pace Car. The Mustang would also win a Tiffany Award for design excellence – a unique honor for an automobile. But even with all of the thinking and planning and awards, no one would have predicted that the Mustang was going to sell over a half million units in its first year of production.

1966 Mustang convertible   **Brad Bowling**

Speaking of the first-year Mustangs, the question of whether they are 1964-1/2 or 1965 models is a matter of semantics and whether you own one. Traditional practice in the auto industry has always been to officially consider a midyear car a "next-year" model. That makes it a new car, rather than a year-old vehicle. So all Mustangs built prior to the fall of 1965 carry 1965 serial numbers and data plate coding. From the factory's view, there are no 1964-1/2 models. But, certain distinctions are unique to early cars. Under the hood, the engine choices were a 170-cid in-line six or the 260-cid "Falcon" V-8 and generators were used. The door handles were attached with C-clips. The length of the front fender nameplates changed slightly. The design of the door lock buttons changed. So it is possible to physically distinguish a 1964-1/2 model from a car sold after Ford's 1965 model-year began on October 1, 1964.

At first, the Mustang came as a $2,368 coupe or a $2,722 convertible. Both rode a 108-inch wheelbase and measured 182 inches long. The coupe weighed 2,445 pounds and the ragtop weighed 2,629 pounds. By 1965, Ford's 120-hp 200-cid "Big Six" was the base engine. The optional 289-cid V-8 came in 200- and 225-hp versions, as well as a 271-hp high-performance version. On paper, the Mustang looked very ordinary – but it sold extraordinarily well.

"There is a market out there searching for a car," Ford once said. "Ford Motor Company committed itself to design that car. It carries four people, weighs under 2,500 pounds and costs less than $2,500." This reflects the view that the Mustang was simply a niche-market product and Ford had found the perfect niche. I think the car has more going for it than that. It was a great design and a great product. The Corvair Spyder fit in the same niche, but it didn't have the Mustang's looks or other attributes.

1965 Mustang GT-350   **Phil Kunz**

The Mustang was simply a car that everyone liked. It had broad-based appeal, along the lines of the bright red MG TD roadster that I drive nearly all summer. As I toodle along in my little car, school kids hoot, whistle and wave. At the gas pump, men driving huge pickup trucks ask if it's OK to peek under the hood to see my "lawn mower" engine. When I stop at a fast food joint, teenagers say, "Awesome car, man!" And when I drive the car, I feel like I'm going 100 mph, though the speedometer needle is only half the way there.

If you take all the qualities of the T Series MG and wrap them up in a less archaic package—and give it 1960s technology in place of 1930s technology—with a rear seat—you have the early Mustang. Who among those who lived when the car first arrived can forget that bright Poppy Red color that was so popular those first few years? "Only Mustang makes it happen!" was slogan I remember and it was so true back in 1964 and 1965. Ford sold every one it could build.

1966 Mustang convertible   **Elton McFall**

"Mustang, when introduced, seemed to embody everything that interested the budding youth market," said *Ward's 1969 Automotive Yearbook*. "The car had the styling secret of long hood and short deck, was low enough in price to attract nearly any new car buyer and had an appeal that spanned the generations. For the now-adult postwar baby boom, the car provided individual transportation and also served the mobility needs of a beginning family. The car rose astronomically in consumer interest, bettering the half-million mark for two consecutive years. It would have undoubtedly remained at that level, but for the introduction of competitive sporty cars in 1966 and 1967."

1968 Mustang 2 + 2 fastback   **Jerry Heasley**

For 1965, Ford expanded the line with a fastback. It was quickly whipped up to keep the Barracuda at bay. It wasn't a true pillarless hardtop because it had no rear side windows. There were louvers in that area instead, making it a coupe. Ford circumvented the issue of body-style classification by making up a name and calling it the "2+2." The base six-cylinder version had a $2,553 window sticker and weighed 50 pounds more than the hardtop.

A new grille design, simulated magnesium wheel covers, a five-dial instrument cluster and safety features were standard on 1966 Mustangs. New options included a Stereo-Sonic tape player and a high-performance engine/

automatic transmission option. Also optional were front-wheel disc brakes, GT equipment, an interior décor group and a full-width front seat.

The 1967 Mustang featured a complete restyling. The new body was still on a 108-inch wheelbase, but was 2.7 inches wider and two inches longer than before. The design motifs and the body style offerings were patterned after the originals, but much more stylized. Body panel sculpturing was heavier than before and more rounded than the "flat" 1964 through 1966 style. The vents on the rear quarters were more scoop-like. The new snout-like grille looked as if it was ready to take a bite out of any Camaro or Firebird. News for under the hood was a 390-

1969 Mustang Mach I CJ 428   **Phil Kunz**

1965 Mustang 2 + 2 fastback **David Lyon**

1964-1/2 Mustang two-door hardtop **Brad Bowling**

Once Mustang had competition from GM, it became a game of making the cars and engine options bigger each time the cars were redesigned. While retaining the basic Mustang look and 108-inch wheelbase, the '69 models were nearly four inches longer, as well as a half-inch lower. Ford adopted the GM pattern of selling the car in model-option packages. The Mustang was the base version, the Grande' was the luxury edition and the Mach I was the high-performance entry. The Mach I came standard with the 428 Cobra Jet Ram-Air V-8, while other models offered a 200-cid 155-hp six and 351-, 390- and 428-cid V-8s that ranged from 250 hp to 335 hp. Significantly, the base price tag on the '69 Mach I broke the $3,000 barrier.

As the price went up, the sales and production numbers came down. In 1969, the undisputed leader of America's specialty cars saw its third yearly drop in a row. Total registrations were 259,903 Mustangs, a 15.7 percent drop from 1968 and a 31.5 percent decline from the 1966 total. The biggest threat came from Chevrolet with its Camaro. The party was over for Ford (at least for a while), but it had been a very good one while it lasted.

cid V-8 with 320 hp. All '66 engines were carried over. While the Mustang's overall sales fell, V-8 sales increased 20 percent.

New accent striping and side sheet metal contours highlighted the 1968 Mustang. The lineup remained at three body styles, but power train choices grew to include items like a 427-cid high-performance engine. Starting in April, the 428 Cobra Jet engine was made available. A louvered hood that was optional in 1967 became standard equipment. The grille got a new "floating" pony emblem. New striping packages were added to the options list. Prices climbed higher than ever before, but even base V-8s were still under $3,000.

1960s "solid gold"

1964-1/2 Mustang convertible

6	5	4	3	2	I
$1,400	$4,200	$7,000	$15,750	$24,500	$35,000

Estimated values in today's marketplace taken from the 2006 Collector Car Price Guide.

CHAPTER TWO

1964-1969 Plymouth Barracuda

1967 Barracuda convertible

With the Falcon Sprint and Corvair Monza Spyder selling to enthusiasts in big numbers, Plymouth realized it wouldn't take much to spin off a sporty car based on the Valiant to generate some much-needed sales. The name Barracuda was picked for this "glass-back" version of the recently restyled (by Elwood Engle) compact. It was introduced on April 1, 1964, about two weeks before the Mustang arrived. It was officially a 1964 model and coded as such. A distinction of the base '64 model was use of a 170-cid 101-hp six. A 273-cid 180-hp small-block V-8 (235 hp optional) was used in most (22,300) of the 24,600 cars built. The six sold for $2,365 and V-8s started at $2,496.

The Barracuda rode on a 106-inch wheelbase. The body was 189 inches long and 71 inches wide. The only model offered was the fastback coupe, made by cutting the top off a Valiant and adding a large, hatch-style curved-glass window behind a rakish roofline. The Barracuda included a fold-down rear seat that, when folded, provided wagon-like rear luggage space. While such configurations are common today, they were unusual in 1964.

A three-speed manual transmission was standard, along with a 3.23:1 rear axle. TorqueFlight automatic transmission was optional. The suspension utilized torsion bars, instead of springs, at the front. Outboard-mounted

asymmetrical leaf springs supported the rear. Standard equipment included power brakes, 9 x 2.5-inch drums, 13 x 4.5-inch wheels and 6.50 x 13 tires.

For model-year 1965 only some minor facelifting was done. The Barracuda was treated to technical improvements and offered an increased range of both standard and optional equipment. A new 225-cid 145-hp six was used as base engine, but the 273-cid 180-hp V-8 was a *no-cost* option. In November, a Formula S competition kit that provided true sports car performance was made available. It included a 235-hp Commando 273 V-8, a Rallye Pack suspension, wide-rim 14-inch wheels, 6.95 x 14 Goodyear Blue Streak racing tires, simulated bolt-on wheel covers, Firm-Ride shock absorbers and a four-speed manual gearbox. Barracudas with this package cost below $3,169 and could do 0 to 60 in eight seconds! They carried special "Formula S" badging. One amazing thing about the

Plymouth initially portrayed the Barracuda interior and emphasized it as a spacious family car.

'65 Barracuda was that it was the most popular Plymouth product after just one year on the market. Some 65,000 were built.

Fender-mounted turn indicators, new shell-type bucket seats and a new die-cast metal grille characterized the 1966 Barracuda. New "fish" medallions were on the body-colored center grille divider and the sides. Plymouth also redesigned the taillights. Pin stripes decorated both sides of the body. A newly restyled instrument cluster incorporated a trip odometer, a locking glove box and an oil pressure gauge. A new unsilenced air cleaner sat atop the 273 V-8.

The Barracuda line for 1967 was unveiled on November 25, 1966 and immediately hailed as one of the most beautiful designs since the classic '63 Buick Riviera. The car was longer and wider and had two additional inches of wheelbase. There

The 1968 Barracuda convertible (left), Barracuda S fastback (middle) and coupe (right).

*1969 Barracuda
340 convertible*
Tom Glatch

were now three body styles – the traditional fastback, a new two-door hardtop with notchback styling and a convertible. The Mopar designers went for an Italian-style appearance that retained the split grille, but added European-type road lights and a quick-fill gas cap. The interior came standard with a sports bench seat and bucket seats were an option. For performance-oriented buyers, there was a new 280-hp 383-cid big-block V-8. The 273 remained available, as did the Formula S package for V-8 cars.

"Sports Barracuda" was the new name for the fastback, which now incorporated a folding rear seat and a security panel. The convertible had an upgraded interior with standard bucket seats, a power-operated top and a glass rear window. The new two-door notchback featured a conventional trunk. With the handsome new styling, a bevy of equipment upgrades and prices between $2,449 and $2,779, the '67 Barracudas were real value for the money. Interestingly, this was the first year Plymouth began referring to its pony car as the "'Cuda." However, the term was not yet an official model name.

A new grille and new taillights set the 1968 Barracuda apart from the 1967. A 318-cid V-8 replaced the 273. It had 230 hp. Also new was a high-performance 340-cid V-8 with 275 hp. The hardtop and convertible could now be ordered with Formula S 340 or Formula S 383 equipment packages, as could the Sport Barracuda. A lengthy list of options was offered. And interior trim packages were further refined. New Super Wide Oval Red Streak tires were new, too.

For 1969, a new 'Cuda 340 series was headline news at Plymouth. It came in hardtop or fastback form. The regular Barracuda line continued to offer the same three body styles. Standard in 'Cuda series cars was a four-

speed manual transmission, heavy-duty suspension and heavy-duty brakes. The hardtop was available with a new yellow paisley roof treatment. The 225-cid six was the base engine. V-8s started with the 318 (230 hp) and included the 340-cid 275-hp job and the 383-cid with 330 hp. Cars with both larger V-8s could be Formula S models. Late in the year, a 440-powered 'Cuda was released.

1960s "solid gold"

1965 Barracuda

6	5	4	3	2	1
$1,080	$3,240	$5,400	$12,150	$18,900	$27,000

Add 10 percent for the Formula S option.

Estimated values in today's marketplace taken from the 2006 Collector Car Price Guide.

1967 Camaro Indy 500 Pace Car convertible **Tom Glatch**

1967-1969 Chevrolet Camaro

1968 Camaro Z-28 coupe **David Lyon**

One of the most collectible Chevrolet models of the 1960s—excluding the Corvette—is the Corvette's "baby brother" the Camaro. The 1967 Camaro was Chevrolet's belated reaction to the 1964-1/2 Mustang. It gained instant popularity. In its first year on the market, Camaro production was roughly half that of the Mustang. From 1968 on, the two totals moved closer and closer, although the Camaro never had more assemblies than Ford's pony in the 1960s.

Amazingly, the Camaro was the fourth totally new car that Chevy had introduced since the Corvair bowed late in 1959. Each of the cars – Corvair, Chevy II, Chevelle and Camaro – filled a different niche in Chevy's marketing scheme. While inspired by the "pony car" segment that the Mustang had carved out of the market, the first Camaro was really promoted as more of a "Junior Corvette" that gave the family man with a hunkering for a real sports car the opportunity to buy one with four seats. Chevy first described the Camaro as a "road machine" and promised buyers "wide stance stability and big-car power."

The Camaro rode a 108-inch wheelbase just like the Mustang. At 185 inches long, it was about 1.5 inches longer than Ford's entry. Sport Coupe (two-door hardtop) and convertible body styles were offered. The Camaro had a unitized body with a bolted on front frame section that carried the engine, front suspension, steering and sheet metal components. Its overall appearance included a long hood and short rear deck with the popular "Coke-bottle" shape dominating the design.

1969 Camaro SS coupe **David Lyon**

The Camaro offered buyers 81 factory options and there were 41 other accessories that owners could ask their dealer to install. There were pre-packaged "model-options" (groups of specific extras) that essentially turned the base Camaro into different models. The high-performance SS 350 option included concealed headlights. Strato bucket seats were standard equipment.

Engine choices included a 230-cid six and a special two-barrel version of the 327 V-8. The new Camaro's front sub frame was large enough to hold big-block Chevy V-8s like the 396-cid Turbo-Jet V-8. This meant that 427-cid V-8s could also be accommodated and a small number of 1967 Camaros were converted to 427 power by Yenko Chevrolet of Canonsburg, Pa.; Nickey Chevrolet of Chicago, Ill., Bill Thomas of Anaheim, Calif. (who worked in connection with Nickey Chevrolet); and by Motion Performance of Baldwin, N.Y.

The standard six-cylinder coupe was $2,466 and the counterpart convertible listed for $2,704. Those prices made the Camaro just $5 more expensive than the lowest-priced 1967 Mustang. Barracuda offered the cheapest coupe, but for some reason the Barracuda convertible was the most expensive ragtop of the three brands. The Camaro's base V-8, with 210 hp, cost $105 extra. The 327 also came with a four-barrel carburetor and 275 hp. Also available was the 350-cid V-8 with 295 hp and the big-block 396-cid 325-hp Turbo-Jet V-8.

In December 1966, Chevrolet introduced the first Camaro Z/28. This was a limited-production option package based on a performance-tuned 302-cid V-8 that was "legal" for SCCA racing. The Z/28 small-block served up 290 hp. The package also included drive train, suspension and appearance upgrades to set the Z/28 apart from other Camaros. Production versions of the Z/28 were all two-door hardtops and carried a base price of $3,273. Only 602 were made.

1967 Camaro RS coupe   **Tom Glatch**

1968 Camaro RS convertible

1968 Camaro RS coupe

1969 Camaro ZL1 coupe   **Tom Glatch**

CHAPTER TWO

1969 Camaro Indy 500 Pace Car convertible **Phil Kunz**

1969 Camaro Rally Sport coupe

1969 Camaro SS convertible

1967 Camaro SS 396 convertible **Phil Kunz**

1960s "solid gold"

1965 Camaro Z-28 coupe

6	5	4	3	2	1
$1,700	$5,100	$8,500	$19,130	$29,750	$42,500

*Estimated values in today's marketplace taken from
the 2006 Collector Car Price Guide.*

The Camaro was virtually unchanged as it entered its second model year, although a close inspection would reveal the addition of new front and rear side marker lights and ventless side windows. Standard engines remained the same with the 230-cid six and the 327-cid V-8 carried over. A new option was a 250-cid 155-hp six. Other power options were the same.

The year 1968 was a good one for the Camaro as 235,147 cars were built in the model year. A total of 209,822 new Camaros were registered in the 1968 calendar year compared to 204,862 in the 1967 calendar year and 41,100 in the 1966 calendar year. Camaro sales for calendar year 1968 came to a new high of 213,980 units (2.50 percent of industry) compared to 205,816 (2.7 percent of industry) in 1967. A single 1968 Camaro Z/28 convertible was specially built for Chevrolet general manager Elliott "Pete" Estes.

The last of the first-generation Camaros is considered by many enthusiasts to be the most popular one. The concept behind the new-for-1969 design was to make the Camaro look more "aggressive." The heavily restyled body looked longer and lower. The wheel wells were flattened with sculptured feature lines flowing off them towards the rear of the car and rear-slanting air slots ahead of the rear wheel. At the front of standard Camaros was a grille with 13 slender vertical moldings and five horizontal moldings forming a grid-work surrounded by a bright molding. A badge with the Chevrolet bow-tie emblem was in the center. There were single round headlamps near both outer ends of the grille. The full-width bumper integrated with the body-color outer grille surround and there was a license plate holder in the center of the valance panel. Round parking lights were positioned on either side of the license plate. At the rear were wider taillight bezels with triple-segment lenses.

The restyled Camaro kept the 108-inch wheelbase, but was one inch longer at 186 inches. It was also 74 inches wide—or 1.5 inches wider. The basic models were the Camaro six hardtop ($2,638) and convertible ($2,852) and the Camaro V-8 hardtop ($2,727) and convertible ($2,941). Available option packages included Rally Sport (RS), Super Sport (SS) and Z/28. It was possible to combine options to get an RS/SS Camaro. The 230- and 250-cid sixes returned. The 327 with 210 hp was base V-8. Also available were 250- and 300-hp versions of the 350-cid V-8 and the 396-cid 325-hp big block.

In 1969, Chevrolet was invited to supply a Camaro Indy Pace Car once again. Sales were in a slump, so an Indy Sport Convertible package was created for the public. This option arrived February 4, 1969. Chevrolet literature called it "Midseason Change No. 13" and detailed a long list of package contents including Hugger Orange accents and houndstooth upholstery. Pace car door decals were available with the Z11 Indy pace Car option, but not mandatory.

Camaro club enthusiasts have documented that a Pace Car Sport Coupe was also offered as a promotional model by the Chevrolet Southwest Sales Zone. These coupes were sold in a number of states including Arizona, Oklahoma, Texas and Wisconsin. This Z10 package could be ordered for the Camaro Coupe with RS/SS equipment. Z10 coupes were similar to the Z11 convertible on the outside, but had some interior differences such as black (standard, custom or houndstooth) and ivory

1969 Camaro Z-28 coupe **Phil Kunz**

(standard and houndstooth) interior choices, in addition to orange houndstooth. They also came with the optional woodgrained steering wheel, ComforTilt steering, a vinyl top and other options. It is believed that the Norwood, Ohio factory built 200-300 of the cars.

Production of 243,085 cars was realized in the model year. That represented 2.9 percent of total U.S. industry production and compared to 235,151 cars and 2.8 percent of industry in 1968 and 220,906 cars and 2.9 percent of industry in 1967. Camaro sales for calendar year 1969 came to 171,598 units for a 2.03 percent share of the industry total. That compared to 213,980 (2.50 percent of industry) in 1968 and 205,816 (2.7 percent of industry) in 1967. A total of 172,459 new Camaros were registered in the U.S. during calendar year 1969, down from, 209,822 in

the 1968 calendar year, 204,862 in the 1967 calendar year and 41,100 in the 1966 calendar year.

A 375-hp SS 396 Camaro with the close-ratio four-speed manual transmission and cold-air-induction hood was tested by *Car Life*. The car did 0 to 30 mph in 2.6 sec., 0 to 60 mph in 6.8 sec., 0 to 100 mph in 15.6 sec. and the quarter mile in 14.77 sec. at 98.72 mph. It had a top speed of 126 mph. Several hundred special ultra-high-performance 427-powered '69 Camaros were also created by performance-oriented Chevrolet dealers as so-called COPO (Central Office Production Option) cars. The 1969 Camaro did well in Trans-Am racing, too, capturing top honors in for cars in the over 2.5-liter class. Mark Donohue and Roger Penske were the top Camaro drivers in Trans-Am events.

1968 Camaro SS 396 coupe **Phil Kunz**

CHAPTER TWO

1967-1969 Yenko Camaro

Don Yenko, of Canonsburg, Pennsylvania, became one of Chevy's first factory-authorized dealers to turn the Camaro into a hot rod. During the early 1960s, Yenko had built and sold race-modified Corvettes and Corvairs. His "Yenko Stinger" Corvair pointed the way to the pony car market. Starting in 1967, Don's Yenko Sportscars dealership started modifying Camaros by dropping in new big-block Chevy V-8s in place of smaller stock engines. Yenko upgraded everything from soup to nuts to make a Super Camaro.

After Yenko's dealership mechanics put a few cars together themselves, he set up a Chicago-based distribution network called Span, Inc. to market the cars nationally. Chicago was the home of another factory dealer that was famous for its racing efforts—Nickey Chevrolet. Ex-Nickey mechanic Dickie Harrell was into drag racing at the time, and the Super Yenko Camaro concept was actually something that he had dreamed up. According to Camaro experts, most of the cars probably had the modifications done in Chicago. Yenko added decals, badges and other sprecial features at his dealership in Canonsburg. Other performance dealers, like Fred Gibbs, helped sell the cars.

A 1967 Span, Inc. ad offered the Super Yenko Camaro/410 with a 427-cid 410-hp hydraulic-lifter V-8, a Super GT Hydro (three-speed automaticx) transmission, metallic brakes and other high-performance upgrades. The "410" listed for $4,245. There was a Super Yenko Camaro/450 for the same price. It had a 450-hp version of the "Rat" motor with solid lifters, a close-ratio four-speed manual gear box and other modifications. In addition, there was a "Z/28 Stormer" competition package that carried a

$6,000 price tag. Special individual options available for the Z/28 Stormer included an L-88 Corvette engine, side-exit exhausts and a high-rise intake manifold.

The early 427-powered Camaros assembled by Yenko Sportscars and distributed by Span, Inc., led to the first Camaros with factory-installed 427-cid V-8s. Demand for the dealership-built cars was so strong that Yenko's mechanics could barely carry out enough engine swaps to fill the orders. As a result of this situation, in 1968 Yenko and his father visited Chevrolet headquarters to discuss the possibility of getting '69 Camaros with factory-installed 427s. It was decided to use a specialized Central Office Production Order (COPO) system to get about 100 such cars made for Yenko Sportscars.

Early in the year, Don Yenko and Dickie Harrell went their separate ways. Until the so-called COPO 9561 Camaros became available, Yenko's mechanics continued building other SYC Camaros. About 72 cars were ordered in 1968 under COPO 9737. These cars had a 140-mph speedometer, a positraction rear axle (with 3.73 or 4.10 gearing), dual exhausts and high-performance suspension components. The COPO order specified factory installation of the L78 V-8 (396 cid 325 hp) and four-speed gearbox. Seven cars were not made into 427-powered SYC models. The balance were converted by replacing the 396-cid short block with a 427-cid one. A very rare 1968 was COPO 8008 (serial number 9737-1001). This was the first 427 Camaro built on a factory assembly line. It was a Fathom Blue coupe and the only car sent out without a white nose stripe. Yenko added the white nose stripe later.

If you wanted to order 100 Chevys today and have the engines replaced with a high-performance version, the company couldn't do it – at least not legally. And the fine they'd pay if caught would far outweigh the profit on 100 units. Fortunately, things weren't quite like that in '69. If Don Yenko's dad wanted to plunk down a 100-car order,

Chevy would pull strings to put 427 V-8s in. A COPO order was completed and the 1969 SYC Camaro was created.

The original 1969 Yenkos were produced under COPO 9561. They had L72 engines (427 cid 425 hp), M21 or M22 four-speed manual gearboxes (or M40 Turbo-Hydra-Matic), front disc brakes, a special Z12 ducted hood, a heavy-duty radiator, a special suspension, a 4.10:1 posi rear and a rear spoiler. The Yenkos also ordered a batch of COPO 9737 Camaros that had 15-inch wheels, Goodyear Wide Tread GT tires, a 140-mph speedometer and a beefy one-inch front stabilizer bar. Somewhere between 101 and 201 cars were made.

Yenko's SYC Camaros came in only specific colors: Hugger Orange, LeMans Blue, Fathom Green, Daytona Yellow, Rally Green and Olympic Gold. The cars had a base price of $3,895 including shipping. Available options included front and rear bumper guards ($25), front and rear floor mats ($12), an AM/FM push-button radio ($134), heavy-duty Air Lift shocks ($45), traction bars (450) and chrome exhaust extensions ($38).

On April 19, 1969 a Yenko Camaro with factory-installed headers and racing slicks, driven by Ed Hedrick, did the quarter mile at a drag strip in York, Pennsylvania in 11.94 seconds at 114.5 mph. Drag racing is what these cars were built for and they didn't disappoint.

1960s "solid gold"

Yenko and COPO Camaros

The 2006 Collector Car Price Guide considers the value of the Yenko and COPO Camaros inestimable. In 2005, Barrett-Jackson auctions reported a 1967 Yenko Camaro SS was bid to a $118,800 selling price while two 1969 COPO Camaros also hit six figures. A green original COPO Camaro, originally delivered in Toronto, Ontario, was sold for $145,800 while a low-mileage version, originally from the Atlanta area, was sold at auction for $201,960.

1969 COPO Camaro 427 **Phil Kunz**

1967-1969 Mercury Cougar

1967 Mercury Cougar GT 390 two-door hardtop

Mercury's "Sign-of-the-Cat" car is probably the most collectible model to come from Ford's Mercury Division in the 1960s. It was based on the successful Mustang, but had a three-inch longer wheelbase and fancier body and interior trim. Overall length was stretched even further. The Mustang was 183.6 inches and the Cougar was 190.3 inches − nearly seven inches longer. The standard engine was the 289-cid V-8 with 200 hp. Buyers could add a four-barrel version of the same engine with 235 hp or opt for a GT 390 model with 320 hp.

Only a two-door hardtop was available and it window-stickered at $2,851. Starting in February, for $230 additional, you could get a much more impressive XR-7 version. It didn't look much different outside, except for a model medallion on the rear roof quarter and special wheel covers. Inside, the interior was really something else. It featured a walnut finish dash, leather-and-vinyl upholstery trim and an aircraft-style overhead console with a functional aircraft look. I remember an ad showing a dark green Cougar XR-7 with a tan interior. One look and you wanted to own the car and the interior was oh so cool!

The GT had a firmer suspension with solid rear bushings, stiffer springs, big 1.1875-inch shocks and a fat anti-roll bar. Power front disc brakes, 8.95 x 14 Wide-Oval tires, special I.D. and a low-restriction exhaust system were included. The GT's 1:10 power-to-weight ratio provided driving excitement. Transmission choices included 3- or 4-speed synchromesh or a 3-speed Merc-O-Matic with manual shifting to second below 71 mph or to first below 20 mph. Specific manual gearboxes were used with the 390. A 3.00 "Power Transfer" axle was standard and a 3.25 version was an extra-cost option.

1967 Mercury Cougar Dan Gurney Edition

1967 Mercury Cougar GT

1968 Mercury Cougar XR-7 coupe

1968 Mercury Cougar GTE 7-Liter coupe

1969 Mercury Cougar Eliminator coupe   **Phil Kunz**

The "sign of the cat" soon became famous throughout the automotive world. **Greg Hertel**

The Cougar was a more substantial car than the Mustang. It outweighed its cousin by over 400 pounds. And Mercury did a good job of promoting it as a luxury model. Car magazines of the day must have gotten many free loaners, because they gushed over the XR-7's upgraded personality and performance and helped push the new car towards an upscale clientel. Early statistics showed that the average Cougar owner was 37 years old, attended college and earned about $10,000. One out of every six early Cougar buyers was female.

Like the Mustang, the Cougar was a successful car. Early Cougar sales pushed the Mercury division to all-time sales highs for November and December 1966. In all, 26,470 Cougars were delivered to buyers before the calendar flipped to 1967. Those weren't exactly Mustang numbers, but they were great for Mercury. A total of 48,013 builds were recorded in calendar year 1966. For the model year, production wound up at 150,893 cars, making the Cougar the best-selling 1967 model out of all Mercury Division products.

The 1968 Cougar retained the same styling, but it could now be ordered with an optional bench seat. A 302-cid V-8 replaced the 289 as base engine. The Cougar also got its first real high-performance package. This was the 7.0-liter GT-E, which was an option for both the base Cougar and the XR-7.

Although the Cougar was aimed at the sporty luxury niche, the 1968 GT-E was its first (but not last) step into the muscle car sweepstakes. The option included a 390-hp "E" version of Ford's 427-cid V-8, plus a SelectShift Merc-O-Matic transmission, a performance handling package, styled steel wheels, power disc brakes and a non-functional "power dome" hood scoop. A 7.1 second 0-to-60 mph time was published in the enthusiast magazines.

Putting the 427 in the Cougar was a short-term deal because the engine was discontinued. Later in the 1968 model year the Cougar got the 428 Cobra Jet V-8. To keep insurance agents and bean counters happy, the big-block carried a rating of 335 advertised horsepower. Because it had a longer stroke, the 428-cid engine had an easier time with emission requirements. However, its actual power output was estimated to be closer to the choked down 427E it replaced.

A limited-edition Cougar XR-7G was also offered in 1968. The "G" stood for "Dan Gurney"—an American racing hero who was under contract to Mercury. Gurney piloted Bill Stroppe-prepared 1967 Cougars in the SCCA Trans-American sedan racing series. The rare XR-7G option package was mainly an assortment of "gingerbread" and any engine from the base 302-cid V-8 up. The option included a fiberglass hood scoop, road lamps, a racing mirror, hood pins and a power sun roof (which could also be ordered for other 1968 Cougars). At the rear, four exhaust tips exited through the valance panel. New spoke pattern styled wheels held radial FR70-14 tires. Badges showing a special emblem decorated the instrument panel, roof pillar, deck lid and grille. The XR-7G Cougars were not widely promoted back in 1968 and very few were made, making the survivors highly prized by collectors today.

1969 Mercury Cougar Eliminator coupe

Ironically, the car that most closely predicted the Cougar was the Mustang II prototype.

1969 Mercury Cougar convertible

The '68 Cougar was advertised as, "Pound for pound and dollar for dollar the best equipped luxury sports car in America." Lincoln-Mercury dealers set new all-time sales records in 1968, but buyer interest in the Cougar died down, as it does for many second-year models. A total of 112,166 Cougars were retailed by dealers in calendar-year 1968, an almost seven percent decrease from year one. Model-year production also dropped by 24.6 percent. However, calendar-year production of Cougars dropped just 1.5 percent.

With a new convertible as its headline-news item, the Cougar was completely restyled for 1969. The overall design theme was the same, except for a Buick-like "S-curve" body side feature line and a peak on the center of the hood. The 1969 grille had horizontal pieces that protruded slightly at the center. Standard equipment included retractable headlights, rocker panel strips, wheelhouse moldings and twin body pin stripes. The back-up lights wrapped around the fenders. The taillights were trimmed with concave vertical chrome. Foam-padded vinyl bucket seats and carpeting were standard. The mid-season Eliminator was aimed at muscle car fans and came only as a hardtop.

All of the new Cougars were three-and-a-half inches longer and nearly three inches wider. The new base engine was a 351-cid V-8 with 250 hp. Options included a 290-hp version, a 390-cid 320-hp job and the 335-hp 428 Cobra-Jet V-8. The big engine came with functional Ram Air, which did not boost its advertised horsepower, but you can betcha it boosted how fast the car would go both in the "Stoplight Grand Prix" and in the showroom.

Eliminators included front/rear spoilers, a black-out grille, a hood scoop, Argent styled wheels, side striping, a rally clock and a tachometer. The 351-cid V-8 with 290 hp was standard. Ford's "Boss 302" V-8 was offered in "street" and "race" tunes. The latter had two 4-barrel carburetors. With the 428-CJ you got a scoop, hood hold-down pins, competition handling and hood striping.

The Cougar of the 1960s was never a wildly successful car, but it was a machine that buyers could be proud of owning. The sporty pony car was successful in reviving the performance image that Mercury had once had in the 1940s and 1950s. From the late 1950s until the Cougar came along, the company became best known for building large, flashy cars. The new Cougar model proved that Mercury knew how to make something other than land yachts.

1960s "solid gold"

1967 Mercury Cougar XR-7 hardtop

6	5	4	3	2	1
$ 840	$2,520	$4,200	$9,450	$14,700	$21,000

Add 10 percent for the Formula S option.

Estimated values in today's marketplace taken from the 2006 Collector Car Price Guide.

1969 Pontiac Firebird 400 coupe **Phil Kunz**

1967-1969 Pontiac Firebird

Ford rocked the automotive world with its mid-1964 Mustang and took the industry by surprise. Pontiac wasn't able to field a true competitor until three years later, when it introduced the Firebird on February 23. It was PMD's version of Chevy's new Camaro dressed up with a Poncho-style split grille, different engines and transmissions and a few suspension tweaks.

Pontiac offered the sporty "shorty" in five flavors – base, Sprint, 326, 326 H.O. and 400 – created by tacking options onto the same basic car. The options created distinctive packages that were merchandised as separate models. Bucket seats were standard in all Firebirds. Design characteristics of the 1967s included vent windows and three vertical air slots on the rear fenders.

Sprints featured a 215-hp overhead cam six with a four-barrel carburetor. A floor-mounted three-speed manual gearbox and heavy-duty suspension were standard. A Firebird Sprint convertible cost $3,019 and a coupe was $2,782.

Firebird 326s featured a 250-hp version of the Tempest 326 V-8 with a two-barrel. The convertible cost $2,998 and the coupe was $2,761. Firebird 326-HOs used a 285-hp version of the same V-8 with a 10.5:1 compression ratio and a four-barrel carb. A column-shift three-speed manual transmission, dual exhausts, HO stripes, a heavy-duty battery and Wide-Oval tires were standard. The HO

convertible cost $3,062 and the coupe cost $2,825.

The performance version of the 1967 Firebird was the 400. It featured a 325-hp version of the 400-cid GTO V-8. Standard equipment included a dual-scoop hood, chrome engine parts, three-speed heavy-duty floor shift and sport-type suspension. Prices were about $100 higher than a comparable 326 HO. Options included Ram-Air induction, which gave 325 hp and cost over $600.

In road tests, the stock 1967 Firebird Sprint hardtop did 0-to-60 mph in 10 seconds and the quarter-mile in 17.5 seconds. With the Firebird 400, the times went down to 6.4 and 14.3 seconds. A magazine clocked the Firebird 400 hardtop with the 325-hp V-8 at 14.7 seconds and 98 mph in the quarter-mile.

The Firebird arrived so late in 1967 that Pontiac had no time to make big changes for 1968. The vent windows went the way of the unfortunate dodo and were replaced by one-piece side glass. Suspension upgrades included bias-mounted rear shocks and multi-leaf rear springs. Pontiac built 90,152 coupes (base price $2,781 and 16,960 ragtops (base price $2,996).

The $116 Sprint option included a three-speed manual gearbox with floor shift, an overhead-cam six, Sprint emblems, body sill moldings and F70 x 14 tires. The 250-cid engine had a single four-barrel carburetor and 215 hp.

1967 Pontiac Firebird convertible **David Lyon**

The appeal of the new $106 Firebird 350 option was a 265-hp V-8. The 350 HO option included three-speed manual transmission with column shift, dual exhausts, HO side stripes, a heavy-duty battery and four F70 x 14 tires.

The Firebird 400 ($351-$435 more) added chrome engine parts, a sports suspension, dual exhausts, 400 emblems and a dual-scoop hood. Its 400-cid V-8 produced 330 hp. The Ram Air 400 was about the same, except for its de-clutching fan and *functional* hood scoops. The Ram Air V-8 produced 335 hp and did 0-to-60 in 7.6 seconds. A quarter mile took 15.4 seconds.

Flatter wheel openings, front fender wind splits, new rooflines and a creased lower beltline characterized 1969 Firebirds. The gas filler moved behind the rear license plate and a rectangular Pontiac-style split bumper grille was used. Square body-colored Endura bezels held the headlamps. Headlines were made when the Trans Am arrived March 8, 1969 at the Chicago Auto Show. It was the slinkiest Firebird model-option up to this point.

Standard equipment for Firebirds included vinyl bucket seats, grained dashboards, carpeting, outside mirrors and side marker lamps. The hardtop listed for $2,831 and the ragtop for $3,045. Model-options included Sprint ($121 extra), 350 ($111 extra), 350 HO ($186 extra), 400 ($275-$358 extra), 400 HO ($351-$435 extra) and Ram Air 400 ($832 extra), plus the Trans Am.

The features of each model-option were similar to 1968. The Trans Am included a heavy-duty three-speed manual gear box with floor shifter, a 3.55:1 axle, glass-belted tires, heavy-duty shocks and springs, a one-inch stabilizer bar, power front disc brakes, variable-ratio power steering, engine-air extractors, a rear-deck air foil, a black-textured grille, full-length body stripes, white-and-blue finish, a leather-covered steering wheel and special identification decals. The hardtop had a base price of $3,556 and a production run of just 689 units. Eight convertibles were built and were priced at about $150 more.

1969 Pontiac Firebird coupe **David Lyon**

1960s "solid gold"

1968 Pontiac Firebird coupe

6	5	4	3	2	1
$ 960	$2,880	$4,800	$10,800	$16,800	$24,000

Add 10 percent for the 350 HO and also for four-speed transmission. Add 25 percent for Ram Air Firebird.

Estimated values in today's marketplace taken from the 2006 Collector Car Price Guide.

The Trans Am grew out of the Sports Car Club of America's Trans-American racing series. PMD paid the SCCA a $5 royalty per car to use the name. The T/A was originally planned with a special super-high-performance 303-cid small-block V-8 that would have made it race-eligible. About 25 cars were fitted with the short-stroke 303-cid tunnel-port V-8s, but these were used exclusively for SCCA Trans-Am racing. Production models could have either a 335-hp 400 HO (a.k.a. Ram Air III) V-8 or an optional 345-hp Ram Air IV engine. Quarter-miles times for Trans Ams were in the 14 to 14-1/2 seconds bracket.

Pontiac raced to third place in the auto industry because the youthful performance image it had honed after 1955 was perfectly in tune with sociological changes that occurred in the 1960s. Its challenge for the new decade was to expand that image into every market niche to maintain its "third-best-selling" ranking. The Firebird was designed to give Pontiac a foothold in the pony car niche. At the time it was launched, no one could predict the long life it would have, but the Firebird would survivefor 35 years and accounting for many, many sales.

1969 Pontiac Firebird Trans Am coupe   **Tom Glatch**

1969 Pontiac Firebird Trans Am coupe   **Tom Glatch**

1969 Pontiac Firebird Trans Am coupe   **Phil Kunz**

1970 Dodge Challenger (introduced fall 1969)

The Challenger was Dodge's late-breaking answer to the Mustang and Camaro. It was introduced as a 1970 model and came as a beautifully styled hardtop, a ragtop and a Special Edition (SE) formal-roofed hardtop. A total of 24,875 Challengers were delivered by Dodge dealers during the 1969 calendar year, so in that sense the Challenger does fit into a history of "1960s cars."

The low-profile pony car, that Dodge called a "specialty compact," was built on a 110-inch wheelbase and measured 191.3 inches long. Model offerings included a two-door hardtop, a formal roof hardtop coupe and a convertible. Prices for the six-cylinder base versions ranged from $2,851 to $3,076. V-8s were about $122 extra. All three Challengers were offered in the high-po, V-8-only R/T series. R/Ts included an electric clock, a Rallye instrument cluster, Rallye suspension with sway bars, heavy-duty drum brakes, F70-14 tires, R/T emblems and bumblebee or longitudinal tape stripes.

Base engine in the Challenger was the 225-cid 145-hp slant six. The base V-8 was a 318 with 230 hp. Standard in the Challenger R/T and optional in other models was a 383-cid big-block V-8 with 330-335 hp. Available engines included a 340 with 275 hp or the 426 Hemi with either 375 or 390 hp.

1970 Dodge Challenger R/T hardtop

1970 Dodge Challenger R/T Hemi hardtop   **Phil Kunz**

1970 Dodge Challenger T/A hardtop   **Phil Kunz**

1970 Dodge Challenger T/A Six Pak hardtop **Phil Kunz**

1970 Dodge Challenger R/T 440 hardtop **Phil Kunz**

1960s "solid gold"

1965 Dodge Challenger R/T convertible

6	5	4	3	2	1
$1,520	$4,560	$7,600	$17,100	$26,600	$38,000

Add 10 percent for the Formula S option.

Estimated values in today's marketplace taken from the 2006 Collector Car Price Guide.

1965 Shelby Mustang **Brad Bowling**

1965-1969 Shelby-Mustang

Ford Motor Company used the Mustang to sell accessories – everything from fancy wheel covers to a Cobra performance kit. "Mix a Mustang with a Cobra . . . for the performance rod of the year" said one 1965 advertisement. The Cobra was a powerful sports car that race driver Carroll Shelby had created using a British

1965 Shelby Mustang GT-350 V-8 **Brad Bowling**

AC roadster body and a Ford V-8. To strengthen the relationship between the two cars, Ford asked Carroll Shelby to make the Mustang into a sports car that could compete with the Corvette. Ford sent Shelby 110 stock White 2 + 2 hardtops with no hood or back seat and asked him to "pimp their rides" into a performance machine.

Shelby was given a blank sheet of paper and asked to modify the Mustangs to show the GM and Mopar guys what it was capable of. The first-year Shelby Mustang was released on January 27, 1965. Prices for GT-350 "street" models started at $4,547. The GT-350R competition versions cost $5,950 up. The cars were designed to help create a "hairier" image for the stock Mustang and most buyers were serious enthusiasts who "understood" the car.

There were many modifications throughout the car, but the most important ones were under the hood. Adding an aluminum intake manifold to the 289-cid V-8 upped output from 271 hp to 306 hp. A reworked exhaust system featured Shelby headers jutting out ahead of the rear wheels. A Borg-Warner T-10 four-speed manual gearbox was bolted in. Chassis goodies included a large front stabilizer bar, a one-inch sway bar, adjustable Koni shocks, rear traction bars (also made by Koni) and 15-inch wheels and tires.

The exterior had changes. Shelby added a fiberglass hood with functional air scoops. The side of the car got a blue stripe and GT-350 lettering across the lower body sides. Shelby removed the factory emblems and added a small grille badge with a horse on it. Inside, the rear seat was removed and the spare was bolted in its place. Other interior features included black vinyl upholstery, a three-spoke steering wheel and competition-style seat belts.

To satisfy Sports Car Club of America regulations and make the cars eligible for SCCA racing events, at least 100 cars – including both street driven and racing versions)

CHAPTER TWO

had to be made. Production for the first year far exceeded the minimum. A total of 562 Shelby Mustangs were put together. Twelve were all-out race cars, 36 were "R-code" competition models and 516 were GT-350s.

For 1966, the Shelby-Mustang was more "showroom-friendly" and more emphasis was placed on selling street versions. Black, Red, Green and Blue exterior color choices (all with White side stripes) were added. When buyers of 1965 and early '66 models complained that the fiberglass hoods were not up to snuff, Shelby reverted to steel hoods. A smaller grille emblem was new. A GT-350 gas cap was added. There was also a similar center button on the steering wheel. Eventually, Shelby switched to 14-inch wheels and put the spare in the trunk. The engine and transmission were carried over. The suspension was more like the factory version, but with heavy-duty FoMoCo shocks. Koni shock absorbers were now an extra-cost option.

Carroll Shelby convinced the Hertz Rent-A-Car company to buy about 1,000 GT-350s to rent to business travelers. The idea was that the cars would tempt more customers to Hertz and the Hertz fleet would tempt car renters to buy a Mustang or a Shelby-Mustang. Renting the cars cost $17 per day and 17 cents per mile. They had special GT-350H call-outs and many were done in Black with Gold stripes and trim. Gold striping was also used on most, if not all, of the GT-350Hs finished in other colors. Car renters as a group didn't do real well with the T-10 transmission, so late GT-350 Hs had automatic transmissions. Shelby also built about 10 supercharged '66 GT-350s with 390 hp. A handful of convertibles were produced, including one for Shelby himself.

1968 Shelby Mustang GT-500 KR **Brad Bowling**

Ford was hard pressed to improve on the "classic" Mustang it had introduced in 1964, but had to. The competition was getting very keen. On the exterior, the 1967 Mustang was heftier and more full fendered. A new 2+2 fastback featuring all-new sheet metal was especially low and sleek. The roofline had a clean, unbroken sweep downward to a distinctive, concave rear panel. Instead of louvers, Shelby Mustangs had a functional air scoop on each side of the side of the car and a rear spoiler.

Shelby tried placing the high-beam headlights in the center of the GT-350 grille, but many state laws specified outboard placement. About 200 cars were built with lights in the roof air scoops and ran afoul of state lighting laws. Mercury Cougar taillights were adopted. Many body panels were made of fiberglass. The length of the body increased, permitting use of larger engines.

A 306-hp version of the 289 was standard in the GT-350, but also offered was a new GT-500 that carried a 428-cid 355-hp Police Interceptor V-8 with a "medium-riser" aluminum intake. Shelby moved even further away from the strictly-for-racing format by offering two new Ford transmissions (a C-6 automatic and a four-speed "toploader"), power steering and power brakes. Gone

1968 Shelby Mustang GT-500 KR **Phil Kunz**

1968 Shelby Mustang GT-500 KR

were the GT-350H and supercharged GT-350. A 427-powered 520-hp "Super Snake" was built as a pilot model for a proposed 50-car run that never made it to reality. Around 1,100 GT-350s and 2,000 GT-500s were made in 1967.

Ford owned rights to the Cobra name by 1968 and used it on the Shelby in place of "Mustang." A 302-cid V-8 was under the GT-350's hood. Early '68 GT-500s came with a 427, but the 428 Cobra-Jet engine was substituted later on in a GT-500KR version. The Shelby KR package ("King of the Road") was available as a coupe or ragtop. It included a fiberglass hood, fiberglass front panels, functional air scoops and engine air extractors. The instrument panel carried a large tachometer and speedometer, but other gauges were console-mounted. Bucket front seats, vinyl upholstery and thick carpets were standard. Other content included a fake wood dash, heavy-duty suspension, staggered shocks, E70-15 Goodyear Polyglas tires and a limited-slip differential. Large, but ineffective air scoops were attached to the body sides to cool the brakes.

Although it was not the fastest car ever made, the GT-500KR was the fastest Shelby-Mustang made up to its time. Some racers registered ETs below 13 seconds and top speed was around 130 mph. The fastback was base-priced at $4,473 and ran about $4,900 with a nice selection of options. Production counts were 404 GT-350 convertibles, 402 GT-500 convertibles, 318 GT-500KR convertibles,

1,253 GT-350 fastbacks, 1,140 GT-500 fastbacks and 933 GT-500KRs. The fastback was now promoted as the "Sportsroof."

1967 Shelby Mustang GT-500   **Phil Kunz**

An all-new Mustang arrived in 1969 and an all-new Shelby followed. The new grille was empty, except for a tiny Cobra emblem. The fog lights were now below the front bumper. A new fiberglass nose protruded above the grille. There were scoops to take in and extract engine air and cool the brakes. New body side graphics were seen. Coiled snake Cobra emblems decorated the sides of the Sportsroof or front fenders of the convertible. A slightly taller rear spoiler was fitted. T-bird taillights were used. The 302 was the base GT-350 engine, but a 351-cid V-8 was optional. The GT-500 used the CJ-428 big block. In 1970, Shelby added two black center stripes and a black front spoiler to leftover '69s and sold them as 1970 models. Two-year production total included 1,085 GT-350 fastbacks, 194 GT-350 convertibles, 1,536 GT-500 fastbacks and 335 GT-500 convertibles.

1968 Shelby Mustang GT-500   **David Lyon**

1968 Shelby Mustang GT-500 **Phil Kunz**

1966 Shelby Mustang **Brad Bowling**

1960s "solid gold"

1965 Shelby GT-350 fastback

6	5	4	3	2	1
$2,600	$7,800	$13,000	$29,250	$45,500	$65,000

Estimated values in today's marketplace taken from the 2006 Collector Car Price Guide.

1968-1969 AMX

By the mid-1960s, American Motors Corporation was losing momentum. AMC had done wildly well during the early-'60s compact car boom. It was "ahead of the curve" in marketing small, cheap-to-operate cars. When the demand for such vehicles took off around 1958, AMC quickly raced to third rank in industry sales. Unfortunately for AMC, the trend didn't last. By the mid-'60s, compact car sales were dropping. Buyers then wanted specialty cars and luxury cars. This shift in demand spelled doom for Studebaker and left AMC clinging on as the only large independent automaker. To claw its way back to health, AMC needed image cars. Realizing that Chevrolet's Corvette was the "gold standard" in this area, AMC launched its own no-back-seat sports car and called it the AMX (American Motors Experimental). It was a winner!

The AMX was a hard car to pigeonhole because it's so unique. It seemed to fit best in the "pony" category, although it was not a true pony with a rear seat. It was derived directly from the Javelin, so it was not an all-out sports car. With a 390-cid V-8, the AMX packed muscle, but it was not a classic mid-size muscle car. The AMX had a 97-inch wheelbase and a length of 177.22 inches, a width of 71.57 inches and a height of 51.73 inches. Tread widths were 58.36 inches front and 57 inches rear. It weighed just over 3,000 lbs.

Reclining bucket seats, full carpeting, wood-grain interior trim and E70-14 Goodyear Polyglas tires were standard. Also included was a four-speed gearbox and heavy-duty suspension. AMXs built in 1968 had a metal dashboard plate bearing a special serial number from 000001 to 006175. The first 550 cars, built in 1967, lacked this feature.

The 1969 AMX 390 V-8 engine

AMX/ GT show car

V-8The AMC had a "ready-to-roll" look and V-8 power to back it up. The base 290-cid V-8 produced 225 hp at 4700 rpm. Options included a 343-cid V-8 with 280 hp and a 390-cid 315-hp V-8. All engines carried four-barrel carburetors and true dual exhaust systems. To go even faster, you could order AMC Group 19 performance parts for dealer installation. The hardware included aluminum intake manifolds, hi-lift cams, roller rockers, Detroit Locker rear ends with various gear ratios, side pipes and rear-wheel disc brake kits.

1969 AMX 390 **David Lyon**

By the time the AMX bowed at the Chicago Auto Show on February 24, 1968 it was famous. Craig Breedlove used a pre-production version to set 106 National and International speed records. He also was officially timed at 189 mph at Bonneville and made an unofficial run at over 200 mph.

When car magazine test drivers got behind the wheel of the AMX, they went bananas. *Mechanix Illustrated* said: "The AMX is the hottest thing to ever come out of Wisconsin and I forgot to tell you they have it suspended so that you can whip through corners and real hard bends better than with many out-and-out sports cars." In March 1968, *Car and Driver* wrote, "This is no Rambler, you guys."

1968 AMX 390 **Phil Kunz**

The AMX was America's first steel-bodied two-seater since the '57 T-Bird and it was a bargain compared to Chevy's Corvette. The number at the top of the window sticker was $3,245 compared to $4,663 for a 1968 Corvette coupe. That didn't mean you were likely to see AMXs on every street corner (unless you lived in Kenosha, Wisconsin). After all, two-seat cars have a small market to begin with and the AMX didn't arrive until midyear. The '68 production total was only 6,725 cars. However, the AMX brought new customers into AMC showrooms. In the long run, that was what the company needed to sell cars.

For 1969, the AMX was virtually the same on the outside, but the interior had a new larger tachometer, a 140-mph speedometer, front seat headrests and slightly different door panels. Buyers who ordered automatic

1969 AMX 390 **Phil Kunz**

1969 AMX 390

transmission got a center console while those who ordered a four-speed got a Hurst shifter. There was also a new passenger-side grab handle. Leather upholstery was added to the options list. Twelve new exterior colors were available. In the spring, the three "Big Bad" colors were introduced – Orange, Green and Blue.

The most interesting and sought after AMX was the SS. Only 52 — or by some reports, 53 — AMXs were sent to Hurst for drag race "legalization." The AMX SS had the 390-cid V-8 fitted with an Edelbrock aluminum cross-ram intake, twin 650-cfm Holley four-barrels, Doug's headers and other modifications. It was conservatively advertised at 340 hp. The suggested retail price of $5,994 seems a steal now, but was nearly *twice* the regular 1969 price.

The AMX was the official pace car for the Pikes Peak Hill Climb. Ten to 12 AMXs, all Frost White with red stripes and red interiors, were used as courtesy cars by select participants of the race. Only one of these cars is known to exist. It was used by Bobby Unser during the week prior to the race.

The 1969 production total was 8,293. This was the highest annual total for AMC two seat models. The 1970 AMX was made to "look tougher" according to AMC. The toughest part was that it was the last of the two-seat models and only 4,116 were made. Those cars are not within the scope of this book.

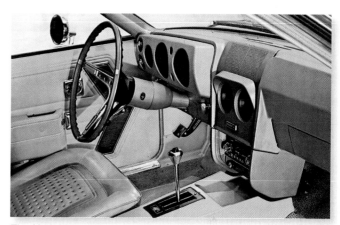

The 1968 AMX 390 interior

1968 AMX 390

1960s "solid gold"

1968 AMX fastback

6	5	4	3	2	1
$ 840	$2,520	$4,200	$9,450	$14,700	$21,000

Add 30 percent for Craig Breedlove edition.

Estimated values in today's marketplace taken from the 2006 Collector Car Price Guide.

1969 AMC Javelin SST two-door hardtop

1968-1969 Javelin

American Motors' Javelin was Dick Teague's good-looking answer to the Mustang and all its clones. It succeeded in tapping into the youth market, where AMC's fastback, the "Charger"-like Marlin had failed. There was a reason. It was an example of great industrial design. The four-passenger pony car was marketed in two hardtop models, the Javelin and the SST. Unlike the AMX, the base Javelin engine had six cylinders. The Javelin six sold for $2,482 and the SST six was $2,587. Adding the base 290-cid 200-hp V-8 to either model cost $105.

The Javelin rode on a 109-inch wheelbase and was 189 inches long. In addition to the 232-cid 145-hp six and the base V-8, buyers could order a 225-hp version of the 290, plus a 343-cid 280-hp V-8 or a 390-cid 315-hp V-8. According to AMC expert Larry G. Mitchell, it was after the AMX came out that the 390 was put in Javelins. Why not? The 390 had the same outside dimensions as the 290 and 343 and fit very easily. "This engine doesn't show up in factory literature because it came out so late, but it makes sense," Mitchell says. "After all, it was just a question of taking the engine from this pile or that pile."

Car and Driver got its hands on the original Javelin "390" and used it in a comparison test printed in March 1968. "Our Javelin was the first 390 ever built," the magazine said. "But its long suit was its handling. It felt very much like a British sports car." Out of the six cars tested—Javelin SST, Camaro SS, Mustang 2+2 GT, Cougar XR-7, Barracuda Formula S and Firebird 400 HO—the SST was the favorite of everyone on the test crew as far as handling.

Car and Driver noted that the engine option was so new that "AMC hasn't had any time to play with the 390, at least officially, so we didn't expect the car to tear up the pavement." This proved to be an accurate assessment, as it was the slowest of the six pony cars with a 15.2 second quarter mile at 92 mph. Part of the blame fell to AMC for limiting early 390s, like the *Car and Driver* test car, to only a three-speed manual transmission supplied by Borg-Warner. For comparison, a "Go-Package" Javelin with the 343-cid 280-hp and four-speed gearbox (that *Motor Trend* said was one of the best production units around) was good for an 8.1 second 0-to-60 time and a 15.4 second quarter mile.

The 1968 Javelin SST tested by *Car and Driver* had a manufacturer's suggested retail price of $3,943 with the 390 Go-Package. Its curb weight was 3,560 lbs. Other Javelin performance extras included front disc brakes, a special handling suspension (with a big sway bar and heavy-duty springs and shocks), 5-1/2-inch-wide wheels, traction bars and quick-ratio power steering.

While Pontiac's GTO was selected as *Motor Trend* "Car of the Year," the magazine offered category awards in 1968. It picked the Javelin as the winner in the sports-personal category saying that it exemplified "the most significant achievement for an all-new car and is the most notable new entry in (its) class."

Motor Trend liked the Javelin so much that it carried out a "Light-ning" project in a car that it called the Javelin SL (for Super Light).

As the name implied, the editors started with a stock, off-the-showroom-floor "Jav" and turned it into a completely modified, lightweight bomb that any enthusiast could duplicate without much difficulty. By removing accessories they cut 306 lbs. from the car, which was fitted with a 390-cid V-8. In the "1/2-mile drags" the car covered the distance in 23.96 seconds and had a top speed of 102.22 mph.

With an Offenhauser aluminum intake, hood scoop and some chassis mods, the Javelin SL did half-mile runs at 118.26 mph in 23.35 seconds. Later, at the Orange County Raceway, with its headers uncorked, the car did the quarter mile in 13.97 seconds at 104.25 mph! Only one Javelin SL was built. Production of other versions included 29,097 Javelins and 26,027 SSTs.

AMC did start racing Javelins during 1968. AMC hired Corvette racer Jim Jeffords to head a racing effort in SCCA competition. Drivers Peter Revson and George Follmer joined the team. A pair of the cars came in second and fourth in their second Trans-Am race at War Bonnet Raceway early in the season. Later, they broke the track record for sedan racers at Mid-Ohio Raceway. Although no all-out victories were registered that first season, the Javelins showed that they were at least competitive. Doug Thorley, one of the biggest names in drag racing, also campaigned a Javelin funny car. In addition, there was a privately sponsored Javelin that ran in NASCAR's GT races of that era.

For 1969, Javelins got a twin-venturi grille and a few mechanical upgrades, but no major changes. Engines again started with a six and V-8s were optional. The 290 continued to offer 200- and 225-hp editions and the latter came with an optional Hurst-shifted four-speed. The four-speed could also be linked to the carryover 343. The "big muscle" on the options list was the 390/315 V-8. It was available with dealer-installed factory high-performance parts, "Isky," Edelbrock or Offenhauser speed equipment and a Doug's Headers exhaust system. AMC was careful to offer it with stick or automatic.

Javelin SSTs included special trim, reclining bucket seats and added chrome. Originally there were two more or less straight stripes on the beltline. On January 9, these were changed to "C" stripes starting right behind the front wheel opening and running back along the mid-body feature line.

The optional "C" rally stripe was also available on a new Big Bad Javelin introduced in the spring. It came in Big Bad Orange, Big Bad Blue or Big Bad Green and included

Javelins were hot performers in the 1968 racing season.

Famous designer Dick Teague poses with the '68 Javelin.

painted bumpers. Options included E70 x 14 Goodyear Polyglas Red Line tires, mag-style wheels, air conditioning, an "airless" spare tire, an 8-track stereo tape with AM radio, power disc brakes, a 140-mph speedo and big-faced tach, Twin-Grip differential, Adjust-O-Tilt steering, a roof-mounted spoiler, a close-ratio four-speed with Hurst shifter and more.

A "Mod" Javelin came in the same colors as the Big Bad Javelin and many Mod Javelins were also marketed with a Craig Breedlove package that included a spoiler on the rear of the roof and simulated exhaust rocker mountings.

Offered again was the Go-Package, which included a 390 or 343 V-8, heavy-duty springs and shocks, a thicker sway bar, wide wheel rims, Twin-Grip and other goodies. Traction bars were a factory-supplied dealer-installed item. As part of a performance package, buyers could install a pair of overlay fiberglass hood scoops, plus a new air cleaner that AMC claimed added 12 hp to the 390 due to better breathing.

Standard rear-end gears in the Javelin with a four-speed transmission were 3.54:1 and 3.15:1 gearing was a no-cost option. Serious enthusiasts could pay extra for 3.73:1, 3.91:1, 4.10:1 and 5.00:1 axle ratios, as well as a Twin-Grip differential.

Production totals for 1969 included 17,389 Javelins and 23,286 Javelin SSTs. AMC built 17,147 of the 390-cid V-8s, but some were used in cars other than Javelin models.

1960s "solid gold"

1969 Javelin SST

6	5	4	3	2	1
$ 740	$2,220	$3,700	$8,330	$12,950	$18,500

Add 25 percent for the GO Package and add 30 percent for the Big Bad Package.

Estimated values in today's marketplace taken from the 2006 Collector Car Price Guide.

CHAPTER TWO

The 1960s . . . Sports-Personal Cars

Like any other automotive label, the "sports-personal car" could just as easily be called the sports-luxury model or, as Ward's *Automotive Yearbook* often described them, "specialty cars." The "personal" part of the name separates these vehicles from "family" cars. These are mainly two-door body styles with limited seating room in the rear. The "sports" part of the name infers a sporty character, although these cars aren't true slap-the-leather-and-damn-the-wind sports cars.

1964 Thunderbird two-door hardtop **David Lyon**

While the compact car was largely a 1960s phenomenon and the pony car was no doubt a 1960s creation, the concept of the sports-personal car can be traced back in automotive history. Many cars of this same "flavor" were seen in the Great Gatsby era. L-29 Cords and front-wheel-drive Ruxtons with wild striped paint schemes come to mind. The Auburn boat-tail speedster and the Packard-Darrin Convertible Victoria are other examples. Do others see a spiritual link between the 810/812 Cord and the 1963 Avanti?

In the 1930s and 1940s, it was largely independent automakers that hired the most talented practitioners of industrial design to create outstanding specialty cars. Gordon Buehrig, Brooks Stevens, Count Alexis de Saknoffsky and Raymond Loewy were among legends in the field. While major automakers built good-looking, practical cars, it was smaller companies, with hired design talent, that produced the head-turning cars that few could own but many could admire.

During World War II, Detroit's assembly lines turned to war-related efforts and a new car of any kind was precious commodity. Brooks Stevens designed the utilitarian Monart station wagon bodies to fit to old Ford and Mercury chassis. These conversions carried more passengers than the chassis-donating sedans and could be also be used as military ambulances. The sporty-type cars that Stevens loved—and collected—weren't produced for the war's duration.

Practicality ruled immediately after the war ended, too. With labor strife and material shortages, new cars stayed in short supply. When the assembly lines finally started rolling again, the focus was on building *family* transport.

Many manufacturers brought trucks and sedans back first, then phased other body styles back into production. Station wagons were a rarity, since building the all-wood wagon bodies took much longer.

1958 Thunderbird coonvertible

Sporty wood-bodied coupes and convertibles were made, but were quite limited. At a time when a drastic shortage of cars meant any model would bring a premium price, there was little motivation to waste time on specialty models. The first to return were the wood-bodied Chrysler Town & Countrys. They and were followed by wood-bodied Ford Sportsman convertibles plus a very few from Mercury.

From 1950 on, as real material shortages disappeared, automakers created artificial demand for their products. Continuing product improvements were needed to bring customers into showrooms. One way to sell more cars was to promote multi-car ownership. Two-car families started to become more common.

This was also the time of the sports car craze in America. Soldiers serving in Europe during the war had been introduced to British, German and Italian cars that were unlike anything sold here. Some cars made their way to the U.S. with returning veterans. The postwar Lincoln-Continental fit the mold of a sporty-looking car suited for personalized transportation. It had racy European styling and a V-12 engine, though its price was out of reach of most buyers. Detroit reacted with its own designs for a sporty two-seat car. By 1953, Chevrolet's Corvette was on the market and the following year brought the Kaiser Darrin. In 1955, Ford's T-bird bowed.

ONLY FROM OLDS a car like this!

Only Toronado looks this new! Low-slung nose. Fastback fuselage. Concealed headlamps. Massive wheels with 10 cut-outs to help cool brakes. And full-view -ide windows, a functional feature of Toronado's unique draft-free ventilation.

Only Toronado rides this new! Smart setting for your solo in America's most distinctive car! Roomy, easy-to-enter interiors, flat floors carry six in solid comfort. And Toronado's luxurious, sporty seats beg you to buckle up and begone!

Only Toronado drives this new! 385-hp V-8 engine feeds power to front wheels via Turbo Hydra-Matic. Toronado pulls (rather than pushes) you through tight turns. Improves traction, increases road stability. And vibration is almost obsolete!

Another first from Oldsmobile! Toronado, only full-size car with front wheel drive! Engine, transmission, differential and steering are all up front . . . to put the traction where the action is!

Out front in '66

TORONADO

by Oldsmobile

1966 Olds Toronado

American manufacturers found small, two-seat cars to have limited appeal. The sliding-door Kaiser lasted two years, the Corvette struggled to survive and the Thunderbird found success as a large, four-seater. The no-back-seaters sold as well as MGs or Fiats, but not well enough to justify the costs of building them. Similar cars proposed by Buick, Dodge, Oldsmobile, Packard, Plymouth and Pontiac never made it to the assembly line.

As the battleship-grayness of the war years turned to the pastel colors of the 1950s, sports-personal cars experienced a revival as sort of "super-sized" versions of the Corvette-Darrin-T-Bird trio.

The first two-door hardtops to arrive were merchandised specialty cars. They had catchy model names like Bel Air, Catalina, Crestliner, Holiday, Newport and Riviera. Car buyers called them "hardtop convertibles" because they had the look of a ragtop with the convenience of a fixed-position steel roof. Another distinctive model offering was Dodge's limited-production Wayfarer roadster. Mercury, Lincoln and Kaiser created "designer-edition" sedans with a sporty flavor. Kaiser-Frazer toyed with a four-door convertible as well.

Raymond Loewy's award-winning 1953 Studebaker Starliner Coupe captured the sports-personal concept so well that it eventually wound up in the Museum of Modern art. Other cars that fit the bill included the Buick Skylark, the Cadillac Eldorado, the Chrysler C300, the Hudson Italia, the Nash Healey, the Oldsmobile Starfire and the supercharged 1957 Pontiac Bonneville convertible. Still, it was the up-sized, four-place 1958 Thunderbird that cleared the bases and drove the runners home. The "Squarebird" featured stand-apart styling and an aircraft-like cockpit with front bucket seats and a full-length center console. It was like a giant sports car and it was about as personalized as domestic transportation got in that era. Wow!

Pontiac artwork captured the 1967 Grand Prix and other cars in memorable poses in the 1960s.

than $25,000 per year. This allowed people to purchase cars on the basis of desire, rather than need. They could afford to be picky and this increased the demand for stylish cars with special features and equipment.

For years, the Chrysler 300 Letter Car and the "Squarebird" had been available for these buyers and the two cars had filled the bulk of demand. Then the prosperous 1960s inspired competition from the likes of the 1961 Oldsmobile Starfire convertible. In 1962, the Olds Starfire line was expanded to offer a bucket-seat-and-console hardtop, while Pontiac dropped the starting flag on its Grand Prix counterpart. Also in 1962, Chrysler launched a "Sport 300" series that had the look of the Letter Car, but not the same distinction or limited edition status. It lacked the Letter Car's performance hardware and wasn't a real sports-personal car. Four more Chrysler 300 Letter cars (H, J, K and L) would be offered in 1962, '63, '64 and '65.

The cork finally popped in 1963 when GM introduced two milestone cars – the Corvette Sting Ray and Buick Riviera – which were then joined by an unexpected treat from Studebaker called the Avanti. The independent from South Bend, Indiana was already involved in the sports-personal field with its sleek GT Hawk hardtop, but the Loewy-designed Avanti had a design that was startlingly new and considered a classic from day one. A new from bumper-to-bumper Grand Prix, a cleaned-up Chrysler 300 and a modernized cigar-shaped T-Bird also joined the grouping.

The 1958 Thunderbird defied gravity! While all other American cars except the American Motors Rambler and American dropped like lead balloons, the sporty Ford saw its sales climb to 53,400 – nearly as high as the combined total of 1955, 1956 and 1957 T-Birds. Its share of total Ford output climbed from 1.3 percent to 3.8 percent. The "Squarebird" would have been an even bigger home run, had it not been for a temporary economic recession that spurred increased interest in small, foreign economy cars. This sudden market shift lasted several years and kept the lid on a ready-to-explode sports-personal segment.

By 1963, that lid was finally ready to blow. The American economy had fully recovered and demand for sporty equipment like bucket seats, floor shifts and consoles steadily increased. It was the strong economy that really drove the car market towards the upscale sports-personal cars. In the early 1960s, the children of America who had grown up the grim Depression Era and the lean times of World War II now were seeing disposable wealth growing by $25 to $30 billion a year, which was enough by itself to buy all the cars, trucks, tires and parts made in a year!

More than half of America's families earned $7,000 per year and 25 percent had incomes higher than $10,000. More than three million households made more

1964 Thunderbird convertible and two-door hardtop

After an ill-timed flirtation with downsizing in 1961 and 1962, the 1964 cars got longer wheelbases, more body length and larger engines. V-8s with more than 400 cubic inches were installed in only 2.6 percent of U.S. cars in 1961, but 6.2 percent in 1964. More than a quarter of all domestic cars built in 1964 were two-door hardtops. Over a million vehicles made here came with factory air conditioning. Nearly 17 percent or 1,227,000 featured bucket seats. All of these factors reflected the growing sales of sports-personal cars. "Plush interiors adorned with wood grain steering wheels, bucket seats, offering all the comforts of air conditioning, stereo tapes and speed control devices – these are the signs of the times," said *Ward's Automotive Yearbook*.

1955 Chrysler C300 two-door hardtop

Changes in the 1964 sports-personal cars were modest. The T-bird was the exception. A major restyling modernized the car and help it fight its new competition and it used the slogan "unique in all the world" to set itself apart. The Starfire and Grand Prix were cleaned up just a bit, while the Riviera had minor changes. Studebaker's GT Hawk and Avanti soldiered on. In 1965, the Avanti was revived as former Studebaker-Packard dealers Nat Altman and Leo Newman kept it alive as the Vette-powered Avanti II. It was built in a section of the old factory.

In 1965, the dramatic fastback Marlin arrived as AMC's attempt to gain buyer attention. The following year, Chrysler followed its unique Valiant-based 1964-1/2 Barracuda compact fastback with the full-size Dodge Charger. Both the Charger and Marlin attempted to break into the sports-personal car field. The Riviera retained its classic styling and Chrysler offered its last Letter Car – the 300 L – with completely new styling. There was little to separate it from the non-Letter 300 except an illuminated "L" medallion in the center of the grille, an upgraded interior, high-performance suspension and tire equipment and a 413 V-8 with a special cam and dual exhausts. T-

birds were mildly facelifted and included unique sequential taillights, while front disc brakes were a new option. Also treated to an all-new look was a longer Grand Prix.

Consumer interest in cars that offered something more than basic transportation was spreading throughout every segment of the marketplace in 1966 and the sports-personal car niche was no exception. *Ward's* called the specialty car "the most dynamic force in the automotive industry." The sports-personal cars offered high-spirited engines, precise handling and luxury. They were built for pleasurable motoring.

A totally restyled Buick Riviera made the scene in 1966. Other GM models like the Corvette and Grand Prix were modestly, but nicely updated. Chrysler's Letter car was now as much of a memory as the Studebaker GT Hawk. T-bird fans were treated to a pair of new vinyl-topped Sport Coupes with landau irons. The big news was Oldsmobile's fresh-from-the-styling-studio front-wheel-drive Toronado, which sparked a revolution in both styling and engineering. The final-edition Marlin had few changes including a new extruded aluminum grille and a longer list of standard equipment. Newman and Altman continued to turn out a few Avanti IIs.

The 1967 sports-personal cars carried higher price tags, which were necessary to offset the cost of adding 17 items of government-mandated safety equipment. AMC switched its Marlin fastback to a six-inch longer wheelbase. A totally new entry in the market segment was the front-wheel-drive Cadillac Eldorado. The Buick Riviera had a restyled grille and stainless rocker panel trim. This was the last year for the so-called "midyear" Corvette with the original

1964 Buick Riviera two-door hardtop

Sports-Personal Car Production By Model Year

	1960	1961	1962	1963	1964	1965	1966	1967	1968	1969
Thunderbird	92,843	73,051	78,011	63,313	92,465	74,972	69,176	77,956	64,931	49,227
Chrysler 300 (1)	1,212	1,660	593	450	3,672	2,828	--	--	--	--
Riviera	--	--	--	40,000	37,958	34,586	45,348	42,799	49,284	52,872
Grand Prix	--	--	30,195	72,959	63,810	57,881	36,757	42,981	31,117	112,486
Toronado (2)	--	--	--	--	--	--	40,963	21,790	26,456	28,484
Starfire (2)	--	7,600	41,988	25,549	16,163	15,260	13,019	--	--	--
Corvette	10,261	10,937	14,531	21,513	22,229	23,562	27,720	22,940	28,573	38,762
Avanti/Avanti II (3)	--	--	--	3,834	809	45	59	66	100	92
Marlin	--	--	--	--	--	10,327	4,547	2,545	--	--
Hawk	4,287	3,708	8,787	3,958	1,772	--	--	--	--	--
Eldorado	2,461	1,450	1,650	1,825	1,870	2,125	2,250	17,930	24,258	23,333
Total	**111,064**	**98,406**	**170,755**	**233,401**	**240,748**	**221,586**	**239,839**	**229,007**	**224,719**	**305,256**

Note 1: Chrysler 300s are Letter Cars only.

Note 2: The Starfire and Toronado overlapped as Oldsmobile's sports-personal car in 1966.

Note 3: 1963-1964 Studebaker Avanti; 1965-1969 Avanti II.

Sting Ray body. The Thunderbird was completely restyled and broke the mold with a four-door hardtop version. The Toronado got a new frontal treatment and a Deluxe model. Pontiac released a one-year-only Grand Prix convertible to complement the newly restyled hardtop coupe model.

Probably the most changed of 1968's sports-personal cars was Chevrolet's Corvette, which had a swoopy new seven-inch-longer body. The design was highly influenced by Bill Mitchell's outstanding Mako Shark Corvette show car of 1965. The Riviera again got a new frontal treatment and some interior revisions. A new 472-cid V-8 was under the Eldorado's hood, which was 4.5 inches longer.

T-bird shoppers were offered a new four-door Town Sedan with the "baby-carriage" roof treatment, as well as a big 429-cube motor. Pontiac gave the Grand Prix a contoured roofline and a bold new front end. Total production of sports-personal cars dropped for the third year in a row.

A new Grand Prix made headlines in the sports-personal market segment in 1969. With production of 112,486 units, this milestone Pontiac design turned the whole category around by itself. After three years of trending downward, model-year output for the group climbed by close to 80,000 cars.

1962 Corvette **Tom Glatch**

1960-1969 Thunderbird

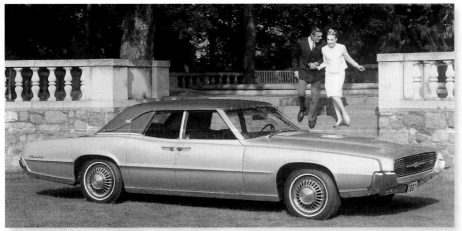

1967 Thunderbird Landau four-door hardtop

The 1960 model was the last Squarebird. It rode on a 113-inch wheelbase and a 352-cid 300-hp V-8 supplied motivation. The manufacturer's suggested as-delivered price was $3,426 for the 3,799-pound two-door hardtop and $3,860 for the 3,897-pound convertible. Ford sold about seven hardtops for each convertible, so it was clear that T-bird buyers were more interested in the personalized nature of the car than its sports car tradition.

When I was young, I tended to be forgetful. Nearly every afternoon, my mother would send me to pick up a few items at a grocery store. To make sure I didn't forget what I was after – or lose the money – she would pin a note and a dollar or two to the inside of my jacket. Usually, it was the 1959 Thunderbird, parked by a house on the route to the store, that distracted me. Off-White, with Red bucket seats and a long center console with a "Buck Rogers" look, it was a dream machine.

By the time I reached Adonizzio's Market, I rarely remembered what mom had sent me there for, but I knew that when I grew up, I was going to drive a car like that T-bird! My 10-year-old mind knew I'd get there. It was worth it. Owning a car like that 'Bird must be the key to happiness.

Completely re-engineered and restyled for the first time, the four-passenger Thunderbird bowed as a 1958 model in February of 1958. The car was an immediate and enormous success with its 53,400-unit production run almost matching the total number of T-birds made up to that point. By 1960, Ford was selling five times as many T-birds as it had when the car held two people. Today these cars are best known to collectors as "Squarebirds."

If the Squarebird was a Buck Rogers machine, the cigar-shaped 1961 Thunderbird was Sputnik on wheels. The gigantic circular taillights resembled a jet engine exhaust

1963 Thunderbird two-door hardtop

1962 Thunderbird two-door hardtop

1961 Thunderbird Indianapolis 500 Pace Car

The classic look of the Thunderbird was further accented in 1964 with a longer hood, a shorter roofline and all-new sculptured side panels. Wider spaced and higher set headlights and a fully-integrated bumper and grille contributed to the leading sports-personal car's distinctive appearance. The massive rear bumper enclosed rectangular taillights. Options included, a swing-away steering wheel and reclining front bucket seats and seat belt retractors. Hardtop and Landau models had a Silent-Flo ventilation system with a vacuum-controlled rear vent. A 300-hp 390 was the only engine. The T-bird had a 113.2-inch wheelbase and stretched 205.4 inches end to end. It was 52.6 inches high and 77.1 inches wide. Production climbed towards 100,000 units in 1964.

New features for 1965 included grille and trim, front disc brakes, "movie marquee" turn signals, a dome light for convertibles, keyless locking and reversible keys. On the standard equipment list was the 390-cid 300-hp V-8, power steering, power brakes and a swing-away steering

outlet. A stroked 390-cid version of the old 352 was the sole engine in this "Battleship Galactica." These low-slung cars were eye catchers and the fact that nothing else on the road looked like them emphasized their "personalized transportation" image. They were cool!

The 1962 and '63 T-birds didn't change much. A few styling details were tweaked and a 340-hp "Thunderbird Special" tri-carb 390 was released. Landau and Sport Roadster models were added to the hardtop and convertible. The Landau was a hardtop with the "baby carriage" roof treatment and the Sport Roadster was a ragtop with a fiberglass cap covering the rear seat to make it into a giant "two-seat sports car." The Sport Roadster included wire wheels. It was expensive at $5,439 and rare as it didn't sell well. Ford turned out just 1,882 of them and the '63s were the rarest with 455 built. The tonneau cover fit later T-Birds, and was offered as a dealer accessory then.

1963 Thunderbird Sports Roadster

1965 Thunderbird two-door hardtop

wheel. Ford advertising often stressed an aircraft theme for the Thunderbird and a cockpit-inspired interior helped drive home the fact that this was a car designed for the driver's personal taste.

Two new models, the Town Landau and the Town Hardtop, were added to the Thunderbird line for 1966. The Hardtop also returned and the convertible was back for its last appearance. Very few buyers opted for the open car and they were extremely rare. The "town" look was created by eliminating the rear side window and extending the pillar to the front window. New options included a 428-cid V-8, a Stereo-Sonic tape player, a fingertip-controlled Auto Pilot speed control system (integrated into the steering wheel) and overhead console to hold the "idiot" lights that monitored various systems.

A complete restyling for model-year 1967 replaced the convertible with, of all things, a four-door Landau. Naturally, it was designed to be distinctive with "suicide"-style door hinging and a 117-inch wheelbase. Two-door models like the Coupe and Landau Hardtop Coupe had a 115-inch wheelbase. By giving buyers of four-door cars the opportunity to be a T-bird owner, Ford boosted production by some 8,800 units, but only temporarily.

Minor styling changes were made to 1968 and 1969 models, but after the initial surge of enthusiasm for the four-door Thunderbird, its popularity dropped from 25,000 units to under 16,000. And the two-door models of these years also proved unpopular. It seemed as if FoMoCo had changed the Thunderbird into a luxury version of the standard Ford. The look of these cars still resembled a Galaxie or LTD of the same vintage. While buyers wanted luxury in their Thunderbird, they still preferred a car that was more sporty and personalized.

1967 Thunderbird Landau two-door hardtop   **Elton McFall**

1964 Thunderbird Sports Roadster

1962 Thunderbird convertible

1960s "solid gold"

1963 Thunderbird Sport Roadster

6	5	4	3	2	1
$1,640	$4,920	$8,200	$18,450	$28,700	$41,000

Add 10 percent for the 390-330 hp engine.

Estimated values in today's marketplace are taken from the 2006 Standard Guide to Cars and Prices.

1963 Thunderbird Landau two-door hardtop   **Cappy Collection**

1962 Thunderbird convertible

1962 Chrysler 300 H two-door hardtop

1960-1965 Chrysler 300 Letter Car

The 300 Series Letter Cars – nicknamed "Beautiful Brutes" – were first conceived as Chrysler's reaction to the Corvette and Thunderbird. Highland Park did not have the money to create a two-seat sports car, but engineer Bob Rodgers, who had a passion for the Mexican Road Races, realized that Chrysler could reach into its parts bin and whip up a full-size specialty car without spending a bundle. Using a New Yorker body, an Imperial grille and some "export" equipment employed on the Chryslers that ran in Mexico, Rodgers' 1955 C-300 ("Chrysler 300 hp") was a limited-edition high-performance car with a Hemi, two four-barrel carbs, automatic transmission, leather seats, racing tires and a top speed in the 150 mph range.

In 1956, the name was revamped to Chrysler 300 B, styling was modestly changed and 340 or 354 hp was put on tap. The more powerful version was for racing and those cars used a Dodge stick shift and other components. A longer, lower, wider "Forward Look" evolved in 1957, when the model name was 300 C. Power was now at 375 and 390 hp was optional. The 1958 Chrysler 300 D was

1960 Chrysler 300 F two-door hardtop

virtually identical and came with 380 or 390 hp. For 1959, someone decided to jazz up the facelifted 300 E with a little more body trim. The big news was the new 392-cid "Golden Lion" wedge V-8. It also had 380 hp, but not all the same kick.

One of the prettiest and most potent of all 300 Letter Cars was the 1960 with its advanced styling and all-new unit-body construction. Styling traits included a massive air scoop front grille, canted tail fins that were integrated into the overall design and a minimum of body ornamentation. The 300 model added a great looking crossbar grille, power swivel seats and a 413-cid V-8 with a ram-tuned intake manifold. Two versions were offered – a 375-hp "long ram" engine and a 400-hp "short ram" version. On the outside, the ram tubes were the same size, but the more powerful setup had internal modifications that shortened the effective length of the tubes and boosted power.

1965 Chrysler 300 L two-door hardtop

1963 Chrysler Sport 300 convertible

this point, the hardtop listed for $5,411 and the convertible was $5,841. A total of only 1,617 Chrysler 300 Gs were made, including a mere 337 convertibles.

Only 523 Chrysler 300 H models were made in 1962, including 123 convertibles. This was actually a good year for Chrysler as they refused to follow the trend to downsizing. When an economic recession ended sooner than expected the company's stubbornness led to a much-needed sales bubble. The Letter Car didn't sell because Chrysler expanded the line with a "Sport 300" model that had the basic looks of the limited-edition model, but the not the same performance hardware. Buyers opted for the look-alike lower-priced edition. The "H" used a 380-hp 413. A 305-hp 383-cid V-8 came in the Sport 300.

Available in two-door hardtop format only, the 1963 Chrysler 300 J sported new Virgil Exner styling and continued to rely on a crossbar grille for identity. A leather interior, a "square" steering wheel and a "J" on the body medallions identified the $5,280 Letter Car. This year the ram-tube-equipped 413 carried a 390-hp rating. Only 400 of the 300 J Sport Coupes were made.

The short-ram version is often written about as if it was a regular factory option, but it was actually a limited-production item made for just 7 to 10 racing or special-production cars fitted with a French-built four-speed Pont-A-Mousson transmission. The 300 F continued traditions

1965 Chrysler 300 L convertible

by winning the first six places in the Flying Mile competition at Daytona Speed Weeks with a top speed of nearly 145 mph. Illinois hardware store owner Greg Zeigler set a new record with one of the 400-hp four-speed cars. That Chrysler 300 F was purchased by collector Bob Macatee who still owns the 11,000-mile Letter Car.

The 1961 Chrysler 300 G was still considered a sports-personal car by those who appreciated brute horsepower in a luxury automobile. This year the crossbar grille was flipped so it was narrower on the bottom than on the top and the headlights were canted like the taillights. A ram-tuned induction system with dual four-barrel carbs was again standard and produced 375 hp. A four-speed manual gearbox was no longer used, but you could get a floor-shifted three-speed manual transmission with non-synchro first gear. At

Demand for Chrysler 300 Letter Cars had always been inconsistent and 1964's Chrysler 300 K proved the point. The 1963 J had been the rarest of all Beautiful Brutes, but the K turned out to be the most popular with 3,647. This is even harder to understand when you see the two models together. For the most part, they are the same car. The convertible was back, but only 625 were built, so it was mainly hardtops that sold. Ram induction was now listed as an option.

The 1965 Chryslers were completely restyled and lengthened by nearly three inches. Curved side glass was another new design feature. The push-button automatic

1964 Chrysler 300 K convertible

1961 Chrysler 300 G convertible

transmission was no longer used. This was the final year for the Letter Series high-performance specialty car. It closely resembled the standard 300 Series and was a problem, at least for Letter Car sales.

You could spot an L easiest at night with its medallion in the center of the grille that carried the letter "L" and lit up when the headlights went on. The non-letter 300 now used a four-barrel 315-hp version of the 383 V-8. The Letter Car had a single-carb 413 with 360 hp. Other small distinctions included a painted insert in the upper body molding, a damascened insert between the taillights, special interior appointments and appropriate Letter Car medallions. Production for the model year included 2,405 hardtops and 440 convertibles.

Chrysler 300 models built from 1966 on were all of the non-Letter Car variety. They are wonderful automobiles – a joy to drive and own. They don't really fit in the category of a sports-personal car any more than a Chrysler New Yorker would. The main difference is simply based on the idea that a "sports-personal" car has that certain something that makes it special and sets it apart from the pack. From 1960 to 1965, that single letter after the 300 model name meant you had a sports personal machine.

The Chrysler 300 Letter Car was truly a product of the 1950s and had its grandest Hemi-powered hour during that decade. The Wedge-powered Letter Cars of 1959 and the early 1960s are less of a race car than were the first four machines, but they rock when it comes to Chrysler design individuality. With their swivel seats, "fish bowl" instrument panels and spare tire embossments, these sporty speedsters are about as "personal" as automotive transportation gets.

1963 Chrysler Sport 300 convertible / Indianapolis 500 Pace Car

1960 Chrysler 300 F convertible

1960s "solid gold"

1960 Chrysler 300 F convertible

6	5	4	3	2	1
$2,680	$8,040	$13,400	$30,150	$46,900	$67,000

Estimated values in today's marketplace are taken from the 2006 Standard Guide to Cars and Prices

1966 Buick Riviera two-door hardtop   **Jerry Heasley**

1963-1969 Buick Riviera

Buick had used the Riviera name on its postwar hardtops. The two-door hardtop was described as a "Riviera Coupe." When the mid-century four-door hardtop arrived, it was called the Riviera Sedan. The 1963 Riviera came only as a hardtop coupe and it was far different than the earlier. For one thing, instead of being just a unique body style, it was a totally unique car. Second, it brought leading-edge design to Buick, probably for the first time. Third – and directly related to point two—was that it changed the entire image of Buick Motor Division.

Fittingly, the Riviera began as a project directed by GM styling chief Bill Mitchell to revive the LaSalle, a Cadillac companion car of the late-1920s through 1940 that was famous for being the first car to come out of GM's Art & Colour design studio. In 1955, Buick stylists Ned Nickles – the father of the fabulous 1953 Skylark–designed

an experimental car called the LaSalle II. Public reaction to this car convinced GM management that it needed a sports-personal car to compete with the Thunderbird. When Cadillac deferred, the development program was assigned to Buick and Buick's own Riviera name was selected to replace LaSalle.

Mitchell was a great talent in car design and the Riviera was among his crowning achievements. With its Rolls-like razor edge feature lines the Riviera had a hint of classic car styling that blended perfectly with up-to-date motifs like a long hood-short deck configuration and restrained use of bright metal trim. And it was one of those iron-fist-in-a-velvet-glove cars with Buick "nailhead" V-8 power under its hood. The first Riviera could get through the standing-start quarter mile in 16 seconds and look good doing it. And it handled well, too.

The 1963 version came in one model priced at $4,333 and weighing just under 4,000 pounds. It had a 117-inch wheelbase and was 208 inches long. The 404-cid V-8 produced 325 hp. It pushed power through a two-speed Turbine Drive automatic transmission. Standard equipment included front and rear bucket seats, a center console, deep-pile carpeting and a smoking set. The Riviera was aimed at Buick's most affluent buyers and only the Electra 225 convertible was more expensive (by $35).

1966 Buick Riviera two-door hardtop

1966 Buick Riviera two-door hardtop **Jerry Heasley**

For 1964 the Riviera looked about the same, but it had a new die-cast grille, frameless glass windows and fender lamps that glowed when the headlamps were on low beam. Under the hood you could add a 425-cid 340-hp V-8 with a single four-barrel carb as an option. Also available was a dual-carb 360-hp version of the bigger motor. The multi-carb option shaved a half second off the Riviera's quarter-mile time and pushed it to 90 mph in that distance. It could outrun a T-Bird. A new Super Turbine 400 automatic transmission was used. This was a three-speed twin-turbine Hydra-Matic unit.

The most noticeable change in the 1965 Riviera was a switch to hideaway headlights. The vertically mounted dual headlights hid behind fender grilles when not in use. A larger rear bumper housed the tail and back-up lights. In early December 1964 Buick initiated production of a performance-packed Riviera Grand Sport with the 360-hp V-8, riding and handling options. It could do 0 to 60 mph in seven seconds. It had a top speed of 125 mph.

Completely restyled as a modified fastback model, the 1966 Riviera introduced the Circulaire ventilating system that eliminated the need for vent windows. Fresh air entered the car through a hood grille and exited via a grille at the rear window ledge. GM said the change eliminated the hassle and wind noise associated with "ventipanes." The new Riviera was longer in the front and had an even shorter rear deck. A longer new 119-inch wheelbase was used and length was 211.2 inches. The 401 was base engine, the 340-hp 425 was an option and you could still get a dual-carb upgrade kit from your Buick dealer. Buick's calendar-year sales marked a 20.6 percent gain over the 38,602 sold in 1965.

General Motors used many future styling cues in the 1955 La Salle II four-door hardtop.

1968 Buick Riviera two-door hardtop

CHAPTER THREE

The 1956 Buick Super was an example of the Riviera styling in that decade.

A restyled grille graced the front end of the 1967 Riviera. It emphasized "negative space" and had a bright horizontal center molding. The parking lights were redesigned. New stainless steel moldings brightened up the rockers. Also new was a padded instrument panel. New options included front disc brakes and automatic level control. A new 430-cid 360-hp V-8 with a quadrajet carburetor was under the hood. There were no engine options.

While retaining its basic lines, the 1968 Riviera sported a deep-set plastic grille, new front fender and hood contours, redesigned bumpers and recessed taillights. Optional stainless steel moldings could be added to the lower body sides. Hidden headlights were retained. The 430 V-8 was carried over without major changes. Overall length increased a bit due to the heavier new bumpers. The Riviera was losing some of the design "cleanliness" it was known for. By this time the Riviera had a $4,615 base price and weighed over 4,300 lbs.

Retaining its classic image, the '69 Riviera had a new grille and a new hood ornament. Side marker lights were added to the front fender and new back-up lights were located in the rear bumper. A new feature was a center console with a side-mounted gearshift lever that remained below the top of the console during operation. Calendar-year sales of 53,389 Rivieras was a four percent gain over the 50,880 units sold by Buick dealers in 1968. Model year production of the sports-personal model rose seven percent.

During the 1960s, the Buick Riviera offered everything that was hot in the marketplace: sporty two-door hardtop styling, a bucket seat interior, high-performance V-8 engines, specialty model appeal, a rich array of standard equipment and all of the optional amenities that any car buyer could want. While never capturing quite the same sales volume as the Thunderbird or Grand Prix, the Riviera was a very popular entry and a profitable car for Buick.

1963 Buick Riviera two-door hardtop

Note the low center of gravity. Combined with specially tuned front and rear suspension systems, it gives you a whisper-quiet ride that's almost feline in its sure-footedness. Engine, with 445 ft.-lbs. of torque, literally loafs at freeway speeds, has tremendous reserve power.

THE RIVIERA
by Buick

America's bid for a great new international classic car

Note custom look inside. 4 bucket seats. Driver's seat—adjustable up, down, backward, forward—and the 7-position steering wheel for more driving comfort, both optional at extra cost.

The Riviera is the culmination of a five-year program by General Motors and Buick to introduce an American car of internationally classic proportion and quality.

The new automobile combines the best of old-world craftsmanship and coachwork with the high precision art of modern technology. The result is an automobile of the caliber one might expect to see priced at twelve thousand dollars on the international market, offered here for less than half that cost.

If you would like to drive the new Riviera and experience a sensation that words alone cannot describe, we suggest you see or telephone your nearest Buick dealer soon.

The heads of many in the automotive world turned with the introduction of the 1963 Buick Riviera.

1960s "solid gold"

1963 Buick Riviera two-door hardtop

6	5	4	3	2	1
$ 960	$2,880	$4,800	$10,800	$16,800	$24,000

Estimated values in today's marketplace are taken from the 2006 Standard Guide to Cars and Prices

1964 Pontiac Grand Prix **Tom Glatch**

1963-1969 Pontiac Grand Prix

Pontiac's first stab at a sports-personal car was the 1957 Bonneville. In 1957 especially, and in 1958 to a high degree, the Bonneville was a true specialty model. It was Star Chief fancy and Chieftain-sized to make it extra rich and sporty at the same time. In 1959, the excitement of the model name was capitalized on by making a Bonneville series. These cars were big and rich, but weren't as unique as the first two Bonnevilles. Pontiac took the original concept to create the Ventura, a small (now Catalina) car with the fancy Bonneville-type interior. The most powerful "Tempest" V-8s could be added to Ventura models as optional equipment.

The Ventura never generated tons of sales, but the concept had potential. In 1962, a limited edition Grand Prix moved into the sports-personal slot. This car also was a Bonnevillized Catalina, but with its unique Grand Prix identity. The "GP" had extremely clean body side styling, attractive checkered flag badges, an eye-catching anodized grille, solid color vinyl (called Morrokide) upholstery, standard front bucket seats, a center console and a colorful tachometer. This model retailed for $3,490 and buyers quickly scooped up 30,195 of them.

The standard engine in that first Grand Prix was a 303-hp version of the well-known 389-cube Poncho V-8. Pontiac's performance-minded buyers could opt for a 353-hp 421 V-8 with a Quadrajet carburetor or a 370-hp edition of the big engine with Tri-Power. The 120-inch Catalina wheelbase was used and both cars were 211.9 inches long. The GP was basically a Thunderbird for about $1,000 less. It created a sensation in the upper, sports-luxury strata of the medium-price-car class. The GP also helped bring customers to Pontiac dealerships in 1962. The company's dealer stock of cars averaged a 17 day supply versus and average of 37 days for the auto industry as a whole. *Ward's Automotive Yearbook* described the first GP as an "ultra two-door hardtop."

1963 Pontiac Grand Prix

The 1961 Ventura was a beautiful yet powerful car from the Pontiac Division of GM. **John Gunnell**

The '63 Grand Prix was restyled and retained the clean look with no side trim. The new grille emphasized negative space with flat black finish that made the few bright accents standout. The parking lamps were enclosed in the grille. Two unique GP touches were the use of grilled-over taillights mounted on the deck lid and a concave rear window treatment. Standard equipment included special solid color Morrokide upholstery, a wood-grained steering wheel, woodgrained dashboard trim, bucket type front seats and a center console with a vacuum gage. Grand Prix badges were seen on the rear fender sides. Bright moldings accented the rocker panels.

1966 Pontiac Grand Prix

"If you think the Pontiac Grand Prix gets by just on good looks, you've got some driving to do," warned a 1964 Pontiac advertisement. The long, low and wide look of 1963 was carried over. Deeply recessed grilles, rectangular front parking lamps and GP letters on the left-hand grille were new for 1964. The thin roofline and concave rear window were carried over to enhance the specialty Sports Coupe's distinctiveness and eye appeal. Twin bucket seats (front and rear), a center console, deep-pile carpeting and a floor shifter were standard. The 303-hp Trophy V-8 was still standard fare, but options up to 421 cid and 370 hp were available at extra cost. Buyers could select an optional four-speed gearbox or Hydra-Matic Drive. A drop in sales this year was due mainly to strike-related factory closings. Demand for GPs also was hurt by the new GTO and Catalina 2 + 2.

1962 Pontiac Grand Prix

The 1965 GP had a one-inch longer wheelbase and 1.6-inch longer overall length, a twin air-slot grille (with a unique, vertically divided, aluminized insert that incorporated rectangular parking lamps), vertical headlights, visor-like cut-back front fenders, a V-shaped hood with a prominent center bulge and curved side glass. The fin-shaped crease along the lower body side was trimmed with a wide stainless steel molding. The letters "GP" appeared on the left-hand lip of the hood and Grand

1969 Pontiac Grand Prix

1967 Pontiac Grand Prix convertible

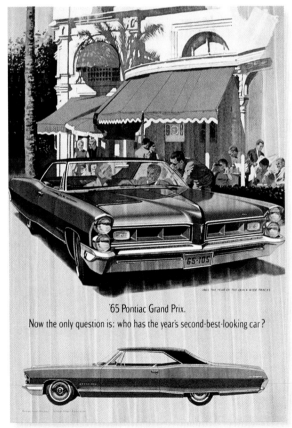

1965 Pontiac Grand Prix

Prix lettering was placed on the front fenders. A badge for further identification was placed on the sides of the rear fenders.

Styling changes for 1966 were subtle. Headlight extension caps provided a more integrated frontal appearance. The GP was distinguished by a wire mesh grille with rectangular parking lamps, "GP" front fender identification and long V-shaped emblems on the ribbed lower body panels. A monochromatic interior of deeply-piped Morrokide was featured. Standard equipment was the same as in 1965, except Strato Bucket seats were new. The same base engine was used.

An integral bumper-grille, recessed wipers, a crisp horizontal belt line and flared sculpturing between the doors and rear wheel openings were new-for-1967 GP design traits. Pontiac's sports-personal car also featured retracting headlights, front parking lamps hidden behind slits in the wedge-shaped front fenders and twin-slot taillights. Fender skirts and lower body accent moldings were seen as well. There were GP letters on the left-hand grille and Grand Prix rear fender lettering. Offered this year only was a GP convertible for $3,813 and only 5,856 of the ragtops were sold.

Only the GP Sport Coupe returned in 1968. Standard equipment included padded bucket seats with contoured backs and armrests, a center console and a 400-cid 350-hp four-barrel V-8. A 265-hp two-barrel "economy" V-8 could also be had. New styling elements included a peripheral front bumper, long horizontal bumper-integrated taillights, a down-swept rear deck and a new instrument panel. A "GP" badge appeared on the left-hand grille and on the right-hand corner of the deck lid. Engine badges were seen on the rocker panel moldings. When they didn't say 400, they identified a 376-hp 428.

The new-generation 1969 Grand Prix hardtop was built on an exclusive 118-inch wheelbase, three inches shorter than before. Overall length was reduced more than six inches. The GP was distinguished by an extra-long hood and short rear deck lid. It had a V-shaped grille, individually mounted headlights, an in-the-windshield radio antenna and flush outside door handles. The instrument panel wrapped around the driver in true aircraft style. You felt very "up close and personal" in this sports-personal car. An SJ option—named for the great classic Duesenberg— included a large-vale 428-cid V-8 that churned out a healthy 370 hp.

Leading the specialty car parade in 1969, the GP looked as if it had finally found its real identity as a smaller, even-more-personal rendition of the American sports coupe. Registrations for this new car topped the 1968 version by 88.5 percent (92,834 compared to 42,259). When set apart from other Pontiacs—like the Thunderbird was from other Fords—the GP found its greatest success to date.

There's really only one way to go Wide-Tracking in '68. Aren't you glad?

Pontiac's monopoly on Wide-Tracking goes unchallenged for the tenth consecutive year. However, success has not led to complacency on our part—as the '68 Grand Prix captured below so elegantly illustrates. For instance, the Grand Prix is endowed with upholstery of rich, supple Morrokide or combination cloth and Morrokide. Its doors and dash are adorned with Carpathian burled elm vinyl. And thick nylon-blend carpeting lies underfoot. But don't let Grand Prix's opulence and beautiful, sweeping lines dull your sense of adventure. For 350 hp from a 400-cu.-in. V-8 coupled to dual exhausts hints that this personal luxury car is equally at home in the world of concrete and asphalt. Grand Prix even comes with bucket seats, rich console and stick shift—floor-mounted, of course. But enough talk. Wide-Tracking is something that's meant to be experienced. And the only way you can go Wide-Tracking is to see your Pontiac dealer. Naturally.

Other equally handsome practitioners of the art of Wide-Tracking: Bonneville, Catalina, Brougham, Executive, Ventura, GTO, Le Mans, Tempest and the Five Firebirds.   Pontiac Motor Division.

Pontiac's 1968 Grand Prix gained a more luxurious appearance.

1960s "solid gold"

1963 Pontiac Grand Prix

6	5	4	3	2	1
$ 920	$2,760	$4,600	$10,350	$16,100	$23,000

Add 30 percent for 421-cid engine option and add 10 percent for aluminum wheel option.

Estimated values in today's marketplace are taken from the 2006 Standard Guide to Cars and Prices

1968 Olds Toronado   **Elton McFall**

1966-1969 Toronado

1967 Olds Toronado

The 1966 Toronado was innovative and it reintroduced front-wheel drive to America. Cars like the Ruxton and the Cord had offered front-wheel drive in the 1920s and '30s and it had last been seen on the 1937 Cord. Some European cars, like Citroen, used this drive system, but no automaker had combined front-wheel drive with a powerful engine like the Oldsmobile V-8. Some doubted the Toronado would drive suitably or last a long time. Today, we know front-wheel-drive is well suited to U.S. roads and reliable. Toronados were reliable. Bob Johnson of Amherst, Wisconsin, still drives his original, 20,000-mile Toronado and says it drives perfectly.

In the fall of 1965, there was no other car like the Toronado on the market. It featured a sleek, ground-hugging body. With a 119-inch wheelbase, the Toronado was 211 inches long from bumper to bumper. It measured 78.5 inches wide and stood just 52.8 inches high. Only the 1966 Corvair and Mustang were lower – and not by very much. Power in the Toronado came from a 425-cid V-8 that put out 385 hp and 475 foot-pounds of torque. The car weighed 4,496 pounds, about as much as a top-of-the-line Oldsmobile 98.

The 1966 Toronado had a long hood, a short rear deck and a modified fastback roof. The grille consisted of horizontal slats running across the front end. A new ventilation system eliminated the need for vent windows. Retractable headlights and a torsion-bar front suspension were incorporated. With no driveshaft hump, the front-wheel-drive Oldsmobile sat six people. According to Don Vorderman, writing in *Automobile Quarterly*, "A radically different look has been achieved with a minimum of fuss. There are no loose ends, no unresolved lines. The result is logical, imaginative and totally unique."

The Toronado was merchandised in standard and deluxe versions and sold reasonably well. Olds dealers made 33,204 calendar-year deliveries. The 1966 model took *Motor Trend's* "Car of the Year" award, *Car Life's* Award for Engineering Excellence and even came in third in Europe's "Car of the Year" competition. On March 16, 1966, a Toronado became the 100 millionth GM vehicle built in North America.

The Toronado was a driving machine easily capable of comfortable, safe cruising in excess of the century mark. Its top speed was in the 135-mph range. In his book *Cars of the '60s* automotive writer Richard M. Langworth described it as "probably the most outstanding single model of the 1960s." *Ward's 1966 Automotive Yearbook* called the Toronado, "Certainly the highlight of the year in both engineering and styling combined."

1966 Olds Toronado

1966 Olds Toronado

While sharing the bulk of its styling with the original version of 1966, the 1967 Toronado had a new grille featuring a cross-hatch pattern and new flush-with-the-hood doors for the retractable headlights. Buyers also found it had a slightly softer ride quality. Oldsmobile added front disc brakes to the options list and the use of a dual-circuit brake master cylinder was adopted. Now, if you lost braking action on two wheels, you still had two left with brakes. Oldsmobile also did something about the wide, heavy doors on the Toronado. A spring-operated "assistor" made it possible to swing them open with less effort. Options included bucket seats and a horizontal racing stripe.

Oldsmobile had its third best sales year in history in 1967, but the bulk of the business went to the mid-sized F-85. Toronado sales for the calendar year were 35.7 percent below the first-year deliveries. Calendar-year production of the front-wheel-drive model was held to 50 percent of the 1966 level and the number came in at 18,444 versus 37,420 in the first year. As in 1966, all Toronados were built at Oldsmobile's "home" plant in Lansing, Michigan.

A bolder looking split-in-two grille characterized the 1968 Toronado, which still used the original body introduced two years earlier. The taillights were moved into the rear bumper. Trim features were also updated. The 425-cid engine was replaced with a new 455-cid V-8 that came in two more-powerful versions. Both used a single four-barrel carburetor. The first produced 375 hp at 4600 rpm. It came linked to a three-speed automatic transmission. The more powerful engine produced 400 hp at 4800 rpm. It was actually part of the W-34 option package that also included a special cam and valve springs, a cold-air induction system, low restriction dual exhausts, a Y70 paint stripe package and a performance-calibrated Hydra-Matic 425 automatic transmission. Only 111 cars with the W-34 package were made. Lower axle drive ratios were also used in 1968. Toronados proved their performance potential by placing first, second and third in the Pike's Peak Hill Climb.

Oldsmobile set records in 1968, which became its best sales year in history up to that point. The company's total deliveries rose 17 percent and the Toronado showed a 26 percent gain with calendar-year sales of 26,826. The 100,000th front-wheel-drive Oldsmobile was built on Friday. November 29, 1968 in the division's main plant in Lansing, Michigan. Early in 1986, an electrically-heated rear window became optional. It was quieter and better than a blower.

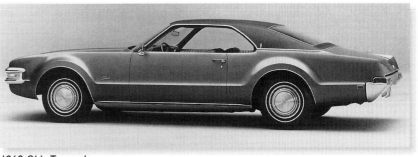

1969 Olds Toronado

CHAPTER THREE

The Rocket Action Cars are out front again!

1967 Olds Toronado

With three and a half more inches of overall length (214.9 inches total), the 1969 Toronado was a considerably larger car. The extra length was used to stretch the rear quarters and deck lid out more than before and to provide a more "formal" styling theme. There was no change to the 119-inch wheelbase. A new grille with an elongated egg crate pattern (instead of 1968's honeycomb pattern mesh) was used. The interior had a much richer look and ride quality was improved. The same engine options were back.

For 1969 Toronado sales hit 27,547 cars for the calendar year, a 2.7 percent increase over 1968. According to the Oldsmobile Club of America's Toronado Chapter, an estimated 2,800 cars got the W-34 option package in 1969.

1960s "solid gold"

1966 Oldsmobile Toronado Custom

6	5	4	3	2	1
$ 740	$2,220	$3,700	$8,330	$12,950	$18,500

Estimated values in today's marketplace are taken from the 2006 Standard Guide to Cars and Prices

1960-1969 Corvette

1962 Corvette **Tom Glatch**

If you told someone in the 1950s that the Corvette would become a luxurious sports-personal car, they probably would have laughed. The original 1953 Corvette

1962 Corvette with hardtop in place **David Lyon**

was designed as an American sports car. When purists scorned the car's Powerglide transmission, smooth styling and other ammenities, Chevrolet hired Zora Arkus-Duntov as chief engineer and saved the "'Vette" by giving it a harder edge and a gutsier flavor. It became a true world-class enthusiast's machine.

Corvette's character changed in the 1960s. The fiberglass-bodied Chevy started the decade as a bugs-in-your-teeth roadster and ended it as a Grand Touring car. Big-block V-8s were available to provide all sorts of go power, but go-fast Corvettes were designed more for the drag strip than roads with scary S-curves. Corvettes came out of the decade different than when they went in.

The 1960 Corvette looked much the same as the 1959 model. A new rear sway bar improved the car's handling. The only model listed was a convertible with a $3,563 price tag, available with a snap-on hardtop. The Corvette came with a tachometer, a small-block V-8 engine, dual exhaust, carpeting, seat belts, an outside rearview mirror and an electric clock. A 1960 Corvette with its base 283-cid 230-hp V-8 could go from 0-to-60 in 8.4 seconds and do the quarter mile in 16.1 seconds at 89 mph. There were six optional 283 V-8s up to 315 hp, one with dual four-barrel carbs and four with fuel-injection.

The "Route 66" television series, featuring Martin Milner and George Maharis driving their 1960 Corvette across the country, debuted this season. The popular show was an ongoing advertisement for Chevy's only two-passenger job. The "M" boys became famous and so did the car they drove as many people under 30 dreamed of owning a 'Vette and driving it coast to coast.

The 1961 Corvette sported a hood badge showing crossed racing flags over a "V." It symbolized the car's V-8 performance. There were five engines available, one (230 hp) with a single four-barrel, two (245 and 270 hp) with dual-quad carb set ups and two (275 and 315 hp) fuelies. A refined, thin, vertical and horizontal bar grille and a new duck-tail rear end treatment with four cylindrical taillights

1968 Corvertte L 89 coupe **Tom Glatch**

quickly set the new Vette apart from its predecessor. This design foretold the Sting Ray—and also added trunk space. The exhaust pipes now exited under the car, rather than through bumper ports. It was the last year wide whitewall tires were available and also the last year a contrasting color could be ordered from the factory for the concave side coves.

The most noticeable changes for 1962 were cleaning up the side coves (no more tinsel), a flat black grille and ribbed chrome rocker panel moldings. Colors were solid only this year. Engine offerings dropped to four 327-cid versions in place of 283. Three engines used a single four-barrel carb and one was a fuelie. Standard output was up to 250 hp and the fuel-injected 360-hp option was tops. A 1962 Corvette with the latter motor and a 3.70:1 rear axle could go from 0-to-60 mph in 5.9 seconds, do the quarter mile in 14.5 seconds at 104 mph with an estimated maximum speed of 150 mph!

The dramatically new 1963 Corvette Sting Ray evolved from a racing car called the Mitchell Sting Ray. Bill Mitchell replaced Harley Earl as head of GM styling

in 1958. He thought it was important to race the 'Vette, so he persuaded general manager Ed Cole to sell him the chassis of a 1957 Corvette SS "mule" for $1. Mitchell had designer Larry Shinoda create a body for the Sting Ray race car inspired by the sea creature of the same name.

Oohs and aahs went to a "split-window" fastback coupe. Shinoda created the "split-window," which Mitchell loved, though Duntov was against its vision-blocking look. The style was offered only one year and is very collectible.

On both ragtops and coupes, the front fenders had two long non-functional louvers resembling brake-cooling ducts. The rear deck resembled the 1962 model, but the rest of the car was totally new. Hide-away headlights were housed in an electrically-operated panel and enhanced the car's aerodynamics. The recessed fake hood louvers were decorative only. The interior had circular gauges with black faces. Firsts included optional knock-off wheels, air conditioning and leather seats. All four engines were based on the 327 offering 250, 300, 340 and 360 hp. The 360-hp job carried Rochester fuel injection.

This 1960 Corvette once was owned by actor Burt Reynolds. **Tom Glatch**

The L-79 Corvette had a 350-hp 327-cid V-8 and four speed transmission. **Tom Glatch**

Styling was cleaned up a bit for 1964. The previous year's distinctive rear window divider was replaced by a solid piece of glass. The fake hood vents were eliminated and the roof vents were restyled. A three-speed fan was available in the coupe to aid in ventilation. A quartet of 327-cid V-8s was offered again with 250, 300, 365 and 375 hp. The top engine option was fuel injected.

Three slanting louvers on the sides of the front fenders, a blacked-out grille with horizontal bars and different rocker panel moldings were the main styling changes for 1965. A new hood without indentations was standard. A new midyear option, the 396-cid "big-block"

V-8, used a hood with a funnel-shaped "power blister." The instruments were changed to a flat-dial, straight-needle design with an aircraft look. The seats had improved support and Corvettes now had one-piece molded inside door panels. A four-wheel disc-brake system was standard. Fuel injection was phased out at the end of the year. New options included side exhausts and a telescoping steering wheel. The 327 came in 250-, 300-, 350-, 365- and 375-hp versions (all with a four-barrel except the 375-hp fuelie) and the 396 produced 425 hp.

A plated, cast-metal grille with an "egg crate" insert, ribbed rocker panel moldings, chrome-plated exhaust bezels, spoke wheel covers, a vinyl-covered headliner and lack of roof vents characterized the 1966 Corvette. The front fender sides again had three slanting vertical air louvers. Corvettes equipped with the new 427-cid V-8 came with a power-bulge hood. The base 327 was up to 300 hp. A higher-compression version hit 350 hp. The big-block 427 came in 390- and 425-hp editions.

Some consider the clean-styled 1967 to be the most handsome "midyear" Sting Ray. 427s had a large front-opening air scoop over the center bulge instead of a funnel. Five functional vertical fender louvers slanted forward. Minor interior changes included moving the

1965 Corvette 396 convertible **Tom Glatch**

1965 Corvette L-79 convertible **Tom Glatch**

1963 Corvette Sting Ray "fuelie" Z06 coupe **Tom Glatch**

1969 Corvette L 79 engine **Tom Glatch**

parking brake from the dash to the console. A new foam-and-fiber headliner was used. Four-way flashers, "lane-change" signal lights, larger interior vent ports and folding seat-back latches were new. Two round taillights were on each side and the back-up lights were moved to the center of the rear. The optional finned aluminum wheels were redesigned with a one-year-only, non-knock-off center. Two 327 and six 427 engines were offered. Two of the big-blocks were rare – the 16-built 435-hp Tri-Power L89 and the 20-built 560-hp four-barrel L88

The Corvette got its first major redo since 1963. "Corvette '68 . . . all different all over," said Chevy. The Sting Ray name was not used. There was a new tunnel-roof coupe with a removable back window and a two-piece detachable "T-top." The convertible's optional hardtop had a glass window. The hidden headlights were now vacuum-operated. The wipers also disappeared. Except for the rocker panels, the sides were chrome-free. Push-button door handles were new. The blunt rear deck contained four round taillights with the word "Corvette" printed in chrome in between. The wraparound, wing-like rear bumper and license plate holder treatment resembled the '67 models. Engine selections were about the same, except the 425-hp 427 was gone.

After a year's absence, the Stingray name (now spelled as one word) re-appeared on the front fenders of the 1969 'Vettes. The back-up lights were now integrated into the center taillights. Front and rear disc brakes, headlight washers, a center console, wheel trim rings, carpeting and all-vinyl upholstery were standard equipment. Eight engines were again supplied. Small-block cars got a new 350-cid V-8 that came in 300-, 350- and 370-hp versions. The large-block monsters were all 427s with 390, 400, 430 and 435 advertised hp. The aluminum head version was rated conservatively. In addition, the "430-hp" L88 option was up around 560 hp again, but Chevy played down the real number and officially used the 430 hp rating.

1966 Corvette 427 convertible **Tom Glatch**

1967 Corvette L 71 convertible **Tom Glatch**

1960s "solid gold"

1967 Corvette Sting Ray convertible

6	5	4	3	2	1
$2,320	$6,960	$11,600	$26,100	$40,600	$58,000

Add $4,500 for air conditioning. Add 30 percent for 390-hp 327 engine, 50 percent for 400-hp 427 engine, 70 percent for 435-hp 427 engine. Add $3,000 for a hardtop. The L88 and L89 Corvettes are inestimable. In 2004. a 1969 Corvette L-89 convertible sold for $169, 560 at Barrett-Jackson's Scottsdale auction.

Estimated values in today's marketplace are taken from the 2006 Standard Guide to Cars and Prices

1963-1969 Avanti and Avanti II

Designer Raymond Loewy stood proudly next to the 1963 Avanti he designed.

The Studebaker Avanti was conceived as a way to save the South Bend, Indiana automaker. Industrial designer Raymond Loewy guided a team of talented designers in the production of a Euro-styled Grand Touring car that could change Studebaker's musty and stodgy image. Studebaker president Sherwood Egbert asked for a closed four-seat car with an aerodynamic shape. He got a milestone design that survived the company.

Loewy hadn't worked for Studebaker since his 1956 redesign of the Hawk series. So he gathered designers John Ebstein, Robert Andrews and Tom Kellogg at a house in Palm Springs, California and sat down to write a new chapter in automotive styling history. What his crew came up with was a startlingly different look that literally stopped people in their tracks on seeing an Avanti in the 1960s. Loewy's scale model went to production nearly unchanged.

In profile, the body resembled a horizontal Coke bottle, narrow in front, bulging over the front wheels, then tapering in the center and flaring out at the rear. It had large glass areas and a flat roof with a built-in roll bar. The front fenders were angular, with flat edges. There was no grille. The front consisted of V-shaped flat panels that slanted forward at the bottom and carried large headlamps in large, square, bright-finished housings. The hood had an asymmetrical hump. Inside were bucket seats and aircraft-like interior layout with lots of crash padding.

Three engines were offered for 1963: the base R1, the supercharged R2 and the seldom-seen and expensive R3. The R1 was a nice, if somewhat unexciting 280-cid 240-hp V-8. The highly-promoted R3 was rare. The R2 was readily available and only $210. While it lacked the brute force of other muscle cars, the use of a small, supercharged V-8 and the clever use of existing Studebaker parts created a car with fast acceleration and great handling.

The Avanti got a publicity boost from a successful assault on existing American speed records. In August 1962, an R3 established several new marks including a 168.15-mph two-way Flying Mile. Early in 1963, a near-stock four-speed R2 averaged 158.15 mph through the measured mile. *Road and Track* reported a 7.3-second 0-to-60 mph time for the four-speed R2. In addition to being fast, the Avanti was rare. With a model-year run of just 3,834 units, Studebaker's sports-personal car was a true limited-edition vehicle.

Studebaker didn't have the resources to make alterations in the 1964 Avanti. There wasn't even a distinct end to the production of 1963 models. The changes that were made were kind of phased in. Round heater, defroster and vent knobs were a characteristic of most—but not all—1964s. The majority of cars — some say all but the first 59 built — had square headlight housings.

1964 Studebaker Avanti

1963 Studebaker Avanti

Performance options for 1964 included a new R4 engine. The R1 was the base 289-cid 240-hp four-barrel V-8 with a 10.25:1 compression ratio. A lower 9.0:1 compression ratio accompanied the supercharged 289-hp R2 engine. With 304.5 cubic inches, the supercharged R3 developed 335 hp and was used in only 10 cars. Even rarer was the 280-hp dual-quad carbureted R4, which was installed on only one car. To promote the 1964s, Andy Granatelli returned to the Bonneville Salt Flats in Utah with a fleet of Avantis. He broke his own record by driving an R3-engined car 170.78 mph. Studebaker President Sherwood H. Egbert managed to turn in a 168-mph pass.

Unfortunately, Egbert was more successful at piloting the Avanti than he was piloting the company's course. In December 1963, Studebaker-Packard closed its factory in South Bend. Some Studebakers continued to be built in Hamilton, Ontario into the 1966 model year, but Avantis were not. When the last of the 809 models made in 1964 was constructed, the *Studebaker* Avanti was done for.

The dramatic interior of the 1964 Studebaker Avanti still looks modern 40 years later.

1964 Studebaker Avanti

CHAPTER THREE

These shells influenced investors to independently produce the Avanti II after Studebaker ended production of the car.

Avanti II

Nate Altmen, a Studebaker dealer in South Bend, had a spot in his heart for the Avanti and decided to try to save the car. Nate tried to get other American automakers interested in it, but had absolutely no luck. He decided to team up with his partner Leo Newman and build the car in South Bend. In February 1964, Newman & Altman bought six buildings that were part of the old Studebaker factory. They contacted Avanti body maker Molded Fiberglass in Ashtabula, Ohio, and found the company still had some 150 Avanti bodies left.

Altman appointed former Studebaker chief engineer Eugene Hardig vice president in charge of engineering and continued to put together a financing arrangement to get the company going. On July 1, 1964, all rights and equipment needed to make Avantis were purchased. On July 22, 1965, the first Avanti II was finished. The following August 2 the $7,000 car had its public introduction in South Bend.

Studebakers were still being manufactured in Canada, but no one knew how long that would go on, so a Chevy engine was selected for the Avanti II. The 327-cid V-8 was taller than the Studebaker engine, so the fenders were modified.

The Avanti II was available in a wide variety of personally-picked colors and buyers were invited to supply their own interior fabrics or choose from about 400 options. Each car was built for the individual buyer and each job was priced accordingly. There was no set assembly schedule and the people who built the cars were told to take their time needed to do the job properly. The company had little luck selling the cars through dealers. Owners then were offered a commission to "sell" other owners. In the end, direct sales seemed to be the best way to go.

According to the *Standard Catalog of American Cars 1946-1975*, a total of 45 Avanti IIs were sold in 1965, followed by 59 in 1966, 66 in 1967, 100 in 1968 and 92 in 1969. By 1969, the 350-cid Chevrolet engine was made an option. Newman & Altman and their heirs continued producing the Avanti II in South Bend until the early 1980s. In October of 1982, real estate developer Steve Blake bought the company and ran it until March 1986, when it was sold to Michael Kelly. John Cafaro purchased Avanti II in 1988 and kept it alive until 1991. A small number of Avanti IIs were produced between 2000 and 2004 and there is a new 2005 model. The important point is the timeless design that looks as modern today as it did in 1963.

1968 Avanti II

1960s "solid gold"

1963 Studebaker Avanti Sport Coupe

6	5	4	3	2	1
$1,000	$3,000	$5,000	$11,250	$17,500	$25,000

Estimated values in today's marketplace are taken from the 2006 Standard Guide to Cars and Prices

The Marlin, along with the Barracuda from Plymouth, had buyers thinking of new angles in 1965.

1965-1967 AMC Marlin

The 1965-1/2 AMC Marlin had the hot fastback look of the Mustang 2 + 2, but what was going on here? Ramblers were supposed to be e-c-o-n-o-m-y models . . . not sports-personal cars. They were supposed to supply basic, cheap transportation, not upscale luxury and fancy trappings. The Marlin looked different because it was designed to change what the initials AMC implied.

The Marlin roofline bowed on the 1964 Tarpon show car, which used the compact Rambler American's 106-inch wheelbase. The Tarpon was aimed at Plymouth's Valiant-based Barracuda and the new Ford Mustang, but the AMC brass blew Dick Teague's design up in size and put it on the mid-size Rambler Classic chassis. From the beltline down, the two cars had the same body.

This was a logical decision in 1965. As the American economy had grown healthy again, cars were growing,

too. The AMC powers that be thought they needed to compete with the Thunderbird, the Buick Riviera and the Pontiac Grand Prix, rather than the Mustang. The 112-inch-wheelbase Classic had been restyled and grew about 5 inches longer. It had distinctions from the four-inch-longer Ambassador, which had more individual styling.

Available only in the single body style, the Marlin six listed for $2,841 and weighed 3100 pounds. Instead of stressing go-power, the Marlin emphasized comfort and roominess. It featured an Ambassador instrument panel and could be optioned with individual reclining front seats or slim bucket-type seats with a center console or center cushion. Base engine was the same new 232-cid 155-hp Torque Command in-line six used in the Ambassador.

By adding $90, the Marlin buyer could get a car with the smallest of two Gen-1 AMC V-8s. This was a mild

The Marlin was heavily influenced by the 1964 Tarpon show car built on the smaller American platform.

287-cid 198-hp version. Priced a bit higher, around $82 above the small V-8, the second engine was the 327-cid 270-hp V-8 that had been around since the days of the '58 Ambassador.

A three-speed manual transmission was standard. Cars without bucket seats could get overdrive or a three-speed Flash-O-Matic transmission. Cars with a console and bucket seats had an interesting Twin-Stick overdrive option offering five forward speeds. You could also get a Shift-Command Flash-O-Matic that could be shifted manually. AMC retained torque-tube-drive. There were coil springs at the rear. Power disc front brakes and flanged rear drums were standard. Though no screamer, the 327 Marlin was sporty enough. Mechanix Illustrated's Tom McCahill reported 0 to 60 mph in 9.7 seconds. The 1965 Marlin got 10,327 orders in the short run after its February 1965 debut.

The 1966 Marlin received a new grille and no longer carried the Rambler name. Some previously standard features like power steering and brakes became optional. This allowed AMC to cut the list price to $2,601 for the six and $2,707 for the V-8. Unfortunately, Dodge introduced the Charger in mid-1966. It used the same formula featuring a fastback body on an intermediate chassis. The Charger easily outsold the Marlin, which found only 4,547 customers.

Styling-wise, the 1967 Marlin was cleaner and smoother looking. A new front-end treatment incorporated rally lights into a horizontal grille. The rear fenders had a "Coke bottle" shape characteristic of other sporty 1960s cars. AMC's "big fish" was even bigger than before, gaining six inches in wheelbase to 118 inches. Overall length got a 6 1/2-inch stretch. This added approximately 350 lbs. and did little for the car's power-to-weight ratio. A brand new 343 V-8 was an option designed to offset the added size and weight.

A big-engined 1967 Marlin gave "Joe Lunchbox" a ticket to ride in a sporty two-door fastback with a five-liter V-8 for just over $3,000. The big 343 was a bored-out version of the AMC 290 and cost just $91 extra in a Marlin.

It had a single four-barrel carb and generated 280 ponies at 4800 rpm with 365 ft. lbs. of torque at 3000 rpm. While it wasn't the hottest car-and-engine combination on the road, the power was up, up, up from last year's 327-cid V-8.

Hot Rod wrung out a Marlin with this engine and naturally compared it to the Dodge Charger. The car turned in a 0-to-60 mph time of 9.6 seconds and a 17.6-second quarter mile at 82 mph. The writer compared this to the performance of a Charger with the base 383-cid two-barrel V-8. The same article mentioned a 343-cid 320-hp heavy-duty equipment option for the Marlin, indicating a hairier engine was available on special order. If any cars were sold this way, they are extremely difficult to find today.

Unlike the Mustangs, Barracudas and Chargers that it competed with, the 1967 Marlin did not come standard with bucket seats. They were $177 extra. A center console, priced at $113, was mandatory when the reclining buckets were ordered. Even vinyl upholstery was optional at $25. By the time a Marlin was all dressed up, the price tag was in the $3,500 range. Pretty sneaky.

Perhaps it was predictable that AMC would run into problems marketing such a big car to anyone, let alone sporty-car buffs. The company had firmly established the image of being an expert in the small-car field. So the Marlin actually represented a double leap—one into performance and the other into personalization. When the jump was first made, the Marlin got off to a good start, but It bottomed out at 2,545 units produced in 1967.

While the Marlin wasn't a commercial success, it became a unique and rare automobile. Total production of cars was under 20,000 and those sold with the optional "big" V-8 were in the low hundreds. Survivors are hard to find.

1966 AMC Marlin fastback

The new Marlin showed its large glass window and canted roofline
first when it was introduced in 1965.

1960s "solid gold"

1965 AMC Marlin fastback

6	5	4	3	2	1
$ 580	$1,740	$2,900	$6,530	$10,150	$14,500

Estimated values in today's marketplace are taken from the 2006 Standard Guide to Cars and Prices

1962 Studebaker Gran Turismo Hawk

1960-1964 Studebaker Hawk

Saturday at the supermarket was always my favorite day in the 1960s. The night shifts during the week were rough. I lived in Staten Island, N.Y., but I went to high school in Brooklyn. That was a bus ride, a ferry ride and three stops on the subway in the morning. In the afternoon it meant subway to the ferry, ferry to the Island, and bus to work, then two buses home after the stored closed at 9 pm. On Saturday my dad drove me to work in the 1957 Chrysler Saratoga, I got to work eight hours and the lady with the shiny jet-black Studebaker Grand Turismo hardtop was certain to show up. What a gorgeous car! It was so pretty that it made working weekends worth it.

You just didn't see many Studebaker Hawks on Staten Island and this car always looked like it was brand new. I'm sure that the owner went to the car wash every Saturday morning, before coming to visit us at the Food Farm. It was almost as if she shined the car just to show it off. I don't think it was ever left in the parking lot where a stray cart could scratch it. It was always parked in the fire lane up front. She must have known no fire marshal would ticket such a car!

1961 Studebaker Hawk   **David Lyon**

It's amazing to think the stylish-in-the-1960s GT started life as the 1953 Loewy Starlight Coupe and that another industrial designer – Brooks Stevens – gave it such a great facelift that it looked far from an almost "teen-age" design. In 1956, the car was updated with a classic-looking radiator grille (because Studebaker dealers were selling Mercedes-Benz cars at the time.) In 1957, someone (Raymond Loewy had been "fired" by then) decided to graft on concave tail fins. They aged quickly, but at first the fins seemed like a pretty good idea. They modernized the car to 1957 trends and squeezed a few more years out of body molds Studebaker couldn't throw out.

The automaker also turned the Hawk into a real deck of cards in the late 1950s, with Power Hawk coupes, Sky Hawk Hardtops and Golden Hawk specialty cars. In 1957, the six-cylinder and small V-8 series offered a Silver Hawk coupe and a Silver Hawk hardtop, while the Silver Hawk coupe and the Golden Hawk hardtop available with the big 289-cid V-8. In 1958, the six-cylinder Silver Hawk hardtop vanished. In 1959, only the Silver Hawk coupe was left and it came with a six or the 259-cid V-8. Only 7,788 were made and no wonder – it was hard to figure out what you wanted and how to order it.

1963 Studebaker Gran Turismo Hawk

1964 Studebaker Gran Turismo Hawk

For 1960, the coupe became just the Hawk. Imitation louvers were used on the front edge of the fins along with Hawk emblems that stood out against a red background. The six-cylinder Hawk was sold only outside North America. The V-8 version was also a coupe – not a hardtop – and the 259 V-8 was standard. You could get the 289 at extra cost. When Studebaker counted how many it made, no one was smiling. Only 227 sixes and 4,280 V-8s departed the factory in South Bend, Indiana. For 1961, things stayed the same, but the numbers were worse: 266 sixes and 3,708 V-8s. It was time to simplify things and somebody called Brooks Stevens in Milwaukee.

The new Gran Turismo Hawk was one of the great industrial designer's best projects. Stevens blended the best aspects of the renowned Loewy coupe with the classic elegance of Mercedes. It was the perfect marriage of the design characteristics of the world's oldest automaker with a great shape from America's oldest builder of wheeled vehicles. Actually, the work involved was basic and simple. Stevens smoothed out the front fenders, shaved off the fins and replaced a 1950s-style turret top with a pure 1960s formal roofline. By tastefully highlighting the design with bright metal and a neat interior that out-Chryslered Chrysler, Stevens wound up with a profile that could drive any grocery boy wild.

Production of the Hawk more than doubled in 1962 to 8,787 cars. Unfortunately, Studebaker's ill health couldn't support the car's showroom momentum. Simply put, Studebaker had fewer showrooms in 1963, when 3,958 GT

Hawks were produced. By 1964, the production count was down to 1,772 cars. And that was the end of the road for the GT – and for Studebakers built in the U.S. Production continued for a few more years in Canada, but everyone knew it was over.

The Hawk was given a serious facelift by the famed Brook Stevens, here with his creation which was christened the Gran Turismo Hawk.

1960s "solid gold"

1962 Studebaker Gran Turismo Hawk

6	5	4	3	2	1
$ 880	$2,640	$4,400	$9,900	$15,400	$22,000

Estimated values in today's marketplace are taken from the 2006 Standard Guide to Cars and Prices

1963 Studebaker Gran Turismo Hawk

1967-1969 Front-Wheel-Drive Eldorado

1967 Cadillac Eldorado

The 1967 Cadillac Eldorado was a completely new front-wheel-drive six-passenger coupe. It was described as a "sports-styled" automobile and the first car to combine front-wheel-drive, variable-ratio power steering and automatic level control. The new Eldorado used the standard Cadillac V-8. It replaced the Fleetwood Eldorado Convertible and had its own shortened 120-inch wheelbase.

Built off the Oldsmobile Toronado platform and sharing the same basic body shell, the all-new Eldorado was shorter and lower than even the smallest Cadillacs, but could provide full six-passenger seating because of its drive train layout. Concealed, horizontally-mounted headlights were featured. An improved fresh-air system eliminated the need for front ventipanes. The rear windows slid back into the roof structure. The typical assortment of Fleetwood extra equipment was standard on Eldorados as well. The hardtop coupe carried a $6,277 price and weighed 4,570 pounds. It had a 120-inch wheelbase. Overall length was 221 inches. The tread widths were 63.5 inches front and 63.0 rear.

The 429-cid Cadillac V-8 was fitted to the Eldorado's front-wheel-drive platform with changes in the oil pan, exhaust manifolds, accessory and drive belt layout and engine mount system. It had dual exhaust, but a single outlet muffler and tailpipe arrangement. The engine was rated for 340 hp. The Eldorado shared 1967 Cadillac technical changes such as Mylar-backed circuitry, a bigger power brake booster, a slide-out fuse box, an improved automatic headlight dimmer and braided rayon brake hoses. It was the only model in the line to offer the front disc brake option.

To produce front-wheel-drive Eldorados, a new dedicated assembly line was set up towards the end of the summer of 1966. Thanks to the popularity of the new sports-personal car, Cadillac sales for a single month passed the 20,000-unit level for the first time in the company's history. From the start, the Eldorado was viewed as the ultimate Cadillac. It made money from day one. Model-year production hit 17,930 units and helped give Cadillac a strong 2.6 percent share of total U.S. production. The attention-getting "Eldo" also helped build showroom traffic and sell other Cadillacs. Calendar-year production was 20,822 Eldorados. Cadillac dealer sales were recorded as 19,799 Eldorados.

The 1968 Eldorado had the front parking lights located to the leading edge of the fenders, where they were changed to a vertical mounting. To accommodate recessed windshield wipers, the hood was lengthened by 4-1/2 inches. On the rear fenders, small round safety lights were now affixed. The design of the lens for the front cornering lights (formerly vertically ribbed) was modified. Eldorado equipment included power rear vent windows, power front disc brakes and retractable headlights. Gone from the rear roof pillar, but not the hood and deck lid, were the wreath and crest-style Fleetwood emblems.

Interior trimmings included diamond-pattern cloth-and-vinyl upholstery or Deauville cloth upholstery with vinyl bolsters in four color choices or genuine leather. Rosewood appliques decorated the dash panel.

The new 472-cid V-8, with 525 pound-feet of torque, made it possible to spin the Eldorado's front-driven wheels on smooth, dry surfaces. The big V-8 had a 4.30 x 4.06-inch bore and stroke, a 10.5:1 compression ratio, a single Rochester four-barrel carburetor and dual exhausts. It generated 375 hp at 4400 rpm. Spring rates were slightly lowered to give a more cushiony ride.

1968 Cadillac Eldorado

1968 Cadillac Eldorado

Despite a 21-day United Auto Workers strike at the Fisher Body Fleetwood plant in Detroit in November, the hot-selling Eldorado helped keep the nose pointed up at Cadillac. Model-year production hit a record for the fourth year in a row and included 24,528 Eldorados. The Edorado's share of the total U.S. car market increased from 0.2 to 0.3. Calendar-year production included 23,136 Eldorados. Dealer sales for the calendar-year were 22,616 Eldorados.

The front-wheel-drive Eldorado continued to be offered as a single model in 1969. Production of the Eldorado was transferred from the Fleetwood plant in Detroit to the Fisher Body plant in Euclid, Ohio. It remained a six-passenger, two-door hardtop riding a shorter wheelbase than standard Cadillacs. A new cross-hatch grille was used and was now separated from the headlights. The dual headlights had become part of the body design and were fully exposed and stationary. The base price was $6,711.

A fifth straight Cadillac yearly sales record was set and calendar-year deliveries went over 250,000 cars for the first time in history. Eldorado sales climbed 17.6 percent. Model-year production of 23,333 Eldorados was counted. Cadillac dealer sales for the calendar-year were 25,497 Eldorados.

1969 Cadillac Eldorado

1969 Cadillac Eldorado

1960s "solid gold"

1967 Fleetwood Eldorado

6	5	4	3	2	1
$ 760	$2,280	$3,800	$8,550	$13,300	$19,000

Estimated values in today's marketplace are taken from the 2006 Standard Guide to Cars and Prices

1969 Cadillac Eldorado

The 1960s . . . Luxury Cars

In the early days of motoring all cars were a luxury. Then Ford's spindly Model T put a car within reach of most American families and the automotive industry started building vehicles for every purse and purpose. Over the years prior to World War II, more that 5,500 separate brands of automobiles hit the market. At the top of the heap were the luxury cars designed to transport the rich and famous to the boardroom or the beach.

To illustrate their stature among such a wide range of product, the earliest luxury automobiles were large in both size and power. Dominating this market segment were the three Ps – Packard, Pierce-Arrow and Peerless. The 1930 Pierce-Arrow Custom Eight Limousine rode a 144-inch wheelbase, cost $5,160 and used a 132-hp straight eight engine. The most expensive 1930 Chevrolet sedan had a 107-inch wheelbase, a $675 price tag and a 40-hp overhead-valve six.

The true luxury cars of the Depression Era were really something. Buyers visited a salon or showroom to order a chassis with an engine, hood and radiator, but no body. Then custom coachwork was selected to fit the chassis. The resulting car may have been one of very few exactly like it and could – as in the case of one special Duesenberg – cost up to "Twenty Grand." The result was paint, upholstery and equipment that was specifically selected for that car!

By the time World War II broke out these "Grand Classics" were vanishing. Duesenberg, Franklin, Marmon, Peerless, Pierce-Arrow and numerous other independent luxury carmakers had gone the way of the Great Gatsby. Alone was Packard and the luxury cars associated with the major automakers – General Motors' Cadillac Division, Ford's Lincoln branch and the Chrysler-built Imperial. Nash and Hudson had fairly luxurious models, but they competed more with Buick and Oldsmobile than Cadillac, Lincoln and Imperial.

During the 1950s, Cadillac was able to continue its role as the dominant player in the luxury-car niche. Packard produced some beautiful competitors, but could not survive on high-end sales alone and couldn't crack the "downstream" market without damaging its upstream image. Both Lincoln and Imperial lost their way as the decade rolled on. Cadillac seemed to do everything just right. It kept its luxury image without growing stodgy, because it was GM's leading innovator. The company used its most expensive model to showcase the "all-new" features coming the next year. This left the impression that Cadillac was always "ahead of the curve" in innovation.

The 10 most expensive cars in America in 1960 fell into the "luxury car" category and offered just 14 body styles among them. Eight of the 10 offered a four-door sedan or sedan-limousine. In addition, there were four four-door hardtops, two two-door hardtops and a pair of convertibles:

1960's Highest-Priced Cars

4D Sedan	4D sedan	4D HT	2D HT	Convertible
Cadillac 60S Brougham	--	$12,000	--	--
Lincoln Limousine	$9,386	--	--	--
Cadillac Limousine	$8,950	--	--	--
Cadillac 8-pass. Sedan	$8,750	--	--	--
Lincoln Formal Sedan	$8,435	--	--	--
Cadillac Eldorado Seville	--	--	$6,817	--
Cadillac Eldorado Biarritz	--	--	--	$6,817
Lincoln-Continental	$6,267	$6,267	$6,037	$6,462
Imperial LeBaron	$5,770	$5,770	--	--
Cadillac 60 Special	--	$5,700	--	--

These are introductory factory retail prices without tax, delivery and handling charges.

1969 Mercury Marquis convertible **Phil Hall Collection**

was at its highest for any year except 1958."

By 1962, there was no doubt that the tides had turned. Strong buyer interest after the introduction of 1962 models in the fourth quarter of 1961 helped set an all-time industry sales record for that particular period. Model-year production in the high-priced-car category leapt to 209,039 units or a strong 3.13 percent of total industry production. Even among the popular compact cars, the fancier models were selling better than the bare-bones bargain-basement specials. Also hitting record levels were sales of "luxury" extras like power steering, automatic transmission, bucket seats and air conditioning.

In 1960, a total of 187,586 cars priced at $4,401 or more were made in the U.S. That total included the luxury car in the first chart plus a sprinkling of "standard" Lincolns and Premieres, Cadillac 62s, all three Imperials, the Chrysler New Yorker convertible and station wagon and the Chrysler 300-F specialty car. To industry observers at the time, it may have looked like the luxury niche was going to be less important in the 1960s, but nothing could have been further from the truth. The 1960 numbers reflected the influence of the 1957 and 1958 recession and that the new compact cars were attracting buyer attention. Who knew that the economy would quickly rebound and that America's taste would turn back towards big cars?

In 1961, the production of cars priced at $4,401 or higher slid back to 178,733 units, but this was more of a reflection of an overall 10 percent decline in auto manufacturing than anything else. In fact, *Ward's 1962 Automotive Yearbook* noted, "Attesting to the growing status of the fine car in the U.S. market, and particularly to Cadillac's 'solid gold' image, the company was the most consistent car maker in the industry during 1961. While production fell 6.7 percent to 148,298 units from record 1960 output of 158,941, the company's share of the industry

"Luxury, Performance and Size Keynote '63 Models" was the headline of an article in *Ward's 1963 Automotive Yearbook* that compared 1963 to the "Luxury Car Years" of 1929, 1941 and 1958. The article noted the lack of major facelifts or price increases for 1963 models "But the major trends in auto marketing which highlighted '62 model sales – the longer look in car length and emphasis on the luxury models – persisted for '63," it advised.

In 1963, *Ward's* expounded on what the terms "prestige" and "luxury" car meant. It described the *prestige car* as one that "is elegantly appointed and improves the estimation of the owners, yet is not extremely high-priced or snobbish. Primarily, one has to think of Cadillac, Lincoln Continental, Imperial and a few others as 'luxury-priced' automobiles." In *Ward's* opinion, the luxury-car market was "static" since it represented only 2.8 percent of total U.S. production. It was also pointed out that what the trade journal called special and sports-type cars were getting

1969 Buick Electra 225 Custom convertible and Custom four-door hardtop

"the luxuries and conveniences once confined exclusively to the very few top-price models."

In the sports-personal category, these were the Thunderbird, Grand Prix and Riviera plus the unique Excalibur. But there was also a tier of "almost-luxury cars" that provided Americans with choices. These included the Oldsmobile 98, the Buick Electra 225, the Mercury Marquis Brougham, plus the even more affordable Chevrolet Caprice, Ford LTD and AMC Ambassador DPL. These cars were much like the Hudson Commodore, Nash Ambassador and Studebaker President that nipped at the heels of Cadillacs, Lincolns and Imperials during earlier eras.

1964 Cadillac DeVille convertible

A 1963 survey of consumers visiting car dealers reflected that the U.S. economy was doing well and that people were becoming interested in bettering their lifestyles and driving more luxurious cars. A truck driver making $9,000 a year was ready to purchase a luxury car. A body shop owner told the polltaker that he bought a new Imperial every other year. An autoworker who built Cadillacs for a quarter of a century told a dealer that he was finally earning enough to buy one. It was like Johnny Cash wanting to bring home a Cadillac, piece by piece, in his lunch pail. Many wanted to climb up the pricing ladder with their new buying power. Those who couldn't afford a Lincoln could get an LTD that seemed nearly as nice.

Other factors were also at play in this era. Cars were getting to be more fun to drive and luxury cars with more features were the most fun. Some folks were buying them for the sheer driving enjoyment. Higher trade-in values pushed the sales of prestige and luxury cars. And well-to-do families were growing larger in terms of people and their cars. The youth market came into play. While buyers 35 and older preferred a Lincoln, younger buyers drove LTDs out of the local Ford showroom. An interesting historical fact is that the top-priced models in nearly every 1963 car line were selling better than the low-priced entries. Car buyers were thinking upscale.

In 1963, the rising sales of almost-luxury and luxury cars made sense based on auto industry figures that showed three-million American households with incomes of more

1960 Lincoln Continental convertible

1961 Buick Electra 225 convertible

1960 Cadillac Series 62 convertible

than $15,000 a year. Also, 150,000 American males under age 44 were making more than $25,000 per year. *Ward's* said, "Income seems to be the principal denominator in the selection of an automobile today, much more so than a person's social status." This reflected the growing youth market.

Sales of the Luxury Three (Cadillac, Lincoln and Imperial) may have appeared static in the early 1960s, but by the end of 1962 these brands were also starting to take off. Between 1962 and 1969, total model-year output in the luxury niche grew by over 100,000 units per year. The annual production totals showed an increase in each of those years, except 1967. In 1960, sales of the Luxury Three's products represented 3.06 percent of total industry output. By 1969, that percentage had grown to 3.64 percent.

"Luxury Three" Car Production 1960-1969

	1960	1961	1962	1963	1964	1965	1966	1967	1968	1969
Cadillac	142,184	138,379	160,840	163,174	165,959	181,435	196,675	182,070	205,475	199,904
Eldorado FWD	--	--	--	--	--	--	--	17,930	24,528	23,333
Lincoln Continental	24,820	25,164	31,061	31,233	36,297	40,180	54,755	45,667	39,134	38,290
Lincoln Mark III	--	--	--	--	--	--	--	--	7,770	23,088
Imperial	17,707	12,249	14,337	14,108	23,285	18,399	13,742	17,614	15,361	22,077
Total	184,711	175,792	206,238	208,515	225,541	240,014	265,172	263,281	292,268	306,692

1967 Ford LTD four-door hardtop

percent. With both Lincoln and Cadillac reporting a boom in 1965 limousine deliveries, Cadillac said it expected to sell 2,200 in 1966, a 47 percent gain from already good numbers. At Lincoln, sales of the Lehmann-Peterson-built cars were doing even better with a 57 percent increase. Lincoln also reported a drop in the median age of the people buying Lincoln Continentals with a median age of 48.3 years old, rather than the traditional 50.

In 1967, Cadillac added the new "sports-styled" Eldorado, making it crystal clear that it should be considered a separate marque. This was a down year for luxury cars. Production of standard Cadillacs was significantly lower, but only because some buyers preferred the Eldorado. The two types of cars together managed a small gain. For the Imperial, model-year production rose 28.2 percent, but was still 4.3 percent lower than in 1965. Lincoln registered a 16.6 percent drop in Continental output.

As you can see, 1964 was a good year for luxury car production. Lincoln and Imperial did particularly well, gaining in calendar-year registrations as well as production. Cadillac registrations fell due to a late-1964 strike that hampered deliveries to dealers. The Buick Electra 225 and the Chrysler New Yorker both had gains in registrations, while the Oldsmobile 98 did not, probably due to the strike. Other signs of good times were reflected in annual industry highlights. In January 1964 it was announced that more 1964 Imperials had already been sold than in all of 1963. A week later, the tire industry put out a press release saying whitewall tires had outsold blackwall tires for the first time. In June, a story was published reporting that over half the engines in U.S. cars were over 300 cid.

With the disposable income of Americans increasing by $25 to $30 billion a year in the middle 1960s, the movement towards fancier cars continued unabated in 1965. Air conditioning gained in popularity as an option and showed the greatest gain in installation rates which jumped from 17.9 percent in 1964 to 23.3 percent in 1965. In the luxury class, A/C was found in 83 percent of Cadillacs, 87 percent of Imperials and 90 percent of Lincoln Continentals. It was also the first year cars were available with a factory-installed stereo tape player (Ford) and a seat warmer (Cadillac). Ford's LTD, Chevrolet's Caprice and Plymouth's VIP were new contenders in the almost-luxury-car class. At the very top, limo sales were up.

Cadillac's calendar-year output went up 1.1 percent in 1966. For Lincoln, the gain was 14.7 percent and for Imperial, 7.5

The luxury-car niche rebounded nicely in 1968. Contributing nearly 8,000 units to the record high production count was a new 1968-1/2 Lincoln model called the Mark III. This was the second Lincoln to use the Mark III designation and reflected Lincoln's desire to obliterate recollections of the 1958 "aircraft carrier" version that was considered a bad memory in 1968. The modern Mark III was aimed at the front-drive Eldorado buyer, although it stayed a conventional rear-wheeler with sportier styling. The Buick Electra, Chrysler New Yorker, Ford LTD and Olds 98 also had a great year. The Ambassador DPL, Caprice and Plymouth VIP fell in output.

Chrysler grew the already-large Imperial by five inches in length. The AMC Ambassador got a four-inch

1967 Oldsmobile 98 Luxury Sedan

The Incomparable IMPERIAL

Within the quiet world of Imperial, there are beautiful refinements in the pleasure a fine car can give. The spaciousness, the comfort, the luxuries surrounding you have no equal. But, the extraordinary silence in motion you will experience is still more significant. For this tells you a new level in quality has been achieved in the Incomparable Imperial for 1964.

IMPERIAL DIVISION CHRYSLER MOTORS CORPORATION

1964 Imperial Le Baron four-door hardtop

longer wheelbase. Despite a drop in model-year production, Cadillac had its fifth successive record calendar-year sales season with a whopping 22.1 percent increase in dealer deliveries. Thanks to strong business surrounding the Mark III model, calendar 1969 ended with Lincoln establishing a new record, too. The Continental posted a 2.2 percent drop in sales, but the sportier model's 197.1 percent gain more than made up for it. The restyled 1969 Imperial was also a major success, with calendar-year sales rising 12.6 percent. For some reason, the cars one notch down from the top like the 98, Electra and New Yorker had a bad 1969 selling season, but the Caprice, LTD and DPL all did well. LTD model-year production nearly doubled!

Not mentioned is the Excalibur, a sports-specialty car created by industrial designer Brooks Stevens and built by his Excalibur Motor Corporation, Milwaukee, Wisconsin. The first Excalibur of the 1950s was a sports racing car, but in 1965 production cars using the name were introduced. They were patterned after the classic Mercedes SSK roadster and used a Studebaker chassis and Corvette engine. Pricing in the $8,000 range put the Excalibur into the luxury-car class, even though it was more of a sports car. After a two-door Phaeton with four-passenger seating arrived in 1967, the Excalibur became more of a specialty luxury car and less of a true sports car. The 1967 Phaeton had a $9,000 price tag, and that increased in 1968 and '69.

CHAPTER FOUR

1960-1969 Cadillac

General Motor's Cadillac division dominated the U.S. luxury car market during the 1960s. No other high-priced-car maker in the country ever came close to Cadillac's sales or production numbers. Cadillac did not overwork its stylists, who moved from the radical '50s into a decade of restrained, but graceful designs. Tail fins shrunk and then vanished. Headlights went from horizontal to vertical to horizontal again. Comfort and convenience improvements were favored over cosmetic revisions. A sporty Eldorado was handled as a separate sports-personal car.

The 1960 Cadillac sported a modest clean up of the 1959 look. Overall, the tradition of evolutionary restyling continued. The tail fins were lowered to create one long sweeping feature line that ran from the hood to the rear of the car. There were five series: 62, 60 Special, 62 Eldorado, 75 and Eldorado Brougham. The Brougham was a five-figure, ultra-luxurious model constructed in Italy with a special 345-hp engine carrying three Rochester two-barrel carburetors. Cadillac prices started at $4,892 for a Series 62 hardtop and ran as high as $13,075 for the Brougham. *Car Life* magazine picked the 1960 Cadillac as its "Best buy in the luxury field."

Cadillac's "Bill Mitchell" styling for 1961 had a crisp, lean look with sculptured body sides. Tinsel was not on Mitchell's radar. Sharp, angular lines characterized the upper body. The five series were 62, DeVille, Eldorado convertible, 60 Special and Fleetwood 75. All models

1961 Cadillac sedan **David Lyon**

now had the 390-cid 325-hp V-8. Eighty-seven percent of all 1961 Cadillacs were hardtops and 57 percent of the hardtops had four doors.

Marking its 60th anniversary, Cadillac made just one major design change in 1962. An entirely new roof was used on five models and gave them what Cadillac called a "classic silhouette." There were 12 models in all. Innovations included a three-way braking system and a front corner lamp that lit the driver's way in a turn. The tail fins were lowered again. Two interesting new body styles were the Series 62 Town Sedan and the DeVille Park Avenue. These short-deck sport sedans were built for wealthy dowagers who had shallow garages.

The 1963 Cadillac continued many of the automaker's traditional motifs with a new grille, hood and deck lid, new body panels and more than 70 technical updates. The tail fins were lower and more crisply tailored. Some models

1961 Cadillac Series 62 convertible

Elegance in action!

1968 Cadillac Fleetwood Brougham (bottom) and
Fleetwood Eldorado (top)

got a shorter roofline and smaller, more formal looking
rear windows. The instrument layout was new and the
dash and doors had wood paneling. New features (some
optional) included a new driveline less sensitive to road
or load variations, an alternator (Delcotron) instead of a
generator, and a 6-position movable steering column.

All 12 of the 1963 Cadillac models used a lighter new
390-cid V-8. Although neither displacement or horsepower
changed, the '63 V-8 was completely redesigned. Quieter,
smoother and more efficient, the new engine was one inch
lower, four inches narrower and 1-1/4 inches shorter than
the 1962 V-8. It weighed 82 less pounds, using aluminum
accessory drives.

Performance took precedence over styling at
Cadillac in 1964. The horizontal grille bar was carried
around the front fender on all 11 models. A 429-cid 340-
hp V-8 was new. Turbo Hydra-Matic drive was another
improvement, along with a completely automatic Comfort
Control heating and air conditioning system. Gone for the
first time since 1956 was the Biarritz name.

A new three-model Calais line replaced the Series
62 in 1965. Four body styles were offered in both DeVille
and Fleetwood livery. Cadillacs got some mandatory design
tweaks. They included a broader new grille and vertically
mounted round headlights. True tail fins disappeared, but
broad, flat rear fenders de-emphasized this direction.

1963 Cadillac Eldorado Biarritz convertible

1969 Cadillac Fleetwood Brougham

1963 Cadillac Fleetwood Sixty Special sedan

Introduced on the Buick Riviera, the frameless window with curved side glass came to the 1965 Cadillac. DeVille hardtops were offered with a choice of four different-colored vinyl tops. The Brougham name returned on the 60 Special. New options included a tilt & telescope steering column for all Cadillacs. On November 4th the 3-millionth Cadillac, a Fleetwood Brougham, was built.

The Brougham option was elevated to model status in 1966. In for a major restyling were the big stretched sedans and limos in the Fleetwood 75 series. Cadillac predicted a 47 percent increase in sales over the 1,500 built in 1965. From 60 to 70 percent of all limos went to the government or businesses, but private sector sales were growing. All models got the annual "new grille, new taillights and move the badges around" treatment. Variable-ratio power steering was new as were optional electrically-heated front seats. Headrests were introduced and a reclining front passenger seat and a new AM/FM stereo radio could be factory-installed at extra cost.

A new body side treatment made the '67 Cadillac look longer and was more sculptured than before. There was also a new formal roofline patterned after a show car called the Florentine. It gave the rear seat passengers more privacy. An instrument board with Mylar printed circuits and a slide-out fuse box were among numerous technical changes. The really big news at Cadillac this year was the Eldorado sports-personal car.

Your 1968 Cadillac may be basically the same as a '67, but don't try swapping hoods. The new model featured recessed windshield wipers, which required a 6-1/2-inch-longer hood to hide them. Since this slightly affected overall length, the deck lid also had to be restyled. Under that bigger hood was a bigger motor – a 472-cid 375-hp V-8. Color and trim got a lot of attention in 1968 with 14 new body hues and a total of 147 upholstery combos including 67 in leather. Inside, Cadillacs had an all-new dashboard design. For the first time in its history, Cadillac Motor Division built over 200,000 cars in the model year.

Cadillacs got the "Eldorado look" in 1969. It included a new fender treatment, a stronger horizontal character line and extended rear quarter panels. This gave a longer appearance, although actual dimensions were unchanged. A new grille had a segmented look with horizontally-mounted square headlights on either side. The hood was stretched another 2-1/2 inches. Cadillac moved Eldorado production to a factory in Euclid, Ohio.

1961 Cadillac Series 62 convertible

1968 Cadillac Sedan de Ville

1966 Cadillac Series 62 convertible

1964 Cadillac Eldorado Biarritz convertible

1960s "Solid Gold"

1962 Cadillac Series 63 Coupe DeVille

6	5	4	3	2	1
$1,040	$3,120	$5,200	$11,700	$18,200	$26,000

Estimated values in today's marketplace taken from the 2006 Collector Car Price Guide.

1960-1969 Lincoln

The 1958 Lincoln introduced a new body and new engine. Both were continued into the first year of the 1960s with only modest changes. The 1958 to 1960 look was promoted as "inspired by the Classic Continental," although it had little in common with the 1940 to 1942 cars. Four different 1960 Lincoln/Continental models were offered, the largest regular-production models of the year. In certain parts of the country, owners were required to place red reflectors on the rear and amber clearance lights on the front. They had a 131-inch wheelbase and 229-inch overall length.

1965 Lincoln Continental four-door hardtop

Interestingly, the 1958 through 1960 Continentals were called Mark III, Mark IV and Mark V models to tie them to the "classic" Continentals like the 1940 to 1948 models and the high-priced 1956 to 1957 specialty car. They were not well regarded in their day (although collectors pay a lot for them now). Lincoln went to a clean-sheet design in 1961 and eventually "disavowed" the big cars as true Continentals by reviving the Continental Mark III designation in 1970.

The 1958 to 1960 Lincoln Capri, Premiere and Continental must be viewed in the context of other designs and their times like the chrome-laden 1958 Olds and the tail-finned 1959 Cadillac. All models used a 430-cid V-8 with 315 hp. Each series included a four-door sedan, a two-door hardtop and a four-door hardtop. The Continentals included a Town Car, a Limousine and a convertible. Prices ranged from $4,807 to $9,386. Model-year production showed them losing popularity with 29,684 built in 1958, 26,906 built in 1959 and 24,820 built in 1960.

1963 Lincoln Continental four-door convertible sedan **David Lyon**

1964 Lincoln Continental four-door convertible sedan

1969 Lincoln Continental four-door convertible sedan

"An outstanding contribution of simplicity and design elegance" is how the Industrial Design Institute described the classic 1961 Lincoln Continental. It was sort of a formalized T-Bird and the two cars shared front end tooling to lower production costs. According to automotive writer Charles Webb, "The 1961 Continental showed the world just how beautiful a production American car could be." It was one of the most influential cars of the decade and its basic styling lasted until 1969. After the Continental arrived, Ford's luxury car had a "Lincoln Look" to compete with the already accepted "Cadillac Look."

The new Continental was Lincoln's only model and came as a sedan ($6,067) and a four-door convertible ($6,713). The open car caused a stir. There had not been a "convertible sedan" built in the U.S. since before World War II, except for a few hundred made by Kaiser and Frazer from 1949 through 1951. Lincoln turned out 2,857 of the convertibles in 1961. With its 22,303 assemblies, the closed sedan made total production a bit higher than in 1960.

With an eight-inch shorter wheelbase, the 1961 Continental was an amazing 15 inches shorter than the 1960 model. Under the hood once again was Lincoln's

immense (at least at that time) 430-cid V-8, but now in a 300-hp state of tune. Standard equipment for all Continentals included automatic transmission, power brakes and steering, power windows and power door locks. A $505 air conditioner was installed in 65 percent of the cars.

Lincoln placed a great deal of emphasis on build quality. The closely controlled production process stressed custom-made quality and manufacturing. The cars had the most rigid unit body and chassis ever produced, as well as the best sound insulation and shock dampening. Stringent product testing was done to maintain the very high quality level. All engines were dyno tested and each car was given a 12-mile road test. Lincoln even sold the Continental with an unheard of 24-month, 24,000-mile warranty.

1966 Lincoln Continental two-door hardtop

From the start, Lincoln said that future Continentals would maintain a high degree of styling continuity and that year-to-year changes would only be done to permit model year identification. The elimination of front bumper guards, the use of a new type of individual headlight trim, a narrower center grille bar and a semi-honeycomb style grille insert (repeated at the rear) were changes for 1962.

CHAPTER FOUR

The steering wheel was raised to increase legroom. Nearly 75 percent of new Continentals had an air conditioner integral with the dashboard.

The 1963 Continental had alterations like a new grille. The rear deck was raised and bright metal trim on the rear of the car was re-arranged. The interior was roomier and had more legroom all around and more rear headroom. There was new upholstery inside, as well as a new instrument panel. Lincoln changed from a two-barrel carburetor to a four-barrel one. Other improvements included replacing the generator with an alternator, thicker brake linings and aluminum brakes drums (in front). Lube intervals went to 30,000 miles (from 6,000).

Lincoln extended the 1964's wheelbase and overall length by three inches. The roof was also five inches wider and the convertible had a new low-contour roof design. These changes increased the car's luggage-carrying capacity. In addition to a new grille and decorative trim, there were extensive changes to body sheet metal. The introduction of new low-silhouette tires permitted the use of new 15-inch wheels. New standard equipment included an automatic parking brake release, a trip odometer, a low-fuel-warning lamp, map lights and reading lights on the sedan. Individually adjustable front seats were a new option.

The 1965 Lincoln Continental had a new hood and grille that made the design look slightly more horizontal. Its larger, wider look set the theme for the rest of the decade. The grille extended into the fender tips where the parking lights and turn signals were mounted. Instead of being offered just in Black and White, the sedan's optional vinyl top now came in Brown, Blue and Ivory as well. Front wheel disc brakes were standard and a transistorized ignition system was optional.

For 1966, "America's Most Distinguished Motorcar" – as Ford billed it – was promoted as being "completely restyled for the first time in five years," although it didn't

1962 Lincoln Continental four-door hardtop **David Lyon**

1965 Lincoln Continental four-door convertible

1963 Lincoln Continental four-door hardtop **David Lyon**

1962 Lincoln Continental four-door convertible **David Lyon**

1960 Lincoln Continental four-door hardtop

look all that different. The big update was a five-inch larger body (on the same wheelbase as before). There was also a brand new body style – a two-door hardtop. Lincoln took advantage of a natural trend towards this sporty model. The Continental needed more cubic inches and got them in a new 472-cid V-8 with 340 hp. Ford said this made Lincoln the most powerful car, although the Imperial had 350 hp, the Olds 98 had 365 hp and the Toronado had 385 hp. Among the 1966 Lincoln's points were more luggage space, a glass rear window for the convertible and a larger-capacity gas tank.

1969 Lincoln Continental Mark III   **David Lyon**

1960s "Solid Gold"

1964 Lincoln Continental four-door convertible

6	5	4	3	2	1
$1,200	$3,600	$6,000	$13,500	$21,000	$30,000

Estimated values in today's marketplace taken from the 2006 Collector Car Price Guide.

1969 Lincoln Continental Mark III   **David Lyon**

1960-1969 Imperial

1965 Imperial Crown convertible

"The flying saucers have landed!" said a character in an Elvis Presley movie when he saw a late-1950s Imperial convertible drive up. Designer Virgil Exner gave the cars a wild, tail-finned look in the '50s and it was carried over in 1960. The front was cleaner and had a new grille made up of fine vertical and horizontal bits. The headlights were somewhat recessed under the overhanging front fenders. An overlapping roof treatment was used. Power came from a 413-cid "wedge" V-8 that put out 350 ponies.

Imperials were served up in four series that included the Custom line with a four-door sedan and two- and four-door hardtops. The Imperial Crown line had the same and a ragtop. Two four-door models with a limousine-like rear window treatment were found in the LeBaron line. Cars in the three lines rode an already-substantial 129-inch wheelbase. An even bigger car was the 150-inch-wheelbase Crown Imperial limousine. Priced at $16,000, this model was custom made from an Imperial two-door hardtop by Ghia in Italy. Only 16 Crown Imperial limos were done up.

1968 Imperial Crown convertible

The 1961 Imperial had moderate styling tweaks. Somebody at Chrysler decided the luxury car needed a "classic" image, so the new model had "free-standing" headlights patterned "torpedo" headlights. The grille had a simpler design and was "centrally placed in the classic car tradition," said Chrysler, though it hardly looked old-fashioned. Definitely not from the 1930s were the wild "shark" fins at the rear. Pricing ranged from $4,925 for a Custom two-door hardtop to $16,000 for a limo. Rare was the $5,759 Imperial Crown convertible, which had a production run of 429 versus the 618 made in 1960. The unusual styling didn't sell well.

For 1962, the Imperial kept the same basic body, but the rear styling theme changed considerably. High rear fenders, with a hint of the '56 models' flat, broad sweep, eliminated the wild fins. The taillights were stuck on the tops of the fenders and looked like a J.C. Whitney accessory item. The front used two grilles with a vertical divider between them. The freestanding headlights were retained. The built-by-Ghia-in-Italy limousine had not a single taker this year.

1967 Imperial sedan

Abandoning the split grille, substituting a flatter roof and adopting minor rear end mods were the main things Imperial stylists were paid for in 1963. Pulling down most of the money was former Ford stylist Elwood Engle, who replaced Virgil Exner. No wonder the new roof had a Lincoln look! A new braking system, power windows, and remote-control rearview mirrors were standard.

Lincoln enjoyed good luck with its "keep-it-simple" approach in the 1960s, so Imperial followed suit in 1964. The model lineup was reduced to four cars in two series, plus 10 Crown Imperial limos put together by Ghia in Italy. Imperial Crowns included the two-and four-door hardtops and the convertible with prices from $5,581 to $6,003. The LeBaron series offered only the $6,456 four-door hardtop. The Ghia limo was $18,500. With an attractive new all-Engel look, the divided grille returned, but the bullet headlights left. The 1964 was influenced by the slab-sided Continental, which Engle had helped design. Sales were the second best in Imperial's long history. Even the convertible registered relatively high production of 922 units.

1963 Imperial Crown four-door hardtop

A new two-piece die-cast grille with rectangular-framed dual headlights protected by a heavy panel of tempered glass was used on the '65 Imperial. The grille had a new mesh-pattern insert. The revised Torque-Flite automatic transmission was quieter and smoother. The interior and instrument panel were trimmed with walnut veneer accents. The instrument board had a new Sentry Signal to warn a driver to check the gauges when high temperature, a low fuel level or low oil pressure was detected. Power vent windows were standard on all Imperials for the first time. It was the last year for the custom-built Ghia limousine, of which only 10 were built.

The 1966 Imperial kept the same array of models as the '65 and body dimensions were unchanged. Updates included a new 440-cid 350-hp V-8 – the biggest Chrysler engine ever – and a new split-bench front seat. This resembled a conventional seat, but was actually two individual seats, each with its own armrest, seat track and adjusting mechanism. The passenger seat had a reclining backrest and a headrest could be added as an extra-cost option.

1960 Imperial Crown four-door hardtop **David Lyon**

1962 Imperial Crown two-door Southampton

1963 Imperial Crown convertible

With the most sweeping styling changes since becoming a separate car-line 10 years earlier, the 1967 Imperial was dramatically different. The new model switched to unit construction, ending the Imperial's tenure as Chrysler's only ladder-frame car. New, rubber-isolated suspension setups were used front and rear. The wheelbase was reduced by two inches, while overall length dropped nearly three inches. A four-door sedan returned to the lineup and front disc brakes were made standard equipment. New was an electrical mechanism that moved the front seat forward when its back was tilted for rear seat entry and an optional front seat that rotated 180 degrees to the rear.

The 1968 revisions were minor like a new grille with a distinctive round emblem and redesigned body trim. The grille wrapped around the fenders so the parking lights could be seen from the sides. An AM/FM stereo multiplex radio was offered for the first time. A stereo tape player could be ordered with the radio. The Crown series had a four-door sedan, two- and four-door hardtops and the final Imperial convertible. In the one-car LeBaron series was a four-door hardtop.

After shrinking a bit in its last redo, the 1969 Imperial went the other way. America's "luxomobiles" were growing and the Imperial had to "bloat up" to keep apace. While the wheelbase remained 127 inches, the new "airplane fuselage" body was five inches longer. A restyled grille and retractable headlights (with a manually-operated fail-safe device) were innovations. New tech stuff included a transistorized voltage regulator, optional fiberglass-belted tires, a more powerful power steering pump and a swing-type gas pedal.

1961 Imperial Crown convertible

1967 Imperial Crown convertible

1961 Imperial Crown four-door Southampton

1960s "Solid Gold"

1961 Imperial Crown convertible

6	5	4	3	2	1
$1,040	$3,120	$5,200	$11,700	$18,200	$26,000

Estimated values in today's marketplace taken from the 2006 Collector Car Price Guide.

1965 Oldsmobile 98 Luxury Sedan

1960-1969 Oldsmobile Ninety-Eight

1965 Oldsmobile 98 two-door hardtop **Elton McFall**

Like most GM cars of 1960, the Oldsmobile looked like a "Kalifornia Kustom" brought to the assembly line. "Star of the Rocketing '60s" the ads called it. There was a "drawer-pull" grille, a little simulated air scoop at the front and a flat, wide, low look to the entire body. The greenhouse was airy and panoramic. Oldsmobile even called the Ninety-Eight two-door hardtop its "Holiday Scenicoupe" after the famous railcars with observation windows.

At the rear of "the Car that Rockets out of the Ordinary" was kind of a flat, shelf-like fin with an aircraft look to it. "Radiantly styled for the rocketing '60s" said another ad. The Olds 98 (you can use the numbers "98" or the letters "Ninety-Eight" and both are correct) was the top-of-the-line, luxury offering for the Lansing, Michigan, automaker. It included a two-door hardtop, a four-door sedan, a four-door hardtop and a convertible. Prices ran from $3,887 to $4,362.

A 394-cid 315-hp Premium Rocket engine with a four-barrel carb was standard in these 126-inch wheelbase cars. A new slim-line Hydra-Matic transmission reduced the size of the transmission tunnel by 20 percent, giving more legroom. Custom Lounge interiors with rich vinyl or leather trim helped set the 98s apart. "Fabric Magic: Fabric and vinyl are married in exquisite inlaid designs, deep-embossed for life by a special process," said GM's Fisher Body Division. Other Oldsmobile features included Roto-Matic power steering, Quadri-Balanced Ride, Vibra-Tuned Stability, Wide-Stance Stability (no one called an Oldsmobile "unstable") and Guard-Beam Frame solidness." The 98 wasn't quite a Cadillac – but you might have called it a luxo-value car. Olds built 59,364 Ninety-Eights in 1960, including the pace car for the year's Indy 500.

Suddenly it was 1961 and the big Oldsmobiles had "Fashion Line Design." The pointy end of the car's profile was at the rear. The front had a glittery "Hollywood" look with the name spelled out like movie marquee lettering. Olds promoted the restyled Ninety-Eight as a "Distinguished

1961 Oldsmobile 98 convertible

1968 Oldsmobile 98 convertible **Elton McFall**

. . . distinctive . . . decidedly new car with more room and more luxury than ever." Another ad claimed, "The Ninety-Eight...speaks for itself, as it speaks for you." Olds promised, "The Action Line in Performance and Design."

For the 98, the 126-inch wheelbase was still in play, but the overall length was 218 inches, compared to 220.9 inches in 1960. That meant the added roominess was all on the inside. "More headroom, more leg room, more knee room" promised the copywriters. The 394-cid "Skyrocket" V-8 was linked to "Hydra-Matic Drive with smooth Accel-A-Rotor Action." Other features included Twin Triangle Stability, designed to bring out the full benefit of rear coil springs.

For 1961, the high-end model was officially listed the *Classic* Ninety-Eight. It had, "The extra sparkle and spice that speeds up your pulse." There were five body styles. Three were "Holiday" (hardtop) models, one was a four-door Town Sedan and one was a convertible. The hardtops included a two-door Holiday Coupe, a four-door Holiday Sedan and a four-door Sports Sedan (with a big back window). Sales of the flagship Olds dropped nearly 25 percent, a situation blamed on the new Starfire luring buyers right on the Olds' showroom floor.

Merrier by the model year, the 1962 Oldsmobiles looked sportier than ever before. Oldsmobile said its new car had, "The most 'Ah' inspiring lines that ever graced an automobile." A fresh new profile was provided by different front and rear styling, and a crisp new, convertible-like roofline.

The Ninety-Eight was, said Oldsmobile, "Where style comes first and quality counts." The '62 version of the luxury model started growing again—back up to 220 inches long. This provided even more room and comfort in the Luxury Lounge interior. Also up was the 394-cid V-8's output rating, which rose to 330 in '62. "Fashioned with flair and exhilarating to drive," said Oldsmobile. It was truly a "daring design, ready to go" and it did with 64,154 cars produced.

1963 Oldsmobile 98 convertible

1960 Oldsmobile 98 Indianapolis 500 Pace Car

1969 Oldsmobile 98 Luxury Sedan

1968 Oldsmobile 98 Holiday four-door hardtop

By giving each 1963 series its own grille, Oldsmobile made them easier to tell apart. On the Ninety-Eight, two slim bright horizontal bars stood out. One was near the tops of the headlights and one was near the bottom. Ninety-Eights also had bright, ribbed underscores on the rocker panels and rear quarters. The body featured new straight-line simplicity (heavy sculpturing eliminated), flatter roof treatments and sharpened metal trim accents. Front body sills were almost eliminated and the dreaded transmission hump in the floor was reduced in size by nearly 50 percent.

Two plush new ultra-luxurious models were added to the 1963 Ninety-Eight series. Olds compared its fancy four door Luxury Sedan to "the most luxurious automobiles on the road today." A Custom Sport Coupe, with a $4,381 price tag, was the other new entry. This sporty luxury car was the only Ninety-Eight to get the hot 345-hp Starfire V-8. The four-door Holiday Hardtop was dropped to help make room for this new dynamic duo. The four other Ninety-Eights were carried over with the same 330-hp 394 V-8 used in the LS.

Olds hyped "bewitching beauty" in the 1963 Ninety-Eight and called the top-of-the-line models "elegant – inviting – sumptuous." Among technical advances was a "sway control" system that resulted in a three-foot shorter turn radius. Self-adjusting brakes and a generator were made standard equipment. A movable "Tilt Steering" wheel was a new option. "No car was ever more appealing," said Olds. "It stands apart in the company of fine cars."

"Here is one of the world's most luxurious automobiles," heralded an ad for the 1964 Olds Ninety-Eight. It was a car with all of the lavish touches you might expect from Oldsmobile's finest offering. Continuing on a 126-inch wheelbase with 222.3 inches of overall length (about an inch longer than in '63) the big Olds continued to use the 394/330 V-8 in five models and offer the 345-hp Starfire version in the Custom Sport Coupe. With "Lines that say 'look' and fabrics that say 'feel'" the '64 Ninety-Eight was lavish motoring inside and out.

The Ninety-Eight was overshadowed in 1964 by the mid-sized Jetstars. The small F-85s were attention getters, too. The Ninety-Eight was a horse of a different color and to keep it from being wiped out by the hotter-selling models, Olds moved it up-market to battle luxury cars. "Ninety-Eight: Starts with luxury and takes off from there," said one ad. Standard equipment included Hydra-Matic, power steering, power brakes, power windows, power seats, windshield washers, special wheel discs, a clock, courtesy and map lights and a padded dashboard.

1961 Oldsmobile 98 Starfire convertible

Enclosed rear wheels emphasized the custom look. Olds called the fender skirts "low-profile fender openings." With production of 70,308 units in model-year 1963 and 68,254 in 1964, Olds had to consider the gussied-up Ninety-Eight a success in the luxury-car niche.

Those numbers were up from the early 1960s and reflected added profits, since upscale buyers usually ordered more options for their cars. A new streamlined body design and a perimeter frame in place of the old X-frame made the '65 Ninety-Eight *the car to be seen in.* So did a new 425-cid 360-hp V-8 (310 hp and 370 hp optional) and a Turbo-Hydra-Matic transmission. One ad focused on getting attention in a 98. "Impressive: Your Oldsmobile Ninety-Eight arriving on the scene. Impressed: Your friends when they see you behind the wheel."

1964 Oldsmobile 98 Starfire convertible

The 1969 Olds 98 was a stretch in the "Youngmobile" ad campaign.

357,000 in '66. Sporty cars and specialty models were the hot ticket in the new-car market and the new front-wheel-drive Toronado seemed to be riding the crest of this movement. So Olds restyled all of its full-size '67s to resemble the Toronado. They had the Toro's in-and-out grille, slab sides and slanting rear roofline. Five inches was taken from the rear deck and added onto the front to approximate the front-driver's long-hood/short-deck image. Production dropped off again, in '67, to 76,189 cars.

In 1968, Olds turned things around, with model-year output of Ninety-Eights rising to 91,747. This year the emphasis was on the youth market and the Ninety-Eight was hyped as the "Most luxurious '68 Youngsmobile from Oldsmobile." An extensive restyling highlighted the Ninety-Eight's cosmetics. It rode a 126-inch wheelbase and overall length was a hefty 223.7 inches.

The technical highlight of the season was a new concept in power train engineering placing less emphasis on speed and horsepower, focusing instead on mid-range performance improvements. It was said to promote better fuel economy, quieter engine operation and better durability. In the Ninety-Eight, the standard engine was now a 455-cid V-8 that used a four-barrel carburetor and produced 365 hp at 4600 rpm. There were no options.

A one-inch longer wheelbase and the addition of a new luxury hardtop sedan made Ninety-Eight new in 1969. The Luxury Hardtop Sedan listed for $4,693 and generated 25,973 assemblies, pushing total production to 116,408. Oldsmobile moved ahead of Plymouth to take fifth place on the sales charts. The 12 millionth Oldsmobile of all time was built late in the calendar year.

The Ninety-Eight was a car of the 1960s with its rich character, huge size, powerful "Rocket" V-8s and large, glittery image. It delivered the goods for Oldsmobile when it came to sales numbers. Although the annual production counts went up and down, there was an overall increase in the appeal of this terrific automobile. In a 1960 trade journal advertisement picturing a Ninetty-Eight four-door hardtop, Oldsmobile told automotive professionals, "You do better as an Olds dealer." Ten years later, the company could remind those same professionals, "We told you so."

The '66 Oldsmobile 98 had the same basic body as the '65 model with a new ice cube tray grille. The rear trim was also restyled. Olds continued to stress its biggest car's richness. The Ninety-Eight was even listed as a totally separate car line in the NADA Official Used car Guide. It was the "one-of-a-kind" Olds and the Ninety Eight was the "luxury car" of the line.

Ads invited car buyers considering the purchase of a 1966 Ninety-Eight to "Step out front in the Rocket-Action Olds." A new Quadrajet four-barrel carburetor helped the 454-cid V-8's "out-front" performance. New options for the year included a tilt-and-telescoping steering wheel, an automatic leveling device and a thermostatically-controlled Comfortron heating-and-cooling system. Model-year production dropped off to 88,119 units, after hitting 92,406 in 1965.

Oldsmobile did a logical thing in 1967. Sales for all of its big cars seemed to be ebbing from 380,000 in '65 to

1960s "Solid Gold"

1964 Oldsmobile 98 Custom Sport two-door hardtop

6	5	4	3	2	1
$ 940	$2,820	$4,700	$10,580	$16,450	$23,500

Estimated values in today's marketplace taken from the 2006 Collector Car Price Guide.

1967-1969 Ambassador

Ambassador DPL two-door hardtop

"We deliver!" was the headline in the ad showing a special red-white-and-blue 1967 Ambassador. It was a U.S. Mail delivery car – one of 3,000 sold to the Post Office that year. AMC called it "First Class transportation."

Despite their postal fleet status, the mail cars were fancy. The Ambassador was AMC's top-of-the-line model. It shared a new body with the mid-size Rebel, but had a four-inch stretch job up front that turned it into a full-size car on a 118-inch wheelbase. Overall length was 202.5 inches.

The '67 Ambassadors were promoted as, "The full-size luxury cars created for today." Vertically-stacked headlights flanked a horizontal bar grille. In the base Ambassador 880 series there were two- and four-door sedans and a four-door wagon. The Ambassador 990 replaced the two-door sedan with a hardtop. The fancy DPL models included a $2,958 two-door hardtop and a rare, last-year-offered convertible priced at $3,143. AMC made 12,552 hardtops and 1,260 ragtops.

DPLs had rally lights mounted deep in a V-profile grille. The DPL interior was as spacious as those found in the most expensive full-size car. "Guests in front and back enjoying over a yard of legroom each" is how AMC described the DPL's passenger accommodations. Ads called attention to the car's fine details: thick-pile carpeting,

an acoustical ceiling, simulated walnut paneling and a "decorator's choice" of luxury fabrics and vinyls. The DPL convertible included individually adjustable reclining seats and the 290-cid V-8.

A 232-cid in-line six with 145 hp was standard in all Ambassador models. Options included a 155-hp version of the same engine. A 290-cid 200-hp V-8 and two versions (235 hp and 280 hp) of a 343-cid Typhoon V-8 were available. Six transmissions, including a smooth, three-speed automatic, were offered. Standard equipment included a road-cushioning four-link rear suspension that did a good job of "gentling" the roughest back roads. AMC described this as the Ambassador's "Red Carpet Ride." *Motorcade Magazine* named the '67 Ambassador DPL the "most improved car of the year."

A two-page ad of 1968 made an "unfair comparison" between the AMC Ambassador DPL and the Rolls Royce

Ambassador DPL two-door hardtop

Silver Shadow. Of course, it made the $2,918 DPL seem like a better deal than the $19,600 British luxury car by explaining the American car's advantages like standard air conditioning and more headroom. It was careful to point out that both cars had unit-body construction, coil-spring seats and deep-dip rustproofing. "We feel you have every right to all the comfort, luxury and value we can give you," the ad explained. "Not everyone can afford a Rolls."

Another humorous AMC ad showed the fancy new-for-1968 Ambassador SST with its available velour seats and a uniformed chauffeur. "To make an appointment for a test ride, visit your American Motors dealers," the copy read. "A number of them have chauffeurs available." Production included 9,700 base Ambassadors, 13,000 DPLs, 21,300 SSTs and 10,700 station wagons. Of 54,700 cars made, only 4,400 had six cylinders.

The SST was the new V-8-only top-of-the-line series. It offered a four-door sedan for $3,151 and a two-door hardtop for $3,172. The base Ambassador came in the same models with a choice of six-cylinder or V-8 power. The DPL was now the mid-range model. It had the same models, plus a station wagon. This year's

1969 Ambassador DPL two-door hardtop

1969 Ambassador limousine **Elton McFall**

grille was modestly changed. It had nine vertical moldings spaced out across it and a more prominent, satin-finish horizontal bar across the center. Gone was the stand-up hood ornament of the '67 model.

The chauffeur was back in 1969. This time he was standing beside his Ambassador SST talking to another chauffeur driving a Cadillac Fleetwood limousine. The message was: "The 1969 Ambassador is the first luxury car for under $4,000 that deserves to be called a luxury car." Its luxury label was based on features like standard A/C, coil spring seats, 100 percent loop-pile carpeting, unit body construction and (in the SST) coach-like seats with velour upholstery. Also mentioned was a big four-inch increase in wheelbase.

This year's grille opening widened in the middle. The grid of vertical and horizontal bars making up the insert was finished in flat black. A bright horizontal molding ran across the center, between the headlights. The "Ambassador" name moved from the hood the left-hand side of the grille. With its new 122-inch wheelbase and 206.5-inch ovedall length, the Ambassador was nearly two tons of steel. The 290-cid 200-hp V-8 was now standard. The 343 Typhoon V-8 came in 235- and 280-hp versions and all-new was a 390-cid 315-hp V-8. This year, the base Ambassador came only as a sedan, while the DPL and SST versions also came in wagon and two-door hardtop models. Model-year production was 76,194 units and the SST was the top seller again.

1968 Ambassador SST two-door hardtop

1968 Ambassador SST sedan

1960s "Solid Gold"

1967 AMC Ambassador DPL two-door hardtop

6	5	4	3	2	1
$ 420	$1,260	$2,100	$4,730	$7,350	$10,500

Estimated values in today's marketplace taken the from 2006 Collector Car Price Guide.

1960-1969 Electra 225

Known to many Buick aficionados as the "Deuce-and-a-Quarter," the Electra 225 represents Buick's big, brawny entry in the prestige-car class. "There's nothing like a new car . . . and no new car like the 1960 Electra 225," said a 1960 Buick ad. With its four ventiports, extra chrome highlights and ribbed body side underscores, the long, low and luscious Electra 225 was 225.9 inches of pure luxury.

1965 Buick Electra 225

Buick stylists had rounded and softened the lines of the 1960 Buicks to get an exciting new decade rolling. Clipping the wild fins of 1959 gave the car a smoother, sculpted appearance. The chrome "vents" on the front fenders were a modern interpretation of the "porthole" decorations that identified 1940s and early-'50s Buicks. They had been the trademark of a brand that offered cars with everything from Chevy-like economy to Cadillac-like prestige.

The Electra 225 was Buick's fanciest model. It rode on the company's longest 126.3-inch wheelbase and used its most powerful V-8. This 401-cid 325-hp "nailhead" (vertical-valve) V-8 was shared with Invicta and other Electra models, but not with any other GM cars. Electra 225s were priced between $4,192 and $4,300. Buick made 8,029 four-door sedans, 4,841 four-door hardtops and 6,746 convertibles in the Electra 225 format.

At the Daytona International Speedway in Daytona Beach, Florida, a '60 Buick was run for three-and-a-half days (10,000 miles) at an average of 120.12 mph. At times the car ran over 130 mph. After this impressive performance feat, Buick decided not to advertise or promote the results of the trial, due to the Automobile Manufacturer's Association (AMA) ban on high-performance.

Buick described its 1961 styling as the "clean look of action." Unbroken character lines swept from the front to the rear of the car accenting lightly sculptured sheet metal. On the upper body sides was a full-length, bullet-shaped contour decorated with the model name up front, ventiports (four on Electra 225s) on the flanks, chrome handles on the doors and thin chrome accents. The 1961

Buick offered more headroom and greater passenger comfort despite being nearly seven inches shorter. Electra 225s had a 126-inch wheelbase and 219.2-inch overall length.

To promote is more efficient size, Buick parked a '61 Electra 225 four-door hardtop in a farmer's hayfield to illustrate the theme "Acres of room." As the ad pointed out, flatter floors were one explanation for the added roominess. Wider doors were also a benefit for Buick buyers. The plushest Buick model had a wide strip of bright trim along the lower body, with vertical "hash marks" behind the rear wheel opening. Electra 225 nameplates graced the front fenders. Calais cloth or leather trim was used. Standard equipment now included a two-way power seat, Super Deluxe wheel covers with gold accents and power windows. The engine was unchanged. The sedan was dropped, leaving the Riviera Sedan (four-door hardtop) and the convertible. Buick made 13,719 of the closed cars and 7,158 of the ragtops.

The big Buick for 1962 carried four ventiports per front fender and featured a rakish, sculptured restyle of its 1961 guise. Crisp clean lines and a completely new instrument panel were among updates. Interior comfort was enhanced by the almost complete elimination of the transmission hump.

New models included hardtop coupes and sedans with a roofline that looked like a raised convertible top. The Riviera four-door hardtop used the previous six-window pillarless configuration. Electra 225s had a group of vertical hash marks just ahead of the rear bumper ends with "Electra 225" spelled out in front of them. The total number of models grew to five: four-door sedan (13,523 made), four-door Riviera sedan (15,395 made), four-door hardtop (16,734 made), two-door hardtop (8,922 made) and convertible (7,894 made).

Buick's largest, plushest, most expensive 1963 model was redesigned. Ads pronounced a "Bold new Buick look." The Electra 225 had distinctive rear fenders that culminated in a sharp edge capped by a satin-finished accent molding housing tri-section back-up lights.

1969 Buick Electra 225 Custom Sport Coupe

1962 Buick Electra 225 two-door hardtop **Jerry Heasley**

Electra 225s had cloth-and-vinyl trim. A Custom vinyl-and-leather interior with front buckets seats and a console, was optional for the convertible and Sport Coupe. Power windows and two-way seat adjustment were standard for convertibles and for closed cars with the optional Custom interior. Standard equipment, in addition to items found on other Electras, included power steering, power brakes, back-up lights, a power brake signal light, a map light, a safety buzzer, Custom padded seats and Super Deluxe wheelcovers.

This season Buick made 14,628 sedans, 11,468 four-door hardtops, 19,714 Riviera sedans, 6,848 Sport Coupes and 6,367 convertibles. The 401-cid 325-hp V-8 was standard again, but a 425-cid 340-hp V-8 was optional. Buick's Turbine Drive full torque converter automatic transmission was used with both engines. Buick ads promised "power steering and brakes, greater road stability, arrow-straight tracking and years of smooth-riding comfort." As in the 1960 ad, the driver wore a tux to let the world know his 2-2-5 was "lux."

Full-size 1964 Buicks had a wider, lower front end appearance due to headlights moved outward in the new die-cast grille. A heavy die-cast metal grille accented the 1964 Electra 225's front end. Four traditional ventiports were found on the front fenders. Wide full-length lower body moldings were used along with a bright deck cove insert. Electra 225 lettering was found on rear fenders and specific full wheel covers were featured. Tuxedo-wearing gents and ladies in stylish evening wear crept back into Electra 225 ads, replacing the businessman.

Most Electra 225s came with fender skirts. Vinyl-and-brocade-cloth interiors were used in closed cars and leather upholstery was offered for convertibles. Base engine for the Electra 225 was the 401-cid 325-hp V-8. The next step up was the 425-cid 340-hp V-8 with a four-barrel carburetor. A rare option was a 360-hp 425 with two four-barrel carburetors.

1967 Buick Electra 225 two-door hardtop

1966 Buick Electra 225 four-door hardtop

1964 Buick Electra 225 convertible

Big Buick's copied the Riviera's smooth look in 1965. This meant a longer hood, a longer and lower roofline and a shorter rear deck. Two-door hardtop models used semi-fastback styling. Another new feature was Riviera-like curved side glass. A distinctive cross-hatch-textured die-cast grille was used at the front of the Electra 225. The hallmark rear wheelhouse skirts and wide, ribbed lower body moldings were retained. The Wildcat now shared the 126-inch wheelbase, but it chased after sporty performance-car buyers while the Electra 225 was still 100 percent luxury car.

Electra 225s had interiors trimmed in cloth fabrics or vinyls, with woodgrain dash accents. Standard equipment included that found on other Buicks, plus Super Turbine automatic transmission, power steering, power brakes, a deluxe steering wheel, two-speed electric windshield wipers with washers, and an electric clock. Convertibles had two-way power seat controls and an outside rearview mirror.

The 1965 Electra 225 sedan, four-door hardtop and Sport Coupe came in a choice of standard or Custom trim, with Customs costing about $180 more. The convertible was exclusive to the Custom series. Custom models could be spotted by a bullet-shaped piece of chrome with a circular badge sitting above the bumper end, just ahead of the front wheel opening. For 1965, Buick put together 31,603 Electra 225s and 35,207 Electra 225 Customs. The total of some 68,900 cars (with exports counted in) compared to some 58,700 in 1964.

Mandatory revisions were made to the grille and the rear end to update the appearance for another year. The cross-bar grille of '65 gave way to a three-tier design. Other small changes were made, but the same key elements were there. When you ordered a vinyl top (about 20.3 percent of all Buick buyers, but it seemed like most Electra 225s had them) you got a round Buick badge on the roof sail panels. "Luxury, luxury everywhere," was how one ad-writing "hypester" described the Deuce-and-a-quarter Custom four-door hardtop. Production rose 32 percent to some 88,200 units. Electra 225 production dropped by over 4,000, but the Custom found nearly 8,000 extra buyers.

A sweeping, contoured line running the full length of the body accented the long, low side profile of the 1967 Buick Electra. The big Buick retained its 126-inch wheelbase and was 223.9 inches long. Power was supplied by an all-new 430-cid V-8 that put out 360 hp at 5000 rpm. The "Nailhead" with its vertical valves was gone. Production for the model year took a big leap from about 88,200 in '66 to 100,300 in 1967. Ads promoted the Electric 225 Limited as "a car even more luxurious than the Buick Electra 225." This "ultimate Buick" was depicted in artistic ads showing sketches couples on trips to London, Mexico and St. Moritz.

Buick's side sweep was the defining styling characteristic of the 1968 Le Sabre, Wildcat and Electra 225 models. Le Sabres had a three-inch-shorter wheelbase than the other models, which shared a 126-inch stance. The Electra 225 was 4.4 inches longer than the 220.5-inch long Wildcat, and that made the luxury model a pretty large car. The 430-cid 360-hp V-8 was used to move the massive machine along. In round numbers, Electra 225 assemblies zoomed, hitting 125,400 cars! It was "a step closer to Buick's 1955 heydays" said *Ward's*. For the calendar year, Buick recorded its second best season in its 65-year history.

"The look is new and beautiful," said a '69 Buick ad. "And it's only the beginning. The 1969 Electra 225 has Buick's revolutionary new suspension . . . upper level ventilation . . . a big 430 cubic inch V-8 . . . a new 60/40 seat . . . an impressive list of GM safety features . . . an energy absorbing steering column . . . and passenger guard door locks." An intrinsic part of the Buick's styling tradition was the sculptured sweepline that extended the full length of the car from the front wheel opening to the

1963 Buick Electra 225 four-door hardtop

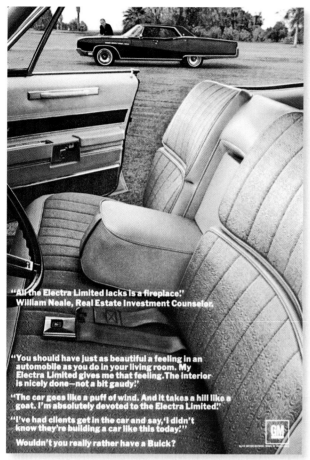

1968 Buick Electra 225 four-door hardtop (interior)

rear bumper. Buick's copywriters said something to the effect that "Buick owners keep selling Buicks for us." They must have done a heck of a job, since the total came in at 43,600 Electra 225s and 115,000 Electra 225 Customs.

The Electra 225 editions were well-suited to the trends of the 1960s towards increased luxury and prestige. It was a simpler age when "the best" meant the biggest and brawniest. While the Electra 225 was never the biggest and beefiest kid on the block, it was often "the best" of the brawny ones that many people could afford. That added up to popularity, dazzle and a decade of sales success. "Wouldn't you rather have a Buick?" ads asked and many buyers said, "Yes!"

1967 Buick Electra 225 four-door hardtop

1960 Buick Electra 225 sedan   **Phil Hall Collection**

1960s "Solid Gold"

1960 Buick Electra 225 convertible

6	5	4	3	2	1
$1,480	$4,440	$7,400	$16,650	$25,900	$37,000

Note: Add 5 percent for the bucket seat option.

Estimated values in today's marketplace taken from the 2006 Collector Car Price Guide.

1965-1969 Caprice

1968 Chevrolet Caprice coupe

In talkng about "prestige cars," *Ward's 1965 Automotive Yearbook* said, "Each succeeding prestige entry, whether it's a 2-plus2, a 4-4-2, an LTD, GTO or a Caprice, not only adds to the proliferation of car models, but also to a growing trend that allows motorists to buy the same basic car for $2,000 or $4,000, depending on options." The trade journal continued, "In other words, a Chevrolet or a Ford today, with very few exceptions, provides the equivalent in styling, engines, handling, riding, comfort and luxury of what once was the sole providence of the most expensive automobiles."

The original Caprice option package arrived early in 1966. It could be ordered only for the Impala four-door hardtop, which normally retailed for $2,850 without extras. Coded as regular production option (RPO) Z18, the Caprice Custom Sedan option included a heavier stiffer frame, suspension changes, a black-accented front grille, a black-accented rear trim panel with a Caprice nameplate, special slender body sill moldings, Fleur-de-lis roof quarter emblems, color-keyed body side stripes, specific full wheel covers and "Caprice" hood and dash emblems. Caprice prices started at $3,028, but could easily climb to $4,000 if many options were added. A total of 40,393 full-size Chevys with the Caprice option were built in 1965.

After bowing as a '65 option, the Caprice name was used on a series of cars in '66. The model lineup included a new Custom Coupe with a special formal roofline and two *station wagon* models. Caprice interiors were plush cloth in the Sport Sedan (bench front seat standard, Strato-back front seat optional), all-vinyl or cloth in the Custom Coupe and all-vinyl in wagons. All Caprices, except wagons, had wood-accented vinyl-and-carpet door panels.

Caprices had color-keyed body side stripes, wide ribbed sill moldings, "Caprice" front fender and deck signatures, wraparound rear taillights with bright horizontal ribs, specific "Caprice" wheel covers and roof rear quarter emblems, twin simulated exhaust ports below the Custom Coupe's rear window and a "Caprice" tailgate nameplate on the Custom Wagons.

Prices ranged from $3,078 for the Custom Coupe to $3,130 for a Sport Sedan to $3,301 for the six-passenger Custom Station Wagon and $3,413 for the nine-passenger Custom Station Wagon. A total of 147,622 Caprices were made. This included 60,660 Custom Coupes, 63,817 Custom Sedans, 13,569 six-passenger Custom Station Wagons and 9,576 nine-passenger wagons.

The smallest engine available in the '66 Caprice was the venerable 283-cid Chevy small-block V-8, that dated back to 1957. Equipped with a single two-barrel carburetor it produced 195 hp. An optional four-barrel version delivered 220 hp. Probably the most common Caprice engine was the 327-cid 275-hp V-8. Buyers could also add the 396-cid 325-hp Turbo-Jet V-8 or even the 427 V-8 in 390- or 425-hp formats.

The Caprice rode the same 119-inch wheelbase platform as other full-size Chevys and was 213.2 inches long (212.4 inches for station wagons). That made it shorter than the Big 3 luxury models – Cadillac, Lincoln and Imperial, as well as cars in the next tier, the Buick Electra 225 and the Oldsmobile 98. Some buyers liked their luxury in a trim package and the Caprice fit more readily into many American's garages.

Among the posh 1967 Caprice's exterior features were front fender lights, front and rear wheelhouse moldings, bright lower body side moldings with rear quarter extensions, color-keyed body side stripes, a belt reveal

1969 Chevrolet Caprice coupe

1969 Chevrolet Caprice four-door hardtop

molding on the Custom Coupe, a black-accented deck lid panel with bright highlight trim, triple-unit taillights with back-up lights in the rear bumper, "Caprice" deck lid signatures, roof side panel nameplates and specific "Caprice" full wheel covers.

Caprice interiors came in cloth, cloth-and-vinyl or all-vinyl, depending on the model. Interior features included a walnut-look lower instrument panel facing (with bright outline), pattern-cloth-and-vinyl door panels, wood-look door panel trim in sedans and coupes (wagons all-vinyl) and a front seat fold-down center armrest (sedans).

The 1968 Caprice again came in two- and four-door hardtop models, plus the station wagon with either six- or nine-passenger seating. Prices varied from $3,078 to $3,413. Production increased to 210,515 units including 107,047 two-door hardtops (Custom Coupes), 73,962 four-door hardtops, 18,000 six-passenger station wagons and 11,506 nine-passenger station wagons.

The Caprice lost a little popularity. The $3,219 Custom Coupe had a production run of 58,108. The $3,271 Custom Sedan had a production run of 61,187. Prices for the six- and nine-passenger wagons were $3,458 and $3,570, with production of 17,622 and 13,325 in the same respective order. A larger 307-cid engine was the base V-8. It produced 200 hp. Other options included the 327-cid in 250-hp and 275-hp versions, the 396-cid 325-hp big-block and the 427-cid 385-hp monster mill.

The 1969 Caprice was the top-rung offering in the Chevrolet full-size lineup. The Caprice-level station wagon was now the luxurious Kingswood Estate.

Prices for the Custom Coupe started at $3,815; for the Sport sedan $3,895 and for the six- and nine-passenger Kingswoods at $4,245 and $4,300, respectively. About 166,900 Caprices were built. Historical sources do not indicate whether or not that number includes Kingswood Estate Wagons.

In historical terms the Caprice was really much more than that. It became a group of models that significantly increased Chevrolet sales, as well as profits. More importantly, it raised the Chevrolet image. After the Caprice arrived, enthusiasts commented that there was no longer a big difference between a Chevrolet and a Cadillac. The Caprice had turned Chevrolet into a "player" in the luxury-car market niche.

Consider an automobile that has the look of hand-rubbed walnut trim on every door; that seats you on deeply tufted fabric and has deep-twist carpeting underfoot; that relaxes you with a bolster center armrest; that cushions and quiets your ride with extra soundproofing, a heavier frame, a stronger body and a softer suspension . . . that is a Chevrolet Impala luxury option so it won't cost you a king's ransom.

Consider it done.

INTRODUCING THE CAPRICE CUSTOM SEDAN BY CHEVROLET
Chevrolet Division of General Motors, Detroit, Michigan

The 1965 Chevrolet Caprice interior showed the car was all about luxury.

1960s "Solid Gold"

1966 Chevrolet Caprice two-door hardtop

6	5	4	3	2	1
$1,040	$3,120	$5,200	$11,700	$18,200	$26,000

Note: Add 35 percent for 396 cid V-8 and 40 percent for the 427-cid engine. Add 15 percent for air conditioning.

Estimated values in today's marketplace taken from the 2006 Collector Car Price Guide.

1964-1969 Excalibur

Brooks Stevens is one of the heroes of mine that I actually got to meet. He was a "car nut" to the core. As a high school student I had studied industrial design at Brooklyn Technical High School and I had dreamed of becoming a car designer. Brooks, Raymond Loewy and Dick Teague were well-known designers at that time and had a lot to do with some of the greatest cars of the 1960s. If you loved '60s cars, you could not do better than counting Brooks among your friends.

The first time we met was at his wonderful car museum in Mequon, Wisconsin. My friend Bill Hebal was having a replica of the first Excalibur built by Raymond Besasie, who crafted body panels for the original. Brooks Stevens was giving Bill advice on the project. I was in awe of the famed designer, but didn't need to be. Another time I stopped at the museum again and Brooks invited me to lunch. We were accompanied by a group of his friends and enjoyed a wonderful lunch talking about sports cars and racing in the early 1950s.

Brooks Stevens was born in Milwaukee on June 7, 1911. He was strongly influenced by his father, William C. Stevens, executive vice president and director of engineering for Cutler Hammer. The senior Stevens invented an early pre-selector transmission. Brooks contracted polio as a child and spent hours each day sketching automobiles. Brooks said his father took him to a shoemaker who made special shoes for him every few months. The shoes helped him walk and, after graduating from the Milwaukee Country Day School, he went to New York to study architecture at Cornell University. He started school there in 1928 and graduated in 1933. He then started his industrial design career. Brooks eventually designed clothes dryers, bicycles, gas engines, boats, bicycles, trains and cars from Jeeps to Studebaker GTs.

1981 Series IV Excalibur

Brooks was involved in sports car racing in the early '50s, starting with his 1952 Excalibur J, a two-seat roadster built on the Henry J. platform. Stevens constructed a pair of these cars, one using a modified Willys F-head four and another with a specially-tuned Henry J L-head six. One of his drivers was the late Bob Gary, who became an automotive historian. Bob always claimed the 1,670-lb. Willys-powered Excalibur reached speeds in excess of 120 mph.

During the 1950s and early '60s, Brooks designed for Studebaker, once a leading automaker. Times had changed in South Bend and Studebaker was floundering. Studebaker president Sherwood Egbert had worked for McCulloch – a company that made superchargers – and Stevens designed the Paxton Panther for him. Egbert knew his company needed something special. In 1962, Stevens suggested the "Mercedes-baker," a hot Studebaker engine in a roadster that resembled a classic Mercedes SSK. Brooks sketched the car during lunch with his sons.

Egbert promised to supply Stevens with a Studebaker chassis. Stevens wanted a supercharged Lark Daytona chassis with disc brakes. One chassis was shipped to Brooks Stevens & Associates and taken next door to their shop. Joe Besasie – a Stevens staff designer – made some drawings and the prototype Excalibur SS was then built by Steve Stevens, metal fabricator Jules Mayeur, sheet metal craftsmen Ray Besasie Sr. and Ray Besasie Jr., and machinist Frank Neuschwanger. The plan was to exhibit the car at the Studebaker booth at the 1964 New York Auto Show.

The Excalibur seemed doomed when Studebaker ceased U.S. production early in 1964 and relocated from South Bend to Hamilton, Ontario. Stevens and his sons trailered the car to the New York Auto Show where it caused a sensation. Brooks, David and Steve Stevens returned to Milwaukee to form the Excalibur Automobile Corporation. They manufactured the neo-classic Excalibur SSK in Wisconsin, using a Studebaker convertible chassis and a Corvette V-8.

Mrs. Brook Stevens, David Stevens and the restored Excalibur I in New York. **Bill Hebel**

1986 Series V Excalibur

Whether the Excalibur is a sports car or a luxury car can be debated. Most collectors agree the boattail Duesenberg speedster is a luxury car. The Excalibur was a custom-made automobile with special features, high-quality construction and a very steep price. The 1965 Excalibur SSK roadster retailed for $7,200 – higher than any Cadillac, except a limousine. It used a large 109-inch wheelbase and ran 167.5 inches bumper to bumper. The 300-hp, 327-cid Corvette V-8 was linked to a four-speed manual gearbox. A total of 56 cars were constructed in 1965.

In 1966, Excalibur Automobile Corporation produced 90 cars (87 roadsters and three phaetons). In addition to the $7,250 roadster, a deluxe "SS" version had long, swooping front fenders, running boards and over-size rear fenders for $8,000. The standard equipment specifications were identical both years. As in '65, a Chevrolet Powerglide automatic transmission was optional. At 2,500 pounds, the deluxe model was a quarter-ton heavier than the original.

The new four-passenger Phaeton was officially added to the Excalibur offerings in 1967. Prices kept going up – the roadster was $7,750, the deluxe roadster was $8,250 and the phaeton was $8,950. Options included a supercharger that boosted the 327-cid V-8 to 400 hp. A luggage rack was $60, a roadster tonneau cover cost $60, a phaeton tonneau cover was $100, a center driving light was $75 and an AM/FM radio, $200. Production came to 38 roadsters and 33 phaetons.

In 1968, prices went up to $9,000 for the roadster and $10,000 for the phaeton. EMC stopped using the Holley carburetor it had adopted in 1966 and used a Rochester four-barrel carburetor instead. The base 327 stayed at 300 hp, but the supercharged version now put out 435 hp. Production of all models rose to 37 roadsters and 20 phaetons.

The last year for the 327-cid V-8 was 1969 when the roadsters retailed for $10,000 and the phaeton price rose to $11,000. Otherwise, very little change took place. Excalibur built 41 roadsters and 44 phaetons.

1960s "Solid Gold"
Excalibur SS

No prices are listed for the Excalibur SS. Crown City Motor Co. of Pasadena, California, recently offered a white 1966 Excalibur SS for $39,995. At the 2003 Palm Beach, Florida, Barrett-Jackson auction, a 1965 Excalibur SS roadster sold for a high bid of $64,260.

1976 Series III Excalibur

1967-1969 Mercury Marquis

The Marquis first bowed as a pricey two-door hardtop. It included a vinyl roof and five, full-length pin stripes on the lower portion of the body. Standard equipment on Mercury's prestige model included power front disc brakes, wood-grain interior trim, deluxe body insulation, an electric clock, a courtesy light group, a spare tire cover and plush fabric-and-vinyl upholstery. The lavish front seats had fold-down center armrests. All this came for just a tad under $4,000 in a upscale machine that attracted a mere 6,510 orders.

Base V-8 in the Marquis coupe was the brawny 410-cid Mercury V-8 with a 4.05 x 3.98-inch bore and stroke. It ran a 10.5:1 compression ratio and a Holley four-barrel carburetor and churned up 330 ponies at 4600 rpm. Anyone wanting to burn just a little more fossil fuel in those days of 37-cents-a-gallon gas could opt for a massive 428-cid mill that came in both 345- (single exhaust) and 360-hp (dual exhaust) versions.

1967 Mercury Marquis two-door hardtop

1967 Mercury Marquis

Mercury added new grillework and bumpers to its '68 models. The rear end was modestly restyled and new upholstery choices were issued. Some hardtop models offered a new fastback roofline, but the top-of-the-line Marquis stuck with the more conservative, formal top. The price was reduced by nearly $300 to spur sales, which fell to 3,965 units. A 390-cid four-barrel V-8 with 315 hp was base engine, replacing the old 410. A 428 with 340 hp was on the options list.

Inspired by the front end design of the Gen II Lincoln Continental MK III, the '69 Mercury Marquis had a new look and a full new range of models. They included a four-door sedan ($3,840 and 31,388 built), a two-door hardtop ($3,902 and 18,302 built), a four-door hardtop ($3,973 and 29,389 built, a rare convertible ($4,107 and 2,319 built) and a four-door Colony Park station wagon ($3,878 and 25,604 built). All shared a new, integrated bumper-grille with a distinctive horizontal-bars motif. Hidden headlight covers blended into the grille.

There was little doubt that this much more impressive Marquis was a true luxury car with a host of features meant to pamper its owners. Dual pin stripes decorated the body feature line above the bright "curb" moldings. Except for two back-up lights, the rear deck panel was a solid row of concave, rectangular, chrome-accented taillights. The interior lavished passengers in deep-pile nylon carpeting and rich upholstery selections. The dash and doors carried burled-walnut paneling and the steering wheel had a wood-tone rim and matching spokes. Standard equipment included convenient courtesy lights and an electric clock.

1969 Mercury Marquis convertible **Phil Hall Collection**

1968 Mercury Marquis **Phil Hall Collection**

Engine options started with the 390-cid 270-hp two-barrel V-8. A 429-cid V-8 with 320 hp was optional. The wheelbase grew an inch to 124 inches, which put the Marquis a bit closer to the luxury-class leaders. Overall length was 224.3 inches, compared to 218.5 inches in 1967 and 220.1 inches in 1968.

In the 1970s, the Marquis would be joined by the Marquis Brougham, with both models continually moving up-market towards the Lincoln bracket. But it all started back in the sensational '60s when prestige cars and luxury models became all the rage with American car buyers. Mercury may not be the most collectible marque, but those who collect Marquis know how easy it is to form an appreciation of these great automobiles.

1969 Mercury Marquis **Phil Hall Collection**

1960s "Solid Gold"

1966 Mercury Marquis two-door hardtop

6	5	4	3	2	1
$ 600	$1,800	$3,000	$6,750	$10,500	$15,000

Estimated values in today's marketplace taken from 2006 Collector Car Price Guide.

1965-1969 Ford LTD

If you were of driving age in 1965, you probably remember the first LTD as the quieter-than-a-Rolls Ford. "At 60 miles per hour the loudest noise in the Rolls-Royce comes from the electric clock," said the *London Daily Mirror*. "Tests carried out by a firm of acoustic consultants show that, at 60 mph, the new Ford is 2.8 decibels quieter than a Rolls."

The first Ford LTD fit the 1960s "prestige car" trend. The initials indicated "Limited" and this plush entry was embraced by upward-mobile Americans. Ford sold 105,729 of the "fancy Galaxie 500s" in the LTD model's first year of production – 37,691 two-door hardtops and 68,038 four-door hardtops.

The new model wore the "Galaxie 500" name on its front fenders, but round LTD medallions on the roof sail panels told the rest of the story. Standard equipment included all Galaxie 500 features, a 289-cid 200-hp V-8, Cruise-O-Matic, thick-padded seats, "pinseal" upholstery, a simulated walnut dashboard appliqué, interior courtesy lights, a lighted glove box, and a self-regulating clock. The two-door hardtop sold for the same price as the Galaxie 500XL two-door hardtop, $3,167. The four-door version was stickered at $3,245.

While the '66 model looked similar to the 1965, there were many differences. The 1966 version had more rounded contours. A new option was a 428-cid V-8 – the engine that came standard in the legendary Galaxie 7-Litre. LTD features were the same. Production for the model year came to 31,696 two-door hardtops and 69,400 four-door hardtops. Of all the upscale models – Caprice, VIP and Monaco – in the "regular-size" field, the LTD was far and away the sales leader. It contributed to a 22 percent gain in Ford's 1966 car business. A completely restyled line of Fords greeted buyers in 1967. LTDs were three inches longer and had softer, more sweeping body lines. An LTD four-door sedan was new. With a $3,298 price it was about $65 less expensive than the hardtop models. The new look featured sculptured side panels and a bi-level, gull-wing grille.

Select Shift Cruise-O-Matic three-speed automatic transmission was standard. This transmission could be shifted like a manual gearbox. A new Convenience Control Panel had lights to warn when fuel was low or if a door was ajar. Also optional was a new AM/FM stereo. This year there was a separate LTD series. Ford built 12,491 sedans, 51,978 four-door hardtops and 46,036 two-door Landaus. The 1968 Ford LTD underwent minor styling changes, including alterations to the side sheet metal. Model-year output included 22,834 sedans, 61,755 four-door hardtops and 54,163 two-door Landaus. Highlights of Ford's 1969 models included 0.6-inch longer and 2.1-inch lower exterior designs, a wider stance for better handling and a roomier interior. The LTD had a new front-end design with hidden headlights. All hardtops had ventless side windows.

"Looks like one of America's most expensive cars?" asked an ad for the '69 LTD Landau Coupe. "Hugs the road with as wide a track as a Cadillac. Has more front legroom and headroom than a Chrysler. Is designed to ride quieter than the LTD that was quieter than a Rolls-Royce."

1960s "Solid Gold"

1965 Ford LTD four-door hardtop

6	5	4	3	2	1
$ 700	$2,100	$3,500	$7,880	$12,250	$17,500

Estimated values in today's marketplace taken from the 2006 Collector Car Price Guide.

1967 Ford LTD two-door hardtop

1965 Ford LTD four-door hardtop

1966 Ford LTD four-door hardtop

The 1965 Ford LTD was promoted as being quieter than a Rolls Royce.

CHAPTER FOUR

The 1960s . . . The Compact Cars

The small car evolved in Europe, where travel distances were short, roads were narrow and fuel was expensive. Small cars had been marketed in the United States, too – from cycle cars made just after the turn of the century (one named the Imp was indicative of their size) to American Austins, Bantams and the Willys 77 and Willys Americar of the 1930s and '40s. In the 1950s it was the Henry J and Aero Willys. Sales of such models, here, were always relatively low.

America was a large country with broad coast-to-coast highways and cheap gas. One could envision a rancher in string tie and cowboy hat, barreling across Texas in an Eldorado ragtop with dual four-barrel carburetors and steer horns bolted to the hood. "Boy, Ah never met a gas pump Ah didn't like," he'd say. "I'm pumpin' it out of my front lawn, so's ah might as well use it up!"

So "small" usually meant "foreign" until 1957, when sales of imported cars – primarily British and German in the U.S.—doubled. The imports' market share moved from under one percent in 1955 to over eight percent in 1958.

Suddenly, America's "Big Three" automakers were watching as foreign car distributors nailed down 10 percent of the market – about 500,000 sales – by the end of 1959. This change caught American car companies "looking the other way." The 1958 Chicago Auto Show's "new" models included the Mercury Medalist, the De Soto Adventurer, a Chrysler-built custom limousine by the Italian coachbuilder

New Import Car Sales in the United States

Year	Sales	Percent of Total U.S. Sales
1949	12,251	0.25
1950	16,336	0.26
1951	20,828	0.41
1952	29,299	0.70
1953	28,961	0.50
1954	32,503	0.59
1955	58,465	0.82
1956	98,187	1.65
1957	206,827	3.46
1958	377,625	8.12

Ghia, the Thunderbird and the Rambler American. Only the American Rambler model was small and did well in the marketplace.

The American was some three feet shorter overall than the *typical* American car. What was "typical?" According to a chart appearing in the *1960 Encyclopedia Yearbook*, changes in American car sizes between 1936 and 1960 charted like this:

1960 Rambler American Super sedan

American Car Sizes 1936 to 1960

Year	Wheelbase	Length
1936	109 in. (9 ft.	185-1/2 inches (15 ft. 5-1/2 in.)
1942 to 1948	116 in. (9 ft.	Longest: 197-3/4 in. (16 ft. 5-3/4 in.)
		Shortest: 195-7/8 in. (16 ft. 3-7/8 in.)
1949 to 1958	115 in. (9 ft. 7 in.)	Longest: 197-13/16 in. (16 ft. 5-13/16 in.)
		Shortest: 195-1/2 in. (16 ft. 3-1/2 in.)
1959 and 1960	119 in. (9 ft. 11 in.)	Longest: 210-9/10 in. (17 ft. 6-9/10 in.)
		Shortest: 210-8/10 in. (17 ft. 6-8/10 in.)

America's second compact — the Studebaker Lark — was similar to the American. Like the AMC model, the Lark was a huge success for its manufacturer. In the last quarter of 1958, the Lark set a production record and the company posted its first profitable period since 1953. By February 1959, Studebaker-Packard sold more Larks than all its 1958 models. Model-year production was 131,508 cars (124,308 Larks) compared to 49,770 in 1958.

By the spring of 1959, magazines were full of stories about small cars that Chevrolet, Ford and Chrysler were developing. In *Motor Trend's* May issue, Bill Callahan spotlighted "Detroit's Smaller Cars" in an article showing artist Bill Motta's vision of Chevrolet's forthcoming Corvair.

Reports said GM's AC Division was already making small oil filters and Buick was building engines with a 10-in. shorter crankshaft. The Big Three said they might cancel their small-car programs because big-car sales were picking up, but turning the pages in those magazines revealed ads for BMW Isettas, DKWs, Toyopet Crown Customs, Opel Rekords and Triumph sedans and wagons. Was there any doubt about the Big Three fielding compacts?

Despite public denials by GM that a small car was slated for production, the Corvair sedan arrived in showrooms on October 2. (It would be January 1960 before the Club Coupe got there). Second to show up was the Ford Falcon Tudor and Fordor sedans, which bowed on October 8. A wagon would join them in March 1960. Chrysler's Valiant (not yet a Plymouth) debuted on October 29. Appearing March 17, 1960, was the Mercury Comet—a big Falcon.

Over the next 10 years, up to 12 compacts and "senior compacts" would be available in the annual model mix. These cars were essentially small versions of big American cars. Many had standard or optional V-8s and far less economy than the gas-*sippingest* European four bangers. The rear-mounted, air-cooled engine in the Corvair tried to be different and succeeded to attract good numbers of sporty-car buffs until the Mustang arrived. With multiple-carb setups, the Corvair was no real economy car. Both Tempest and Chevy II offered four bangers, but didn't catch on.

The American compacts heralded a continuing trend towards smaller cars in the long term, but did not really catch on in the 1960s. They stalled, but didn't stop, imported car sales (see chart). They induced buyers of big, high-profit cars to opt for cheaper ones. By mid-decade, the compacts had sired a new "mid-size" car segment that remained strong into the late '80s. The compacts also supplied a platform for the pony car. By 1970, most compacts were gone or so changed that they no longer fit the definition.

In 1964, the Tempest helped create a new kind of car with its GTO. **Phil Hall Collection**

1960S Imported Car Sales and Market Penetration

Calendar Year	U.S. Sales	Market Penetration
1960	498,785	7.58 %
1961	378,622	6.47 %
1962	339,160	4.89 %
1963	385,624	5.10 %
1964	481,131	6.00 %
1965	569,415	6.11 %
1966	658,123	7.31 %
1967	780,579	9.33 %
1968	985,767	10.48 %
1969	1,061,617	11.23 %

Despite the compacts' long-term failure, U.S. automakers popped corks when the 1960 production and sales totals came in. Calendar-year import sales reflected an 18.8 percent *decrease*. Market penetration was 7.58 percent, the lowest in three years. But Volkswagen sales increased by nearly 40,000 cars. English Ford, Mercedes-Benz, Metropolitan, Opel, Simca, Vauxhall, Ford Taunus and DKW-Auto Union were being hurt most by the American compacts.

Model-year production in the U.S. increased from 5,568,046 units in 1959 to 6,011,481 in 1960, a 7.9 percent gain. Compact car output reached 26.2 percent of industry in 1960 versus 9.1 percent in 1959. The new compacts had hurt most imports and some big U.S. cars, but not Volkswagen.

There was talk of Ford launching an even smaller car, code-named the Cardinal, as a direct competitor to the Volkswagen and Renault. Reports accurately discussed the Cardinal having a 96-in. wheelbase, a cast-iron V-4 and a $1,700 base price. But the Cardinal fell victim to a change of Ford leadership. It had been developed under Robert McNamara, who became Secretary of Defense in the Kennedy Administration. In 1962, with the Cardinal on the verge of production, Lee Iacocca ended the program. Much of the research and pre-production was used on the German Ford Taunus in the mid-'60s. Other rumors suggested a compact De Soto—which appeared as a rebadged Valiant in the South African market—as well as a Corvair El Camino.

For 1961, Buick, Oldsmobile and Pontiac added compacts. The Pontiac Tempest captured a bit of the radical Corvair thinking in its drive train engineering and suspension, while the Buick Special and Olds F-85 were more conventional. Dodge's Lancer was little more than a Valiant clone. Compact cars hit a new record in 1961, but the independent automakers lost market share. While small-car output by the Big Three jumped 21.44 percent between 1960 and 1961, the combined total of Americans, Ramblers and Larks built dropped 24.49 percent.

"Does this Rambler really come with rally stripes?"

"No, but with the new engine it drives that way."

'66 Rambler American

1966 Rambler American convertible

While AMC and Studebaker worried about losing share, other U.S. automakers had their own concerns about small cars. People were buying the lower-priced compact, yet big-car sales declined by close to a million units between 1960 (4,436,643) and 1961 (3,503,826). And though sales of imports declined by 120,000, Volkswagen sales again increased to 177,308.

At the beginning of model-year 1962, the American car market was in a state of flux. Small-car output exploded in 1961, but standard-size cars began to show renewed strength. Automakers were blindsided by this surprising twist in demand. *Ward's 1962 Automotive Yearbook* said, "The car size changes for '62 ran both counter to and parallel to the new sales trend, promising further adjustments in car sizes for '63."

A very quick recovery from a short-lived, early-1961 business recession was the reason for criss-crossing trends. Monthly new-car sales increased through May 1961 and fourth-quarter sales set a record for the period, despite labor contract strikes. Buyers were suddenly turning away from compacts. Sporty hardtops were back in favor, as were sporty features like bucket seats. Big, powerful, gas guzzling V-8s were in.

Most of those who wanted basic transportation were happy with a Volkswagen. Those who preferred a small car with a roomy back seat and a degree of sportiness turned to American-built compact hardtops and convertibles. Buyers often added performance and convenience extras. Some asked why America didn't have a car sized between compact and standard models. Detroit listened and Ford was the first to respond with the '62 Ford Fairlane and Mercury Meteor.

Also arriving in 1962 was the Chevy II, a conventional car designed to go head-to-head with Ford's hot-selling Falcon. Marketed in three series and nine models, with a choice of four- or six-cylinder engines, this "economy" model was designed to get buyers the Corvair missed. The Chevy II was really a Falcon/Rambler/Lark with a 110-in. wheelbase. Chevrolet expected it to double the Corvair's sales with 326,618 assemblies for the model year, but still missed its target.

1959-1961 U.S. Model Year Compact Car Production

Make	Model	Model Year Production		
		1959	1960	1961
AMC	American	58,900	120,603	136,003
AMC	Rambler	145,500	314,440	223,057
Buick	Special	N/A	N/A	87,444
Chevrolet	Corvair	N/A	250,007	297,881
Dodge	Lancer	N/A	N/A	74,773
Ford	Falcon	N/A	435,676	489,323
Mercury	Comet	N/A	116,331	197,263
Oldsmobile	F-85	N/A	N/A	76,394
Plymouth	Valiant	N/A	187,808	133,487
Pontiac	Tempest	N/A	N/A	100,783
Studebaker	Lark	98,200	121,510	61,552
Total		**302,600**	**1,546,375**	**1,877,960**

The remarkable 1963 Olds Jetfire used the Turbo-Rocket V-8 that burned waste gases in its turbocharger.

1962-1964 U.S. Model Year Compact and Senior Company Car Production

Make	Model	Model Year Production		
		1962	1963	1964
AMC	American	125,700	105,300	163,700
AMC	Rambler/Classic	280,400	279,800	146,800
Buick	Special	154,467	149,538	midsize
Chevrolet	Corvair	306,022	266,564	199,387
Chevrolet	Chevy II	326,618	375,626	191,691
Dodge	Lancer/Dart	64,271	153,921	195,263
Ford	Falcon	414,282	345,972	317,435
Mercury	Comet	165,305	134,623	189,936
Oldsmobile	F-85	94,568	118,811	midsize
Plymouth	Valiant	145,353	198,399	200,693
Pontiac	Tempest	143,193	131,490	midsize
Studebaker	Lark	85,900	67,600	33,150
Total		**2,306,079**	**2,327,644**	**1,638,055**

American compacts (except the Chevy II) accounted for a calendar-year production of 1,979,961 cars in the 1962 model year, a 5.4 percent increase from 1961. Sales of standard size cars *increased* 10.4 percent to 3,868,000 while imports fell to 339,160. The pendulum was swinging back toward larger cars. Volkswagen had 192,570 units or 56.8 percent of total imports. It seemed no matter what the Big Three did, VW's popularity grew.

The number of true "compact" cars available in 1963 shrunk as the AMC Rambler became the Classic with a longer 112-in. wheelbase. The Special, F-85 and Tempest grew into "senior" compacts, also using a new 112-inch wheelbase. Dodge transferred its well-known Dart name from a larger car to a car with a 111-in. wheelbase, replacing the Lancer. The Valiant – though heavily restyled – got a slightly smaller 106-in. wheelbase. The only American compacts left with a less-than-110-in. wheelbase were the American, Corvair, Falcon and Valiant. (The 98-in. Corvette and 109-in. The Studebaker Avanti was a *sports* cars, rather than *compacts*.)

In 1964, the Special, F-85 and Tempest became "midsize" cars, as did the new 114-in.-wheelbase Comet. Ford's Falcons retained a 109.5-in. wheelbase. Calendar-year production of genuine compact cars fell by over 100,000 units. The 1964 Corvair, with Gen I styling, was suddenly outselling the Chevy II.

1966 Falcon Futura Sports Coupe

1965-1967 U.S. Model Year Production – Compact and Senior Compact Cars

Make	Model	Model Year Production		
		1965	1966	1967
AMC	Rambler (*)	112,900	93,700	70,000
Chevrolet	Corvair	237,056	103,743	27,253
Chevrolet	Chevy II	130,425	172,485	117,995
Dodge	Dart	206,631	112,920	171,413
Ford	Falcon (**)	227,362	161,762	76,419
Mercury	Comet	165,052	midsize	midsize
Plymouth	Valiant (***)	159,197	138,137	108,969
Studebaker	Lark (****)	19,440	4,648	N/A
Total		**1,258,063**	**787,395**	**572,049**

(*) Includes Rambler American and Rambler Rogue.

(**) Additional 1966-1967 Falcons made in Canada for the U.S. market.

(***) Excluding Barracuda.

(****) Made in Canada.

The 1965 compacts reflected different ideas in styling. In the General Motors stable, the Corvair got smooth, rounded lines and an "Italian" look. Ford and Chrysler products adopted crisper, boxier lines. Rambler Classics became Rebels and left the compact-car field, while the American took the Rambler name and introduced the sporty Rogue hardtop. It was a good year for the Dodge Dart, but most other compacts and senior compacts had lower sales and production. America's economy was solid and tastes were swinging back to big cars. Some compacts grew larger or fancier (or both) and engine sizes went up. The Falcon replaced its 144-cid base six with a 170-cid six. Comets got a 28-amp alternator.

The 1966 season was mainly a year for restyled mid-sized cars (including former compacts like the Special, F-85 and Tempest.) Also becoming a "former compact" this year was the up-sized Mercury Comet. The Falcon and the Chevy II went to the beauty parlor for new "looks." Production totals make it look like the new Chevy II was a winner and the Falcon wasn't, but that's not altogether true. Ford made some Falcons in a Canadian factory, which led to its U.S. production total dropping off. Ford made 55,965 cars north of the border from January 1966 until December, and that U.S. sales in calendar-year 1966 included 155,266 Chevy IIs and 162,965 Falcons. Government-mandated safety equipment was starting to show up on all 1966 American cars, including compacts. This was the last year for the now-Canadian-built Studebaker Lark.

The compact car count was down to six models in 1967. The Dodge Dart – the largest of all U.S. compacts –was the most popular, followed by the Chevy II and the Plymouth Valiant. Most of the compact cars were restyled. Additional safety equipment was required on all cars this year. Naturally, prices had to be hiked.

1964 Corvair Monza Spyder coupe

1963 Pontiac Tempest   **Tom Glatch**

Corvair took it on the chin from the Mustang and Ralph Nader and Chevrolet felt it was time to drop the Corsa series. The Falcon, losing buyers to the Mustang, took on a new look closer to that of its pony-car relative. Plymouth Valiants got a new body with curved side glass and a two-inch longer wheelbase. With nine models, the Rambler American was said to be the only U.S. compact remain available in "all" body styles. You could get two- and four-door sedans, a four-door wagon, a two-door hardtop and a convertible.

The same six compact cars were marketed in 1968 and the big news was the addition of government-mandated safety features on many models. At AMC, the Rambler American continued its pattern of minimum change from year to year. A Rogue hardtop was the sporty version. The history of the Corvair was winding towards its close and sedans were dropped. The Chevy II "senior compact" was restyled and was more Chevelle-like. Only two- and four-door sedans remained. The Dodge Dart was a carryover of the new-for-'67 model, with a high-performance GTX added. Ford's Falcon had only a minor facelift and didn't make any big move in the performance-car direction. Plymouth's Valiant was mainly a clone of the Dart, and Plymouth reserved its performance talk mainly for the Valiant-based Barracuda.

AMC renamed its 1969 the Rambler (instead of Rambler American), but very little else was different on the outside. Mechanical upgrades included a new suspended accelerator pedal with revised linkage and a "Clear-Power 24" battery and DRL-style parking lights that stayed on with the headlights. The last Corvair offered buyers new color options and more comfortable bucket seats. The Nova, once a top model of the Chevy II was now the model's name and featured revised trim and a new instrument panel for '69. Dodge offered a new performance-oriented Swinger model with a standard 340-cid V-8 and four-on-the-floor.

1962 Rambler American 400 convertible

Ford's Falcon got more power and more safety equipment for '69 with a "big-car" grille. The '69 Valiant was updated with a new grille, taillights, trim and a straight-element rear window.

By 1969, compact models represented just 7.1 percent of all new cars registered in the United States – a total of 665,639 units. Americans had been scared into buying compacts by the 1957 recession, but the economy rebounded quickly and the market turned to a trend towards larger cars with more performance and luxury. The compacts had some appeal in the sporty car niche, until the Mustang and other copycat pony cars arrived. The small-car market would be revived in the 1970s spurred by rising fuel prices. It is inevitable that shrinking supplies and rising costs of petroleum will push buyers towards smaller, efficient automobiles as long as they rely on fossil fuels for energy. The compact car craze of the early '60s was truly a hint of what was to come.

1968-1969 U.S. Model Year Production – Compact and Senior Compact Cars

Make	Model	Model Year Production	
		1968	1969
AMC	Rambler (*)	81,000	96,400
Chevrolet	Corvair	15,399	6,000
Chevrolet	Chevy II/Nova(**)	201,005	269,988
Dodge	Dart	191,978	214,751
Ford	Falcon (***)	41,650	71,158
Plymouth	Valiant (****)	110,795	107,208
Total		**641,827**	**765,505**

(*) Includes Rambler American and Rambler Rogue in 1968 and Rambler and Rambler Rogue in 1969.

(**) Redesigned Chevy II becomes better known as Nova.

(***) Additional Falcons were made in Canada for the U.S. market.

(****) Excluding Barracuda.

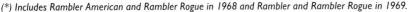

1960-1968 Rambler American and 1969 Rambler

1963 Rambler American 440-H hardtop

The American—built by American Motors Corp. in Kenosha, Wisconsin—was not really a new car. It was a discontinued 1956 model that AMC decided to freshen up and reintroduce in 1958. This "baby bathtub" started as the 1950 "Little Nash Rambler" with body by Italian coachbuilder Pininfarina. The car was popularized in 1958 in the song "Beep-Beep" by the Playmates. The song hit the Top 10 charts the same year the Rambler reappeared as the American. Coming out just after the 1957 economic recession and just before the song arrived, the re-release was perfectly timed and made AMC the only U.S. carmaker to increase sales in 1958. About 30,000 Americans were produced then and more than 76,000 the following season.

The 1960 American came in Deluxe Six ($1,781 to $2,020), Super Six ($1,880 to $2,105) and Custom Six ($2,059 to $2,235) series, all on a 100-in. wheelbase. Larger windows and wider door openings were featured. A four-door sedan was added to the carryover two-door sedan and station wagon. Styling was little changed from 1959. Convenience and comfort got more emphasis. Flashomatic transmission was a $165 option. The old Nash 195.6-cid 90-hp L-head in-line six was the only engine until midyear, when an overhead-valve version with 125 hp was installed in Custom models.

Edmund Anderson restyled the boxy 1961 American. It had a cut-off look with concave sculpturing. Convertible and four-door wagon models were added. It was slightly smaller than before, but wheelbase and basic dimensions were similar. The ragtop came only in the Custom line, but in standard and Custom trim. Freshness made the 1961 American a temporary hit. It was the only compact from an independent automaker to rise in production.

American Custom line models delivered 25 mpg and good performance, but the car had a hard time competing with Big Three compacts in the looks department. Though considered "cult cars" now, these wedge-shaped midgets were thought of as "toads" in their time. After classic car collector Dick Teague joined the AMC design staff in 1961, he set to work prettying up the American.

1960 Rambler American Deluxe club sedan

CHAPTER FIVE

1962 Rambler American 400 station wagon

Teague's '64 re-issue was still a compact, but had a bigger 106-inch-wheelbase. Stretched four inches for comfort and convenience, it had a modified "step-down" platform, lower silhouette, curved window glass, "fine-line" aluminum grille and single headlights. For "sports car" buffs, there was a fastback with a transverse rear crease line. The 195.6-cid ohv six came in 90-, 125- and 138-hp options. There were 10 models and six transmission choices.

This basic design lasted for the rest of the decade. The compact Rambler Classic became the mid-size 1963 AMC Classic. The American and a sporty hardtop version called the Rogue were the only "Ramblers" to survive. By 1966, the base six had 199 cid and 128 hp, while a 232-cid 145-hp "big six" and a 290-cid 200-hp V-8 (introduced at February's Chicago Auto Show) were optional.

1962 Rambler American two-door sedan

The "American" name was dropped and "Rambler" was used for AMC's only '69 compact (with the Javelin and AMX pony cars in that class). Ramblers came as two- and four-door sedans and Rambler 440s came as four-door sedans and wagons. The Rogue was a two-door hardtop with optional 290-cid 200-hp V-8.

A special red, white and blue hardtop called the SC/Rambler was also available in '69. This AMC-Hurst creation had a 390-cid 315-hp V-8, a Hurst-shifted four-speed and a 3.54:1 Twin-Grip differential. It could run 14-sec. quarter miles. Many muscle-car goodies were included. Only 1,512 were built.

1963 Rambler American 440 convertible

1960 Rambler American Super club sedan

AMERICAN CARS OF THE 1960S

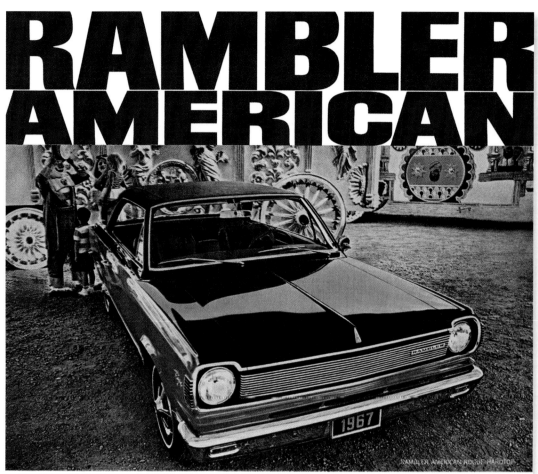

RAMBLER AMERICAN

Now—Typhoon V-8 thunder comes to America's low-priced, economy champ cars. Now Rambler Americans offer five engines to chop hills down to size for you: three powerhouse Sixes (the smallest is a Pure Oil acceleration class winner and Mobil Economy Run mileage champ), and two 290 cu. in. Typhoon V-8s (including a 4-barrel job that delivers 225 hp). Now there are five Rambler American transmissions—including a 4-speed floor stick—plus power disc brakes and a specially tuned suspension that turns bad roads into good roads.

Now there's styling that matches the performance —starting with straight-line grilles, concave tail-lights, and sleek rally moldings. Now there's room you'll find hard to find in other compacts. People-space you just don't get in those little imports. Now there's famous Rambler economy in America's only complete line of compacts: Rogue hardtop or convertible; 440 sedans, hardtop, or wagon; 220 sedans or wagon.

Now every Rambler American gives you these standard safety features: 153.8 sq. in. brakes on Sixes (167.5 on V-8s); Double-Safety brake system; warning signal light to monitor both brake line systems; energy-absorbing steering column and three-spoke deep-dish wheel; padded dash, visors; backup lights; seat belts (retractable in front); shoulder belt anchor plates; 4-way flashers; day/nite anti-glare mirror; and more built-in safety features to help you drive with care and confidence...all built into a solid, single-unit body. Your American Motors/Rambler Dealer sells 9 models of Rambler Americans. See him. He's the only Now Car dealer in town. **THE 1967 AMERICAN MOTORS**

AMBASSADOR · MARLIN · REBEL · RAMBLER AMERICAN

Quality built in—so the value stays in. Read new 5-year or 50,000-mile warranty...see opening page. **5 50,000**

THE NOW CARS

1967 Rambler Rogue two-door hardtop

1960s "Solid Gold"

1963 Rambler American 440-H two-door hardtop

6	5	4	3	2	1
$ 400	$1,200	$2,000	$4,500	$7,000	$10,000

Estimated values in today's marketplace are taken from the 2006 Collector Car Price Guide.

1960-1964 Rambler, Rambler Rebel, Rambler Classic, AMC Classic

1962 Rambler Classic 400 two-door sedan

AMC's Rambler Six and Rambler Rebel, introduced in 1956, rode a 108-in. wheelbase and qualified as compacts. While they didn't fit the "midget car" image like the diminutive American, they added much to sales and the bottom line. The two models combined made American Motors the leading maker of small cars for several years and increased its rank on the 1961 sales charts to third. The Rambler's success was also its downfall, as the niche it carved out soon attracted strong competition from America's "Big Three" automakers.

For 1957, AMC offered the high-performance "Rebel" four-door hardtop with a hot rod version of the 327-cid Ambassador V-8. All Rebels were Silver-Gray with bronze-gold anodized aluminum trim, "Rebel" front fender badges, and a special silver-and-black interior. *Motor Trend* said only a "fuelie" 'Vette could outrun a Rebel from 0-to-60. *Hot Rod* ran 0-to-60 in 9.4 seconds and said a stick-shift Rebel was even faster. The quarter mile took 17 seconds at 84 mph.

The 1960 Rambler came in Deluxe Six, Super Six and Custom Six ($1,918 to $2,571) series, as well as Rebel

Super and Custom Six and V-8 lines, all on the 108-in. wheelbase. AMC promoted two-piece grilles and bumpers to cut repair costs. The grille was heavy die-cast metal for durability. Styling was the same as 1959 and a side-hinged station wagon rear door was new.

For 1961 the renamed 108-in.-wheelbase Rambler Classic was facelifted and given a 127-hp aluminum six. After hyping two-piece designs in 1960, AMC used a one-piece extruded aluminum grille, with the "RAMBLER" name spelled out along the bottom, and a one-piece bumper. The body got new side sculpturing like the American, but small tail fins were retained.

1961 Rambler Custom Cross Country station wagon

In 1962, the Classic's fins were shaved off. It got another new grille, round taillights and a two-door sedan. With other makers downsizing big cars, AMC decided the Ambassador should be a 108-in. wheelbase compact. The aluminum six was reused, but a cast-iron six was optional. The Ambassador offered just a 327-cid V-8. To make the body leaner, the front suspension was revamped. For a hardtop look, aluminum frames concealed sedan body pillars.

The '63 Ramblers were the first AMC products to spring from Dick Teague's sketchpad. This meant a complete top-to-bottom redo with an advanced type of unit-body construction

1962 Rambler Classic 400 two-door club sedan **David Lyon**

1960 Rambler Custom sedan

with 30 percent fewer parts and welds. Classics and Ambassadors got a longer 112-in. wheelbase, but no length increase. They looked lower and more contemporary with a concave "electric shaver" grille and curved side glass. Classics got a semi-automatic "E-Stick" transmission and midyear V-8 option. A "Twin-Stick" transmission was extra. These were nice cars and had an inch longer wheelbase and inch shorter overall length than the "compact" Dodge Dart.

1964 Rambler Classic station wagon and two-door hardtop

Sportier styling and a wider range of styles, including hardtops was seen in 1964. Classic hardtops had a semi-fastback roofline and the choice of a six or V-8. Still on the 112-in. "senior compact" wheelbase was the top-of-the-line "Ambassador 990." It offered new bucket seats with a cushion between them so a third person could ride up front. Available in an up-level Classic 770 line with special "butter knife" body trim was a Typhoon hardtop with a 232-cid six.

By 1965, the Ambassador was stretched to a 116-in. wheelbase and considered the "full-size" American Motors car. That made the 112-in.-wheelbase Classic what AMC then called its "new intermediate-size Rambler." For the Rambler American, the catch phrase was "compact economy king." This meant the Classic, though unchanged, was no longer a "compact."

1961 Rambler Custom Cross Country station wagon

1960s "Solid Gold"

1960 Rambler Rebel four-door hardtop

6	5	4	3	2	1
$ 464	$1,392	$2,320	$5,220	$8,120	$11,600

Estimated values in today's marketplace are taken from the 2006 Collector Car Price Guide.

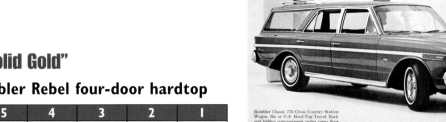

1964 Rambler Classic 770 station wagon

1960-1969 Chevrolet Corvair

1962 Corvair 500 coupe

The Corvair was the first compact from the Big Three – and the most unique. Standard 500 ($1,984 to $2,038) and Deluxe 700 ($2,049 to $2,103) models were offered. The Monza 900 Club ($2,238) came in February 1960 at the Chicago Auto Show. The 108-in.-wheelbase Corvair had a unit-body, rear-mounted, air-cooled "pancake" six and independent swing-axle suspension. Powerglide with a dash-mounted selector was $146 extra. It was just over four-feet high and 15-ft. long. Its flat floor allowed six-passenger seating.

Four-door Corvairs had the flat-top "aircraft carrier" look that GM pioneered on some '59s. The midyear Club Coupe was absolutely huggable with its "bubble" window. I worked in a Staten Island, N.Y. supermarket, Food Farm, with John Biondi who had a two-tone green coupe with three-on-the-floor. To him, it was a sports car with a back seat for his baby daughter.

When the Corvair arrived, I had plans to become a car stylist and the Corvair wowed me with its "leading-edge" design. Its "grille-less" front broke with tradition. The front, side and rear panels were heavily sculptured. The use of wide expanses of glass made it airier than most cars. The Corvair was different from any other car.

Motor Trend named it "Car of the Year" and described the Corvair as "Detroit's VW." Chevy said the sedan could do 0 to 60 mph in 20.6 seconds and the quarter mile in 22.5 seconds at 62 mph. Top speed was 86 mph. *Motor Trend's* Walt Woron compared the Corvair to imports and rated it best in styling, handling and practicality. He rated imports (especially Volkswagen) higher in quality, but liked that the Corvair could be serviced at Chevy dealerships. "In short, Chevrolet has a winner," said Woron.

1964 Corvair coupe

The 1961 Corvair had only minor changes, but it got the Lakewood station wagon, an optional 98-hp engine and an available four-speed gearbox. The 500 and 700 were selling only one-third as many units as the cheaper, more conventional Ford Falcon, but the sporty Monza was carving out a niche. Chevy added a four-door Monza sedan with a vinyl bucket seat interior. Before long market penetration was growing. Most Corvairs (over 139,000) were sold in the $1,901 to $2,000 price group, where there was no Falcon model.

The '62 Corvair took a cut-from-the-bottom-add-to-the-top approach. The 500 Series was now just a Club Coupe. The Lakewood was dropped from the 700 Series. The Monza line got a rare station wagon (2,362 built), a convertible and a Spyder equipment option that included a 150-hp Turbo six and the four-speed. Production climbed

1963 Corvair Monza convertible

over 300,000 for the first (and only) time. In '63, Chevy added a Delcotron (alternator) and self-adjusting brakes. In 1964, both the 500 (Club Coupe) and 700 (four-door sedan) series had just one model. A bigger 164.5-cid 95-hp six was standard and Monza Spyders got the Turbo six.

Completely redesigned for 1965, the Corvair had great new longer, lower, wider "Italian" looks. Club Coupes and sedans were gone. The base 500 line offered two- and four-door hardtops, the now-mid-range Monza line had those plus a convertible. The Corsa was the new flagship and offered just a two-door hardtop and a convertible. Carried over was the standard 95-hp flat six. The Corsa got a four-carb 140-hp version of the same motor. New was a 180-hp turbocharged version of the 164. Frameless, curved side glass was new.

The Food Farm's produce manager – Dominic DeMarci – owned a metallic gold Corsa ragtop with a white roof, bucket seats, automatic transmission and the 140-hp "Turbo-Air" engine. At the time I was driving a '55 Chevy Del Ray coupe

1962 Corvair by Chevrolet

1967 Corvair 500 two-door hardtop

1965 was a wonderful year for car sales in America. Being all-new and good-looking and modern, the Gen II Corvair revived the marque's popularity, but only for its first year. The Corsa performed poorly against the Mustang, which appealed to the same type of buyer, but provided far more power and more stable handling characteristics at a lower price. Corsa production went from 28,654 in 1965 to 10,472 in 1966 and that led to its being dropped by 1967. By 1968, total Corvair output was just 15,399 and by 1969, a mere 6,000 were produced.

Only two Corvair 500 and three Monza models were marketed in 1967. The following year, the four-door

and fantasized about borrowing the Corsa's keys to take a Saturday cruise. One day the keys came flying at me . . . "go over to the New Dorp store and pick up some stuff we need," said Dominic. "They'll have it ready for you."

It was a sunny day and I immediately put the car's top down. I set off on a rather boring route to the other store, filled with slow-moving traffic but thought I could return over Emerson Hill, a steep road with many twisting turns. I envisioned it would be like driving a Ferrari in the Mille Miglia. Little did I know the "stuff" I was picking up was a load of watermelons! "It's a good thing you've got the top down," said the other produce manager. "We'll be able to squeeze them in that way, but try not to go too fast!" The Corsa convertible had a sports car feeling. If the Mustang hadn't come along, Chevy could have sold a million.

1965 Corvair Monza convertible

CHAPTER FIVE

1968 Corvair Monza 500 Sport Coupe

1965 Corvair Monza Sport Sedan

1962 Corvair 700 sedan

1967 Corvair Monza convertible

hardtop was gone from both series, leaving only three models. The same three were carried over in 1969, the final appearance of the Corvair. In mid-May of 1969, Chevrolet offered Corvair buyers a $150 discount coupon to purchase any new Chevrolet, good until 1973. This was seen as compensation for lost resale value caused by the Corvair being dropped.

It is well known that Ralph Nader's 1965 book *Unsafe at Any Speed: The Designed-In Dangers of the American Automobile* hurt the Corvair's reputation. Nader tried to document that automakers were against spending money on safety equipment and used the 1960 to 1962 Corvair's high-strung swing-arm suspension as an example of unsafe engineering. Although Chevrolet had corrected the problem in 1963, GM tried to discredit Nader. The company's practices made headlines and GM president James Roche had to go before a Senate subcommittee and apologize for trying to intimidate him. Later research indicated the Falcon and Mustang hurt the Corvair more than Nader did, but his book was detrimental to the car's sales.

1960s "Solid Gold"

1964 Corvair 900 Monza coupe

6	5	4	3	2	1
$ 552	$1,656	$2,760	$6,210	$9,660	$13,800

Estimated values in today's marketplace are taken from the 2006 Collector Car Price Guide.

1962-1969 Chevy II/Nova

1966 Chevy II Nova SS Sport Coupe **Tom Jevcak**

If the Corvair was Chevy's VW, the Chevy II was its Falcon. It represented an entirely new line of cars four inches wider and 3.5 inches higher than the air-cooled compact on a two-inch longer wheelbase. Though 99 and 44/100ths percent of the car was a conventional big car in a-small-package model, the "Deuce" did have an unusual-for-the-time 153-cid 90-hp four-cylinder base engine and new tapered-plate, single leaf rear springs. These units consisted of a five-foot-long shot-peened steel bars that varied in thickness and width to provide uniform stress distribution. Body-frame integral construction was used.

The model lineup consisted of the Standard 100 two-and four-door sedans and four-door wagon, the same models in Deluxe 300 trim and a top-of-the-line six-cylinder only Nova series with the same styles, plus a two-door hardtop and convertible. Prices ranged from $2,003 to $2,497. Based on the high popularity of the cut-from-the-same-cloth Ford Falcon, the Nova was expected to outsell the Corvair. It did, but not by as much as projected.

There were only detail refinements made to the Chevy II in 1963, including new upholstery materials. The Nova Six two-door sedan was discontinued. Improvements were made to the unit-body with stub-frame system, as well as the suspension. Power again came from the four or 194-cid 120-hp in-line six. Production jumped 15 percent, while Falcon output fell.

The 1964 Chevy II got new self-adjusting brakes and bigger engines, including a 283-cid 195-hp V-8 that made it go faster and hinted at things to come. There was also a 230-cid 155-hp six. The 300 line was dropped and the Chevy II 100 wagon came only in a six-cylinder format. A two-door sedan was reinstated in the Nova line, which lost its convertible. A Nova SS Sport Coupe was added for those interested in high performance. Chevy II output took a tremendous 49 percent hit, much of it due to a crippling 32-day strike that cost Chevy production of 250,000 cars and 56,000 trucks. In addition, the release of the Mustang figured into the equation, as it stole some Chevy II buyers away.

Revisons to the grille and side trim were the 1965 Chevy II's main changes. Sedans got a new roof and window design. These were 11 models in three series, including two station wagons. A mere 376 cars were fitted with four-cylinder engines (down from just 1,121 in 1964). In addition, 108,100 sixes and 16,700 V-8s were built. In the Nova SS

1965 Chevy II Nova SS exterior **Phil Hall Collection**

1965 Chevy II Nova Sport Coupe **Phil Hall Collection**

line, the 4,800 V-8 installations outnumbered the 4,300 six-cylinder cars made. In fact, 12,000 of the V-8s went into Nova and Nova SS models and 3,400 were used in station wagons. It was possible to add a 250-hp (L30) or 300-hp (L74) 327-cid V-8 to a 1965 Chevy II.

Completely restyled for 1966, the Chevy II came in seven models and three series with a lower and wider appearance. There were new rooflines for all coupes and sedans, a new aluminum grille and a more massive front bumper. Seven engines were offered and the top option was the L79 version of the "327" with 350 hp on tap. This "factory hot rod" did the quarter mile in just over 15 sec. and was going well over 90 mph at the end of the run. To fight corrosion, plastic panels were put behind the headlights. Production went up a bit this year.

Styling changes for 1967 included new front fenders, a new grille with a prominent horizontal center bar and revised ornamentation. Still hanging on was the 153-cid four that was used in 648 cars. A V-8 was put into some 26,000 Chevy IIs, including 13,200 Nova and 8,200 (81 percent) Nova SS models. The V-8s offered this year included the 283-cid 195-hp version and the optional 327-cid 275-hp job. Nova production dipped as the '66 styling got old.

Patterned after the Chevelle, the restyled 1968 Chevy II was one of its most popular renditions. It had a longer 111-in. wheelbase and was longer and wider than ever. Things were simplified all around with only one Nova line and two body styles – coupe and sedan. For some reason, Chevy kept the four alive (1,270 were purchased). A larger new 230-cid 140-hp engine was the base in-line

1966 Chevy II Nova Sport Coupe **David Lyon**

1965 Chevy II 100 sedan

1967 Chevy II Nova SS Sport Coupe

1968 Chevy II Nova SS 396 coupe **Phil Kunz**

1966 Chevy II 100 two-door sedan **Dan Lyon**

Dressed up in new exterior and interior trim, the Chevy II became the Nova in 1969. There always was a Nova model but now they were all Novas. Buyers who ordered the SS equipment package got a special hood and front fender louvers. Engine options included one four, two sixes and three V-8s with up to 400 hp. Unlike the short-lived 1966 restyling, this one caught on and production pushed up to nearly 270,000 units in its second year. Not hurting sales was a big ad campaign that pushed low prices – which started at $2,237.

six, but the 250-hp version remained. The V-8s offered this year included a new 307-cid 200-hp version, a 327-cid 275-hp job and a new "350" with 295 hp. Since the new Nova shared its front stub frame with the Camaro, it wasn't long before Chevrolet realized it could install the big-block 396-cid 375-hp V-8. Performance dealers like Don Yenko also fitted a small number of '68 Novas with 427-cid V-8s. The new design pushed production back up and over 200,000 units.

1960s "Solid Gold"

1963 Chevy II Nova two-door hardtop

6	5	4	3	2	1
$ 800	$2,400	$4,000	$9,000	$14,000	$20,000

Note: Add 15 percent for the Super Sport option.

Estimated values in today's marketplace are taken from the 2006 Collector Car Price Guide.

1964 Chevy II Nova two-door sedan

1960-1969 Ford Falcon

1964 Falcon Futura convertible   **David Lyon**

The champion seller of all the compacts was a "small big car" with a 109.5-in. wheelbase and a scaled-down, totally conventional design and engineering package. The 1960 Falcon Six was introduced on October 8, 1959. A full-length sculptured side panel graced the functionally-styled bodies. Tudor and Fordor (Ford's spelling) sedans, priced at $1,746 and $1,803, were offered and a four-door wagon was added at midyear. The Falcon's 90-hp in-line six was designed for 50 percent better gas mileage than standard U.S. engines. Automatic transmission added $159. Production was 435,676.

The 1960 Falcon was a clean-lined, good-looking car with virtually no "tricky" engineering and plenty of room for people and luggage.

Motor Trend compared the "functional styling and engineering" of the first Falcon to the Model A Ford. The front suspension resembled a big Ford's with the springs and shocks repositioned. At the rear was conventional Hotchkiss drive. The Falcon drove like a big car and had no trouble cruising along at 50 to 60 mph or pushing up to 80 mph. Handling was what you'd expect from the average big car of the day. Braking was described as "admirable." *Motor Trend's* Steve Da Costa felt that the Falcon met three of six objectives Ford had established for the car: light weight, six-passenger seating and low upkeep. He said the other design goals—performance, high economy and low cost – needed more work.

1965 Falcon Futura two-door hardtop   **Phil Hall Collection**

The 1961 Falcon got the "don't-mess-with-success" treatment, with few changes other than a new "electric shaver" grille and a Deluxe series including a fancy Futura sedan. The larger 170-cid Comet engine with 101 hp became an option. A double-wrapped aluminized muffler was another new feature. Ford promoted 30 mpg economy and 4,000-mile oil changes. Ford produced 489,323 Falcons and 404,010 of the 144-cid sixes, indicating the car's buyer appeal was mainly for its economy. Most Falcons (235,501) sold in the $1,701 to $1,800 price bracket, one notch up from the market's lowest rung. The second highest number (81,593) were sold in the $2,101 to $2,200 bracket, the top one for the Falcon.

Minor appearance changes in 1962 included a grille with vertical openings, dummy hood scoop trim and different body side molding treatments. A sporty Futura two-door sedan and fancy wood-trimmed Squire wagon

1961 Falcon Tudor sedan

were added. The 1963 Falcon had a slightly revised grille and trim package, but the big trend was toward "T-Bird type" sports-and-performance equipment like hardtop and convertible body styles in an expanded Futura line, a Sprint option and "260" V-8 engine choices. Other Falcons got self-adjusting brakes, a new carburetor, new engine mounts, suspension improvements and optional power steering. This year economy-car demand fell off. Two Falcon Sprints took class honors at Europe's Monte Carlo Rally, while a third one was the winner in Class B at the annual Mobilgas Economy Run.

The 1964 Falcon had its first new look since the model's 1959 launch. It featured a forward-thrusting sculptured body, heavier bumpers and a new grille and hood. The steering wheel, accelerator pedal and brake pedal were all moved. A new suspension provided a softer, more controlled ride. Ford again used a 109.5-in. wheelbase and length grew by one-half inch to 181.6 in. Buyers could get a small six, a big six or the 260-cid 164-hp V-8. The Falcon sired the Mustang, built off the same platform. It stole away some buyers of sporty Falcons.

A horizontal-bars grille made the '65 Falcon look wider. New 14-in. tires on all models but the cheapest created a lower profile. A 170-cid 105-hp six was standard. Two new options were a 200-cid 120-hp six and a 289-cid 200-hp V-8. This was the last year for production above 200,000 in U.S. factories.

The squared-off Falcon of 1964 and 1965 gave way to a larger, convertible-less compact in 1966. Coupes and sedans rode a 110.9-in. wheelbase, while wagons had a 113-in. stance. Length grew 2.7 in. A hardtop was exclusive to the Futura line. The cars had a Mustang-like long hood/short deck look with rear fender contours reminiscent of full-size '65 Fords. A suspended accelerator and foot-operated emergency brake were new. Market trends favored more luxurious cars and a larger Falcon (especially the wagon) made sense, but didn't sell. A "substantial portion" of Falcon production for the U.S. market was switched to Canadian factories. Calendar-year U.S. sales dropped to 162,965 from 201,237 the year before.

For 1967, U.S. model-year production of Falcons hit 76,419, but additional U.S. cars were again made in Canada and not recorded by model year. During the calendar year, 33,527 Falcons (including early 1968s) were made in the U.S. and 75,879 were built in Canada. U.S. calendar-year output was hurt by a strike against Ford's U.S.-only factories. The '67 Falcon had only minor design changes like a new grille, deeply sculptured front fender wind splits and redesigned taillights that incorporated back-up lights. Wider engine choices included a 225-hp 289-cid V-8.

In 1968, the Falcon got square taillights, a new split grille and slight trim changes. This year "289" options were limited to a single 195-hp job, but buyers could also add a

1963 Falcon Sprint convertible

302-cid 230-hp V-8. Falcons were still being built for the U.S. market in both Canada and "the states," so model-year production is a mystery. U.S. sales hit 142,488, a 32.6 percent increase from the year before. Ford announced that model-year output for 1969, at the St. Thomas, Ontario, plant would end in February 1969 to allow the Canadian plant to change to building 1970 Mavericks.

Safety was highlighted in 1969, with a new safety steering wheel and new side marker lights. A full-width anodized aluminum grille made the car seem wider and larger. The Falcon Club Coupe, sedan and station wagon ranged from $2,283 to $2,660, while the same three Futura models, plus a two-door hardtop, were $2,598 to $2,771. U.S. sales came to 97,071. These were the last Falcon compacts, although the name reappeared on a version of the Fairlane/Torino.

1968 Falcon sedan
Phil Hall Collection

1960s "Solid Gold"

1963 Falcon Sprint two-door hardtop

6	5	4	3	2	1
$ 780	$2,280	$3,800	$8,550	$13,300	$19,000

Estimated values in today's marketplace are taken from the 2006 Collector Car Price Guide.

1960-1965 Mercury Comet

1961 Comet sedan **Phil Hall Collection**

Last of the new compacts to appear in 1960 was the Comet. This "Falcon with fins" was a Saint Patrick's Day present for buyers interested in compacts, but not willing to squeeze in the smallest ones. It had been planned as an Edsel successor. The Comet had a 114-in. wheelbase. It was two or three feet shorter than a standard U.S. car and 1,250 lbs. lighter. Models included two- and four-door sedans and station wagons priced from $1,998 to $2,364.

In addition to being the first small Mercury (by a long shot) it was also the first six-cylinder Mercury. The car had a trademark Mercury look to it, although the slanting tail fin treatment was unique. Unlike the Falcon that it was based on, the Comet had lots of bright metal trim. A 144-cid six was standard equipment. Ford-O-Matic transmission was $172. Production hit 116,330 cars.

Mercury made some minor changes for 1961. By the way, the Comet was still promoted as a separate marque at this time. There were four body styles, plus an S-22 trim kit for the two-door sedan. In addition to the standard engine, a 170-cid 101-hp six was available. Production climbed. "Mercury Comet" was the name in 1962. The most obvious appearance change was a flatter, squared-off rear deck lid. A full-width metal rear beauty panel housed dual circular taillights. New rear fenders tapered downwards. All four basic models were in the Comet series. An upscale Custom

line offered a wood-trimmed Villager wagon. The S-22 was the top-of-the-line model with bucket seats. Production began to settle, but still above the first-year number.

Model-year 1963 featured a horizontal-bar grille with three vertical "teeth." A two-door hardtop and a convertible were added to the Custom line. The S-22 sub-series also gained both new body styles. The Villager wagon was now in its own, top-level series with a $2,754 price tag. Also new were optional power steering and a 260-cid 164-hp V-8 option. Other Comet features included self-adjusting brakes, a three-speed manual gearbox with synchros on second and third gears, a counter-balanced hood and extended chassis lubrication. Mercury's "luxury compact" was the division's top seller in 1964 with 44 percent of total sales. The sales total was 115,125 versus 107,450 in '62.

1966 Comet Cyclone

Celebrating its fourth birthday with a complete restyling, the 1964 Comet proved to be a winner in both the looks and sales departments. The look was based on the same forward-thrusting, boxy, truncated body used for the Falcon, but dressed up to make it more Lincoln-like. With a 114-in. wheelbase and 195.1-in. length, it was noticeably larger than its "baby Ford" cousin. The Comet became the "202," the Custom became the "404," the S-22 became the Caliente and a special top-level performance car was the Cyclone Sport Coupe. Engine options included a 170-cid 101-hp six, a 200-cid 116-hp six, a 260-cid 164-hp V-8 and a 289-cid 210-hp V-8. In November, four 1964 Comets specially-equipped for high-speed driving made 100,000-mile reliability runs at Daytona Beach with each car averaging over 105 mph! The cars ran 24/7 for 40 days straight and broke almost every existing speed-distance record.

1961 Comet two-door sedan **Phil Hall Collection**

1964 Comet convertible

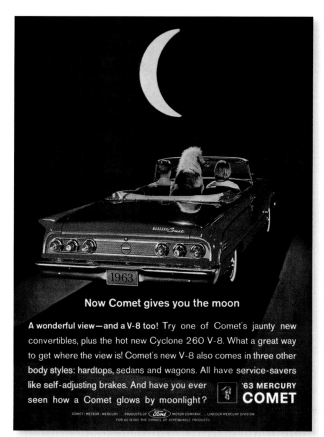

Now Comet gives you the moon

A wonderful view—and a V-8 too! Try one of Comet's jaunty new convertibles, plus the hot new Cyclone 260 V-8. What a great way to get where the view is! Comet's new V-8 also comes in three other body styles: hardtops, sedans and wagons. All have service-savers like self-adjusting brakes. And have you ever seen how a Comet glows by moonlight?

'63 MERCURY COMET

1963 Comet convertible

1962 Comet two-door sedan **Phil Hall Collection**

The '65 Mercury Comet got a new grille flanked by dual stacked headlights. Model offerings were unchanged and prices actually saw a slight decrease, even though a new alternator electrical system was featured. The 200-cid six gained four horsepower and the Cyclone offered a base 200-hp version of the "289" V-8, as well as a 225-hp "Super Cyclone" package and ultimately a 271-hp version that could make the car do 0-to-60 mph in 8.8 sec. The Comet's model-year output dropped slightly from 1964's all-time record. The count came in at 165,052, which still bettered the 1962 and 1963 numbers.

I'd love to tell you some stories about the dark blue Comet "202" four-door sedan that I drove in the mid'60s as my baby food salesman's car, since it was prone to many ailments from oil leaks to a hood that bent across the middle after the two-year-old hinges rusted up. However, we're going to stop our Comet section for this chapter right here, since the '66 and-up models were actually mid-size cars with a 116-in. wheelbase and 196 to 203-in. length.

In 1966, the Comet Cyclone GT convertible was the Indianapolis 500 Pace Car. **Indianapolis Motor Speedway**

1960s "Solid Gold"

1964 Comet Caliente convertible

6	5	4	3	2	1
$ 760	$2,280	$3,800	$8,550	$13,300	$19,000

Estimated values in today's marketplace are taken from the 2006 Collector Car Price Guide.

In 1960, the new Mercurys included the Comet sedan (bottom) and station wagon (top).

1968 Valiant Signet two and four-door sedans **Phil Hall Collection**

1960-1969 Valiant/Plymouth Valiant

The 1960 Valiant was a new Chrysler Corporation compact marketed as a separate nameplate in its first year. Four-door sedan and wagon models were the only offerings in two lines. V-100s were priced from $2,033 to $2,488 and slightly fancier V-200s ran between $2,110 and $2,546. The only engine was a "Slant Six." The Valiant was odd, but not largely innovative. It rode a 106.5-in. wheelbase, the longest of the Big Three compacts. A three-speed manual transmission with floor shift was standard. Push-button automatic transmission was $172 extra. With production of 187,814, the Valiant was a success for Chrysler, and its "conquest sales" car.

Famed stylist Virgil M. Exner wanted his company's small car to be completely different than its full-size models and "new from stem to stern." The Valiant was lower, shorter and narrower than a big Mopar, without looking stubby or small.

Valiant planning started in spring 1957, when a special committee was established to design and engineer a Chrysler economy car. In 1958, a task force of 200 engineers worked in the company's Midland Avenue plant

1961 Valiant V-200 two-door hardtop **Phil Hall Collection**

to finalize the design in 13 short months. The first Valiant was made September 21, 1959 in the Hamtramck, Michigan, plant. Sedans hit the showroom in late October and the wagon came a month later.

Featuring "unitized" body construction, the Valiant was powered by a 170-cid 101-hp Slant Six. This was an in-line, overhead-valve six with the block slanted 30 degrees to the right, allowing the use of long intake manifold runners intended to improve fuel distribution and economy. With all accessories on the left side of the engine, servicing was easier. The engine also had an AC alternator. To make Valiants competitive in the compact car races at Daytona, Chrysler released a "Hyper Pack" engine kit with a four-barrel carburetor that gave the Slant Six 148 hp. These racers were a big hit on television and helped fuel Valiant and Hyper Pack sales.

Standard A-arms were used in the Valiant's front suspension, with oriflow shocks and torsion bars. Outboard semi-elliptical leaf springs were used at the rear. Self-energizing drum brakes supplied stopping power. Attention was paid to insulating the dashboard, floors, roof and rear package tray to quiet the Valiant. The entire lower body half

1962 Valiant Signet 200 two-door hardtop

was dipped in rust preventative, though the cars were still prone to rust. Valiant was the only 1960 Big Three compact to come with factory-installed power steering (used in 7.6 percent) and power brakes (used in 1.1 percent).

The 1961 Valiant became a Plymouth and got a new grille and minor trim changes. A V-200 two-door hardtop model was added and dealer-installed air conditioning became optional. A V-100 two-door sedan was also added and a third seat for the station wagon became optional equipment. To allow smoother operation on lower-octane fuels, the compression ratio of the base Slant Six was lowered from 8.5:1 to 8.2:1. The Hyper Pack option included a 10.5:1 compression ratio. The Valiant accounted for 39.4 percent of Plymouth sales during calendar-year 1961. Its model-year production was 133,487 units.

Outwardly, the Valiant changed little in 1962. The 170-cid Slant Six was no longer available in Hyper Pack form, but the Valiant got the optional 225-cid 145-hp Slant Six that had been available as a "Power Pack" motor for the '61 Dodge Lancer. A 196-hp Hyper Pack version of the "225" that was a '61 option was no longer offered. A new Signet two-door hardtop was released for buyers who wanted a sporty small car. It included a blacked-out grille with a large chrome ring, bucket-type front seats, a padded dash and special wheel covers for just $2,230. The Signet sealed a successful season, as sales rose four percent to 313,219. Model-year production climbed to 145,353 and Valiants accounted for 46.3 percent of Plymouth sales.

Ironically, Valiant's rising share of total Plymouth sales was partly due to one of the company's biggest mistakes of the 1960s. Management decided Valiant's strong showing indicated a buyer preference for smaller, "Euro" styled cars and downsized its large cars. Unfortunately, buyer preferences moved in the opposite direction. Total model-year output fell 4.4 percent, despite the Valiant's 8.8 percent increase.

A totally restyled car greeted Valiant buyers in 1963. The body was two inches longer and bulked up with a wide, flat hood, flattened rear deck and roofline. A feature line ran the length of the fender tops and "veed" back at the front.

1963 Valiant Signet 200 two-door hardtop   **Phil Hall Collection**

1963 Valiant V-200 station wagon   **Phil Hall Collection**

Large, round single headlights flanked the grille. Ragtops were found in both the V-200 and Signet lines. Technical improvements included a strengthened body structure, a new spring-staged choke and many accessories.

The Valiant remained mostly unchanged for '64, but got a higher-mounted front bumper, a reshaped hood lip and a horizontal-bars grille with a protruding center section. Both the 170-cid 101-hp Slant Six and its 225-cid 145-hp big brother had higher compression ratios and fuel and ignition system improvements. Also available was a 273-cid "small-block" V-8 with 180 hp. Buyers interested in more performance added a four-on-the-floor shifter and Sure-Grip differential. Of the 890,298 Valiants made since 1960, a total of 225,245 rolled out of the factory as '64 models, a record for the marque and a 13.5 percent gain over 1963. In the spring of '64, the Valiant sired the all-new Barracuda pony car.

Plymouth used a new crosshatch grille and front fenders without the "veed-back" feature line to clean up the Gen II Valiant for 1965. The beauty treatment included a revised deck lid, new taillights and different body ornamentation. The chrome trim on the front fender copied the old fender sculpturing, but with a narrower V-shape. The big news was a four-barrel version of the 273-cid V-8 that served up 235 hp at 5200 rpm. This was the same engine developed for the

1960 Valiant station wagon   **Phil Hall Collection**

CHAPTER FIVE

177

1965 Valiant 200 sedan **Phil Hall Collection**

Barracuda "S" and moved that slightly heavier car from 0 to 60 in just 8.2 seconds or through the quarter mile in 15.9 seconds. Sales and production of Valiants fell if Barracudas weren't counted.

A redesigned roof, hood and rear panel gave the '66 V100, V200 and Signet a wider and lower appearance. Deep-sectioned bumpers provided extra underbody protection and were said to eliminate stone shields! The three series served up 14 models including ragtops and wagons. Front wheel disc brakes were a new option. Engine choices were unchanged. Sales plummeted again by 13.6 percent, the worst since 1961.

In 1967, the Valiant became a smaller Dodge Dart. Except for grille and trim details, the two cars were styled alike (and looked like clones). The Dart had a longer wheelbase and longer length. It also had exclusive two-door hardtop and convertible models. And Dart coupes were only $170 more than their Valiant counterparts. The 108-in. wheelbase Valiant was available only as a coupe or four-door sedan. Both models came in Valiant 100 and Signet trim. The smaller Slant Six was bumped up to 115 hp. Valiant deliveries dropped 28.8 percent.

Minor changes were made to 1968 Valiants and the compact offered a new 230-hp version of the 318-cid V-8 for buyers who didn't find the 273-cid 190-hp V-8 quite enough. Valiant sales rose five percent from 1967. This up tick contributed to Plymouth's decision to make only minor changes, like a new grille and taillights, for '69. This last 1960s-era Valiant had improved automatic brake adjusters, an upgraded Sure-Grip rear axle, a more efficient power steering pump and a refined air cleaner. Base prices ranged from $2,094 to $2,313, not much higher than 1960.

1967 Valiant 100 four-door sedan **Phil Hall Collection**

1966 Valiant Signet four-door sedan **Phil Hall Collection**

1960s "Solid Gold"

1963 Valiant Signet two-door hardtop

6	5	4	3	2	1
$ 660	$1,980	$3,300	$7,430	$11,550	$16,500

Estimated values in today's marketplace are taken from the 2006 Collector Car Price Guide.

1965 Valiant Signet convertible
Phil Hall Collection

1961-1962 Dodge Lancer/
1963-1969 Dodge Dart

1964 Dart two-door hardtop

Dodge tried to make the best of the situation with minor appearance changes like a fussier grille and a new flagship model called the Gran Turismo. This two-door hardtop included the larger engine. It immediately took 22 percent of Lancer output and a total of 14,075 were made. Drag racers Dode Martin and Jim Nelson stuffed in a big-block 413-cid V-8 and called their Dart the "Golden Lancer." It turned a 12.26-second quarter mile. Model-year output dropped from 74,773 in 1961 to 64,271 in 1962 and production ended in August.

A shrunken Dart greeted Dodge buyers in October 2, 1962. This car would last for 13 years. During October and November of 1962 sales were 116 percent ahead of the Lancer. "During March of 1963 as many as 14,125 of the 1963 model Dart passenger cars were produced," said *Ward's 1963 Automotive Yearbook.* "And in January-March 39,201, indicating substantially improved public acceptance of its new size over the '62 model." That was more than all the Lancers (35,564) put together during calendar-year 1962.

The 1960s would be a delightful decade for the "Dodge Boys" of Detroit. Beginning with the 1960 model year, Dodge entered into battle against the Big Three by launching a line of down-sized 118-inch-wheelbase cars called Darts. These were exciting machines that seemed in tune with the late-1950s trend towards small cars.

The first Darts weren't compacts, which may be why Dodge called its first compact the Lancer. It looked like a Valiant that someone had sent to George Barris for a makeover. When it came back, lots of chrome was gone and J.C. Whitney-style horizontal-bars grille graced the front.

The Lancer had virtually identical specs to the Valiant except in weight, overall length and width. The Valiant weighed 40 pounds more (chrome is heavy), but the Lancer was 5.1 inches longer and almost two inches wider, due to its different bumpers. Both cars came with a 170-cid 101-hp Slant Six and both offered a 148-hp Hyper Pack version, but the Lancer could also be ordered with the mid-size Dart's 225-cid 145-hp Slant Six or a Hyper Pack version of the "225" that produced 196 hp at 5200 rpm.

Lancers came in 170 and 770 series. The "low" series (Chrysler actually used "L" and "H" suffixes to designate them) contained two- and four-door sedans and a four-door wagon priced from $1,981 to $2,356. The 170s had no body side moldings or rocker panel moldings like the 770s. The "high" series had the same models, plus a two-door hardtop. The two-door sedan in the 770 line was called the Sports Coupe. The 770s were $2,077 to $2,451.

Valiants and Lancers sold on the same rungs. Most sales were in the $1,801 to $1,900 bracket, the second most sales were in the $1,901 to $2,000 bracket. Plymouth sold more Valiants than Dodge sold Lancers, but they sold in similar proportions. Chrysler was competing with itself!

1962 Lancer 770 station wagon **Phil Hall Collection**

1962 Lancer GT two-door hardtop **Phil Hall Collection**

LANCER vs. DART

	WB (in.)	Length	Weight	Price	Engine	CID	HP
LANCER	106.5	188.8	2,520	$1,951-$2,408	Slant Six	170	101
DART	106/111	195.9/190.2	2,634	$1,983-$2,512	Slant Six	170	101

Notes: Four-door sedan weight with base engine. Both cars offered the 225-cid 145-hp Slant Six as an option.

Slashes separate passenger car and station wagon data.

The new Dart was hyped as a "king size compact" with looks straight from the Mopar design studios. A wide, flat hood was accented by a concave grille with vertical segments. Large, round single headlights sat in fenders that projected from each side of the grille. The flat roof angled back sharply at the "C" pillars. They flowed smoothly into an equally flat rear deck lid. Dart engines had the same Lancer specs but could be ordered with cast-iron or aluminum blocks. The aluminum-block option was dropped shortly after '63 model production was launched.

Two- and four-door sedans and a four-door station wagon with six-passenger seating were the models in the Dart's standard 170 series with prices running to just above $2,300. Sedans had a 111-in. wheelbase and wagons had a five-inch shorter stance. The high-trim-level 270 series included the same styles, plus a convertible with prices running to $2,433. The convertible and two-door hardtop were available with "GT" front fender medallions. GTs included a padded dashboard, full wheel covers and front bucket seats.

1961 Lancer 770 sedan **Phil Hall Collection**

1961 Lancer 170 two-door sedan **Phil Hall Collection**

1963 Dart two-door hardtop

The re-sized compact – officially called "the medium-sized companion to Dodge" – nailed down 16.69 percent of the corporation's calendar-year output compared to the 11.7 percent racked up by the Lancer. Over the '63 model year, Dodge produced 153,921 Darts, including 28,475 hardtops and 11,390 convertibles.

New body side moldings made the '64 Dart look longer and fancier, while a new grille with fine vertical lines and the Dodge name spelled out across a horizontal center opening added to its slightly more upscale image. Dodge bumped compression ratios for both the 170- and 225-cid Slant Sixes, but claimed no gain in horsepower. A new four-speed manual gearbox was available in nine sporty models. For the first time, a V-8 could be ordered. Dodge used a 273-cid V-8 that produced 180 hp at 4200 rpm and 11.6 percent of Dart buyers selected it. Production included 4,100 Dart six convertibles, 781 Dart V-8 convertibles, 4,882 Dart GT six convertibles, 2,148 Dart GT V-8 convertibles, 33,390 Dart GT six two-door hardtops and 10,349 Dart GT V-8 two-door hardtops. These six sporty models now accounted for 35 percent of Dart production.

To expand the Dart's appeal to "sports car" buffs, Dodge added a two-door hardtop to the mid-range 270 line in 1965. This car drew 10,745 buyers, with most (7,852) opting for one of two V-8s. The 180-hp "273" was the base V-8 and a 235-hp version with 10.5:1 compression was extra. New options included a built-in air conditioner and a vinyl half roof for GT hardtops. Dart production climbed to third, behind Corvair and Falcon, outstanding for a Chrysler product of this era. A shift away from compact cars began during the calendar year and retail sales at Dodge dealerships actually slipped 2.1 percent to 184,319 cars.

There were few changes to the '66 Dart. A new grille had three rectangular segments spaced across the car's front. Power steering was improved and front-wheel disc brakes were a new option. The downward slide in Dart sales continued and they fell to 45.4 percent.

A brand new Dart arrived in fall '66 and it was a winner from the word "go." With wedge-shaped, razor-edged styling that would carry into the 1970s, the '67 Dart saw a 68 percent increase in "builds" between its release and the last day of 1966. The boost turned the Dart into America's best-selling compact car. Curved side glass and delta-shaped taillights were other new features. The standard Slant Six jumped to 115 hp. V-8 options were both based on the same 273-cid "Charger" engine, which again came in 180-hp two-barrel and 235-hp four-barrel versions.

1969 Dart two-door hardtop

All station wagons, two ragtops and two coupes dropped. The Dart series offered two- and four-door sedans, the Dart 270 line offered the sedan and a two-door hardtop and the hardtop and a convertible were the only Dart GT models. Prices ran from $2,187 to $2,732.

The Dart went through minor changes for 1968 with new GTS (GT Sport) hardtops and ragtops carrying a standard 340-cid 275-hp V-8. Engine options were widened with the availability of a 318-cid V-8 with 230 hp and a 383-cid V-8 with 300 hp. The GTS was aimed at the six-second-zero-to-60 muscle car crowd. It could turn nearly 100 mph in the quarter mile! A restyled Chevy Nova was the only compact to out-produce the '68 Dart, but the market niche for small cars continued to narrow. The one millionth Dodge Dart was built late in the first half of 1968. For the model year as a whole, production climbed 12 percent.

Changes for '69 were again in details only. A new Swinger hardtop was available with the 340-cid V-8, a four-speed gearbox, dual exhausts, heavy-duty Rally suspension and wide tires. There were more series than ever – Dart, Dart Swinger, Dart Custom, Dart GT and Dart GTS – and model offerings climbed from 12 to 15. The sales rose 3.4 percent for the calendar year. However, model-year output slid 27.9 percent.

1969 Dart Swinger two-door hardtop

1960s "Solid Gold"

1963 Dart GT convertible

6	5	4	3	2	1
$ 840	$2,520	$4,200	$9,450	$14,700	$21,000

Estimated values in today's marketplace are taken from the 2006 Collector Car Price Guide

1960-1966 Studebaker Lark, Lark Daytona

The 1959 Studebaker Lark arrived in the fall of 1958 and quickly set a production record. In addition, Studebaker turned a profit for the first time since 1953. The 1960 Lark came in Econ-O-Miler VI ($2,393), Deluxe VI ($1,976 to $2,441), Regal VI ($2,296 to $2,621), Econ-O-Miler VIII ($2,430), Deluxe VIII ($2,111 to $2,576) and Regal VIII ($2,331 to $2,758) series. The 1959 styling was used again but a Regal convertible with a power top and heavy-gauge X frame was added. Other models included two- and four-door Deluxe sedans and wagons and Regal two-door hardtops and four-door wagons.

1960 Studebaker Lark sedan

Lark used Roman numerals for its engine designators—VI for the flathead in-line six or VIII for an overhead-valve V-8. Stick, overdrive or automatic transmissions were available. Econ-O-Miler was a 113-in. wheelbase "heavy duty" sedan. All other Larks shared a 108.5-in. wheelbase. Model-year production for 1960 was 122, 649 cars.

A light restyling of the Lark took place in 1961 with Regals gaining dual headlights. The Lark had the shortest overall length of any 1961 American car. In a technical update, the six was converted to overhead valves and 112 hp. A Regal version of the long-wheelbase Econ-O-Miler became the Lark Cruiser.

In the U.S., it was offered as a Cruiser VIII (V-8). Studebaker celebrated its 110th year in business during 1961 and the success of the Lark sparked a temporary revitalization of the pioneering automaker. Unfortunately, the year ended with a strike that idled the South Bend, Indiana, factory from January 2, 1962, until February 12 and cost the company an estimated 9,000 assemblies.

The artistry of industrial designer Brook Stevens was reflected in a 1962 restyling through which all four doors moved to the 113-inch wheelbase. Other changes included a Mercedes-style grille, large circular taillights and elongated rear quarter panels. The upscale Daytona included bucket seats and a 289 V-8. It was available with a four-speed manual gearbox and a sliding roof. Despite the strike, Studebaker's calendar-year unit sales rose 8.4 percent.

For 1963, Brooks Stevens redesigned the "greenhouse" area of the Lark, eliminating its original wraparound windshield, thinning up the roof pillars to give sedans a "hardtop" look and increasing the amount of window glass. The Cruiser model left the lineup. New under-hood goodies included supercharged and non-supercharged Avanti V-8s. There were minor changes to the grille and a completely new dashboard layout. A unique new model was the Wagonaire, a station wagon with a sliding rear roof that increased its utility. On December 9, 1963, Studebaker ceased being America's oldest automaker when the company moved to a modern Canadian factory at Hamilton, Ontario.

Studebaker dusted off its old "Commander" and "Cruiser" nameplates (and added a new Challenger series) for its 1964 offerings that were again restyled by Brooks Stevens. These were essentially facelifted Larks under a different name. The cars were stretched six inches and lowered by one inch. Two-door models continued using the 109-inch wheelbase and four-door models used the 113-inch wheelbase. The sportiest model left was the Daytona convertible. A hot R3 engine was available for high-performance buffs.

1963 Studebaker Lark Daytona two-door hardtop **Phil Hall Collection**

1960 Studebaker Lark two-door hardtop

1962 Studebaker Lark two-door hardtop

There were no styling changes in 1965 but with the closing of the engine plant in Canada, Studebaker sourced its power plants from Chevrolet. The engines available were a 194-cid overhead valve six or a 283-cid "small block" V-8. Fewer than 20,000 Studebakers were made in 1965 and fewer than 5,000 in 1966. After that, the brand disappeared.

1960s "Solid Gold"

1962 Studebaker Lark Daytona V-8 two-door hardtop

1	2	3	4	5	6
$ 580	$1,740	$2,900	$6,530	$10,150	$14,500

Estimated values in today's marketplace are taken from the 2006 Collector Car Price Guide.

1960 Studebaker Lark convertible

1961 Buick Special station wagon **Phil Hall Collection**

1961-1963 B-O-P (Buick, Oldsmobile, Pontiac) Compacts Buick Special

The 1961 Buick Special was once described as "Buick's most auspicious engineering feat. This up-market compact looked like a Buick, except for its scaled-down dimensions, or some 88.88 percent of its big brother. It measured just 188 inches long and weighed 1,600 less pounds than a typical LeSabre. However, it had all of Buick's styling trademarks of the day from a pointed nose to portholes on the front fenders. Special and richer Deluxe models were offered.

Four-door models arrived in showrooms first, with a Skylark hardtop bowing by May 15. The engine was a 215-cid 155-hp aluminum "nailhead" V-8 that weighed only 318 lbs. (It later found its way into Rovers and AMC-Jeep products, before returning to GM.) The Skylark coupe added a four-barrel carburetor to get 185 hp. Bucket seats and a fabric top were Skylark options. A simplified automatic transmission (actually an air-cooled torque converter) was optional. Production was 86,866 units the first year. Total Buick sales rose 12 percent. Of special note was the sale of over 12,000 of the sporty Skylarks.

In 1962, the Special offered an exclusive cast-iron V-6 that produced 135 hp and lowered the price by $100. Before long, about one-third of the cars sold were being built with this economical engine. The Skylark became a two-door hardtop and offered an optional Borg-Warner four-speed manual gearbox. This was an even more popular combination than the original and sales leaped to 42,000 units. Overall sales of all Special models rose by 65 percent.

A Buick advertisement of 1963 called its latest small car the "happy medium-sized Buick Special." That's because it had a four-inch-longer body on the same 112-inch wheelbase. The new body was slightly narrower and had more of the "Big Buick" look than ever before. Standard

1962 Buick Special convertible

1963 Buick Special Skylark coupe

1962 Buick Special sedan

and deluxe versions of sedans, convertibles and station wagons were offered along with the Skylark hardtop and convertible. Engine choices ranged from the miserly V-6 up to a 190-hp V-8.

While Buick's fortunes rose for the year, the popularity of the Special as a so-called "senior compact" fell off a bit. This brought 1964 changes that moved the Special out of the compact niche and turned it into a mid-sized car on a 115-inch wheelbase. From this point, the Special/Skylark story transitions into one of mid-size family cars or mighty "muscle" machines.

1960s "Solid Gold"

1964 Buick Special DeLuxe Skylark coupe or DeLuxe station wagon

6	5	4	3	2	1
$ 720	$2,160	$3,600	$8,100	$12,800	$18,000

Estimated values in today's marketplace are taken from the 2006 Collector Car Price Guide.

1961 Oldsmobile F-85 Deluxe sedan   **Elton McFall**

Oldsmobile F-85

1961 Oldsmobile Cutlass Sports Coupe

October 6, 1960 brought the F-85 into Oldsmobile showrooms across the U.S. Nicknamed the "Pocket Rocket," the new entry in the low-priced field earned 19,800 sales by the end of the calendar year and had Olds management making optimistic forecasts for the future. The car shared the Buick Special's 112-in. wheelbase. Power came from a water-cooled, aluminum V-8 (identical with the Buick's) that weighed 350 pounds and produced 155 hp. The standard series offered a Club Coupe, a four-door sedan and six- and eight-passenger wagons at prices between $2,330 and $2,762. The deluxe line had the same four-door models, but the midyear Cutlass Sports Coupe was a two-door with front bucket seats and a console. Prices ran from $2,519 to $2,897 on the fancier models.

The styling of the F-85 was sculptured, like the Special, but it had a wider look to it. This illusion was created by the use of "flatter" hood-trunk-fender panels and the use of a wide grille with vertical fins and "Oldsmobile" lettering. The F-85 could do 0-to-60 in 13 seconds while giving almost 20 mpg. There was also an optional V-8 with a four-barrel carburetor and 10.25:1 compression ratio that produced 185 hp at 4800 rpm. With V-8s only, the F-85 wasn't a true economy car, but it seemed like one in 1961 since it was small.

Two convertibles for F-85 buyers were new in 1962. One was available in standard trim and the other was a Cutlass model in the deluxe series. The sportier ragtop was a big success, pulling down a 32 percent share of all Cutlass sales. This year's midyear (April) addition for the sports-car set was the F-85 Jet-Fire two-door hardtop, which carried a turbocharged V-8 that

1963 Oldsmobile Cutlass Sports coupe

sporty | performer

...with 185 h.p.
Cutlass
V-8 action !

F-85 Cutlass

BETTER THAN EVER IN EVERY WAY
AND EVERY INCH AN **OLDS**

1962 Oldsmobile Cutlass Sports Coupe

Sharp!

1962 Oldsmobile Cutlass Sports Coupe

Before you buy any low-priced car . . .

Drive the
➤ *F-85* ➤
...it's every inch an
OLDSMOBILE !
OLDSMOBILE DIVISION • GENERAL MOTORS CORPORATION

Once you drive the F-85, you'll *know* this is an Oldsmobile
through and through! Oldsmobile's exclusive Rockette
Engine combines the quick, sure response of a *full eight cylinders*
. . . and the gas savings of advanced *aluminum* design.
You'll ride relaxed . . . with the reassuring control
of new Twin-Triangle Stability, the extra room and
comfort you expect in an Olds! Drive the fabulous F-85 . . .
built for the buyer who wants something better in a smaller car!

1961 Oldsmobile F-85 Deluxe sedan and station wagon

yanked one-horse-per-cube from the 215-cid aluminum V-8. In its brief 1962 stint, the Jetfire generated 3,765 orders and by 1963 would account for some 1,000 sales per month. It helped Olds celebrate its 65th anniversary in August.

On October 4, 1983, Olds launched an up-sized F-85 promoted as "something extra." This "senior compact" had more of the look of a big Olds. Although the wheelbase remained at 112 inches, the body was four inches longer. The engine came in 155-, 195- and 215-hp (turbocharged) versions. The styling was "squarer" and less sculptured than the original version. Sales of this version increased 28.6 percent over the previous model. Rather than leave well enough alone, Olds saw this as a sign that an even larger F-85 would sell even better and was transformed into a "medium-size" car for 1964.

1960s "Solid Gold"

1962 Oldsmobile F-85 Cutlass convertible

6	5	4	3	2	1
$ 680	$2,040	$3,400	$7,650	$11,900	$17,000

Estimated values in today's marketplace are taken from the 2006 Collector Car Price Guide.

Pontiac Tempest

The most innovative and most popular of the three "BOP" compacts that followed the Corvair out of the GM stable was the Pontiac Tempest. The Tempest garnered *Motor Trend* magazine's "Car of the Year" award and many other similar honors. Part of the car's newness was the "Indy Four" engine used in 99 percent of the cars built (one percent came with the optional, Buick-built aluminum V-8). The other big innovation was the use of a rear transaxle, with power plant and axle linked through an unusual, flexible "rope" driveshaft.

Pontiac created the four by cutting its 389-cid V-8 in half. This allowed it to offer the 194.5-cid engine in numerous variations from the base 110-hp version with a one-barrel carburetor up to a 160-hp version with a four-barrel carburetor and special 10.25:1 pistons. The rope driveshaft allowed a flat floor and eliminated the transmission tunnel. Pontiac had actually built its first transaxle prototype in the late 1940s and a picture of a '57 transaxle Pontiac prototype had once appeared in *Motor Trend*. In addition to flattening the passenger compartment floor, the transaxle allowed a lower overall height.

GM-style body sculpturing was used on the 112-inch-wheelbase car, but Pontiac styling trademarks like a split radiator grille gave it a strong brand identity. There was only one series with four models: four-door sedan, two-door Sport Coupe, two-door Custom Sport Coupe and four-door Safari station wagon. Prices for cars with the base engine ran from $2,113 to $2,438. The Lemans Custom Sport Coupe with bucket seats was introduced at midyear. With more than 100,000 Tempests registered in the model's first year on the market, it was far and away the best-selling BOP compact.

When the '62 models bowed on September 21, there was a new LeMans Custom option for two-door models. Two Tempest convertibles were added, including one in

1963 Pontiac Tempest sedan **Phil Hall Collection**

LeMans dress. Other models were unchanged in any major way, but had a slightly busier grille with a grille section in the center that toned down the split-grille image.

My brother Jerry once owned a '62 Tempest Four as a used car – his first car, by the way. It was cheap – and with good reason – it was a lousy car. It ran (barely) every once in awhile, but usually it just took up a parking space and sat. It was noisy and smoky when he did get it going. The interior was falling apart and the headliner sagged down. This must have been in the late 1960s, as he replaced it with a hippie-style paisley fabric that looked really wild. Jerry eventually traded the car for a Fiat 850 Spyder that was even worse. I love my brother, but he's not much of a car guy.

Like Jerry's first car, the first Tempest failed to live up to its promise. *Motor Trend* had written it up as a car that pointed to the direction that the industry was likely to

1963 Pontiac Tempest
Tom Glatch

move in during the 1960s. However, as the 1960s evolved, interest in small cars dried up. Four-cylinder engines never caught on, the rope driveshaft remained a curiosity for all but Porsche fans and the rear-mounted transaxle went largely the way of the dodo. The Tempest name would earn great respect, but on a car that was larger, usually V-8-powered and far more conventional in its engineering make up.

Despite all of this, the "small" Tempest of 1961-1962 received enough positive exposure to wind up a big success. Over 140,000 of them were sold in 1962 and those sales represented 26 percent of Pontiac's business and pushed the company into third place on the industry's hit list. As with the other BOP compacts, the Tempest grew by five inches in '63. It retained its rear transaxle (though many high-performance enthusiasts change this today) for another year, along with the four banger. The LeMans package, which was formerly an option kit, became a separate car line. And, most significant of all, a 326-cid cast-iron V-8 became a popular option.

Popularity of the Tempest tapered off in 1963, but the production counts showed that 38 percent of the cars were ordered with a V-8, 47 percent with bucket seats and 35 percent with air conditioning. Such numbers indicated that the Tempest's appeal was trending towards more performance and sportiness as time went on. Pontiac management read these indicators just right, expanding the role of the LeMans in the '64 model year (when the Tempest grew to midsize) and launching the muscular GTO about halfway through the season. Both of these moves were on the money and made the revised mid-size Pontiac a force to be reckoned with, but its role as a compact car was over.

1962 Pontiac Tempest convertible

1964 Pontiac GTO convertible   **Phil Hall Collection**

1963 Pontiac Tempest Safari station wagon   **Phil Hall Collection**

1963 Pontiac Tempest Sports Coupe   **Phil Hall Collection**

1960s "Solid Gold"

1963 Pontiac Tempest Le Mans convertible

6	5	4	3	2	1
$ 800	$2,400	$4,000	$9,000	$14,000	$20,000

Estimated values in today's marketplace are taken from the 2006 Collector Car Price Guide.

CHAPTER SIX

The 1960s . . . Station Wagons

The evolution of the station wagon between the early 1900s and the 1960s was a striking reflection of middle-class Americans' urge to own fine vehicles and suburban homes. The first "depot hacks" were boxy utility vehicles, but by the late-1930s the richly varnished "woodie" wagon was an icon of stately suburban living. Immediately after World War II, car buyers – especially young, middle-class married couples who were raising families and purchasing suburban homes – turned to the station wagon as an all-purpose vehicle. Station wagon production rose from the early 1950s on, even doubling every three years up to 1957. The sale of these cars – by now made entirely of metal (but sometimes using simulated wood trim) was stimulated by Americans' new suburban life-style. By the late-1950s, the station wagon had evolved to a model selling nearly a million cars a year.

Model Year	Total Wagon Production	Market Penetration %
1951	174,500	3.3 (*)
1952	168,500	3.9
1953	303,000	4.9
1954	310,000	6.5 (*)
1955	580,000	8.2
1956	707,200	11.3
1957	843,500	13.6 (*)
1958	647,000	15.2
1959	937,000	16.9
1960	923,700	15.4
1961	866,800	16.0
1962	924,900	13.8
1963	963,500	13.1
1964	936,969	11.9
1965	968,771	11.0
1966	912,433	10.6
1967	760,094	9.9
1968	860,596	10.3
1969	869,684	10.2

(*) Note doubling in 3-year intervals up to 1957.

The station wagon went through revolutionary changes in the 1950s, after the wood-bodied cars were replaced by the all-steel carry-all. Before long, the steel crate-on-wheels became a "sport wagon," with names like Nomad, Safari, Caballero, Country Squire and Fiesta. There was also a proliferation of station wagons. Ford – the acknowledged "wagonmaster" –offered two wagons in 1949. Both were identical except for engine. In 1959, Ford had a lineup of 12 wagons including plain, mid-range and fancy styles with two- or four-doors and six-cylinder or V-8 power plants.

In model-year 1960, a total of 923,323 station wagons were produced in the United States. Of these, only 113,375 had two doors. The station wagon represented 15.6 percent of all 1960 cars built in the U.S. Ford had the image in the wagon field and it was Ford at the top of the heap with 292,304 made. Chevy's total was 287,705. AMC was third with 174,542 station wagons.

The rarest 1960 station wagon was the two-door style that accounted for 113,375 total assemblies (14,663 GM, 59,803 Ford, 5,123 Chrysler, 28,813 AMC and 4,973 Studebaker-Packard models). Next rarest was the four-door three-seat wagon, of which 157,059 were made (54,516 GM, 50,888 Ford, 34,087 Chrysler, 17,568 AMC and no Studebaker-Packard models). The bulk of production (652,889) was of four-door wagons with two seats. Of these, 218,256 were GM, 181,613 were Ford, 106,394 were Chrysler brands, 128,161 were from AMC and 181,995 were Studebaker-Packard models.

In model-year 1961, the number of station wagons built in the U.S. fell 6.3 percent to 865,356 vehicles. Of these, 483,449 were six-cylinder-powered and 381,907 used a V-8 engine, a trend that would change because many larger, heavy station wagons ultimately got a V-8 as their standard engine. The production total included 65,738 two-door models, 661,142 four-door two-seat models and 138,476 with four doors and three seats. The rarer two-door wagons were still offered by Plymouth (2,381 made), Ford (12,042), Falcon (32,045), Comet (4,199), Studebaker (2,239) and AMC (12,832).

In 1961, the automobile business bounced back from recession and was rolling along at full steam by 1962. Output increased to 924,894 cars. This included 30,978 with two doors, 739,435 with four doors and two seats,

115,226 with four doors and three seats and 39,355 with five or six doors. The latter group included Corvair and Falcon Econoline passenger vans and some AMC wagons. Station wagons accounted for 13.8 percent of all U.S.-built cars in model-year 1962.

Station wagons as a percentage of total 1963 model-year production of U.S. cars notched 13.1 percent of all cars built. That compared to 16.9 percent in 1959, the all-time record year for wagon output. The 1963 total of 963,500 was the highest ever realized. Of that amount, 536,429 had V-8s, 420,481 had a six and 6,551 were four-cylinder Chevy IIs or Tempests. Chevrolet was the leading maker of full-size V-8 station wagons, but Ford made the most V-8 wagons overall if Fairlane and Falcon V-8 models were counted.

In addition to the trend towards more V-8-powered station wagons, 1963 also continued a five-year decline in the number of two-door station wagons built:

Model Year Production of Two-Door U.S. Station Wagons 1959 to 1963

1959	1960	1961	1962	1963
149,896	113,375	65,738	30,978	19,002

Another trend in station wagon sales was a leveling of demand in terms of market penetration. While total model-year production was at an all-time record high, the percentage of total industry sales going to wagons was actually tapering off.

The station wagon market niche continued unabated in 1964. The station wagon's share of total U.S. car sales fell to 11.9 percent, the lowest since 1956. Dropping further in popularity, the two-door station wagon accounted for only 8,744 total assemblies in model-year 1964. Of those, 2,710 were GM products and the rest were FoMoCo models. As far as four-door wagons went, the two-seat variety was built 726,345 times as opposed to 170,061 for three-seat types. In the five- and six-door wagon class were 8,147 GM products, 16,665 FoMoCos, 2,600 Mopars and 4,407 AMC models. That added up to 936,969 total vehicles for the model year, a 2.75 percent decline. The so-called "compact van" was gaining popularity, especially among younger Americans.

Auto sales in America boomed in 1965, so it should come as no surprise that station wagon production hit a record 968,771 vehicles. The station wagon continued to represent a smaller total market share with an 11.0 percent penetration level. The two-door wagon counted 160,509 assemblies, the four-door wagon had 912,761 (including 207,212 with a factory-installed third seat) and the five- and six-door wagons had 39,960. In the fall of 1965, Ford introduced an innovative dual-action tailgate for its '66 station wagon. It could be opened like a door or lowered like a tailgate.

By 1966, the two-door station wagon was gone – at least for a while. Other body style trends continued in mostly the same direction as before. Wagons with a factory-installed third seat saw a modest increase. This reflected buyer interest in fancier and sportier cars. While the station wagon was declining in overall popularity, those who still wanted one were willing to upgrade to fancier, full-featured models. Some wagons of this vintage were virtually luxury cars. Production of five- and six-door wagons – most of which were actually passenger buses – also went up again.

Production of all conventional wagons dropped in 1967, while the five- and six-door versions saw a very modest gain in popularity. Catching on with younger buyers were sporty mid-sized wagons with big engines, bucket seats, mag wheels and even four-on-the-floor. These were small enough to look good and large enough to carry stuff. *Car and Driver* magazine flashed around a Mustang station wagon that it had built. Too bad they never made that cool puppy!

Station wagon business turned around a bit in 1968 with total market penetration rising back to 10.3 percent. Three-seat wagon sales hit a record 284,519. This was the age of the prestige car and the prestige wagon with wood paneling, a roof rack and even a vinyl-clad top made an "anti-environmental impact statement."

For wagon lovers, 1969 was a lot like 1968. The total number of wagons made went up a peg and market penetration went down a peg. Production of fancy four-door three-seat wagons increased by nearly 50,000 units. The number of five- and six-door wagons made increased 47 percent.

In 1966, Ford advertised its "Magic Doorgate" that opened like a door or swung down in traditional tailgate fashion.

1960-1969 Ford Country Squire

The use of the Country Squire name to identify Ford wagons dated back to 1950 when the body was still made of real wood. According to Dennis Bickford, an Iola, Wisconsin restorer who specializes in wood-bodied cars, 1951 was the year a chrome "Country Squire" script was first used on the woodie, but ads from 1950 identify the wagon as a Country Squire.

After 1952, there were other Ford wagons, but the Country Squire was always the fanciest. Until 1954, it was the wagon equivalent of a Crestline model. Beginning in 1955, it had Fairlane trim. By 1957, it was similar to a Fairlane 500. In mid-1959 the Fairlane 500 became a Galaxie and the Country Squire did, too. In 1968, the letters "LTD" turned up on the Country Squire's hood, although it was, apparently, not a real LTD. A sales flyer said the Country Squire with the standard 210-hp V-8 was $3,515.77

1960s "Solid Gold"

1965 Ford 9-passenger Country Squire station wagon

6	5	4	3	2	1
$ 600	$1,800	$3,000	$6,750	$10,500	$15,000

Estimated values in today's marketplace taken from the 2006 Standard Guide to Cars and Prices.

A Country Squire with dual-facing rear seats and the standard 210-hp V-8 was $3,595.87. The same brochure clearly stated "there are *three* models of LTD by Ford for 1968, the 2-Door Hardtop, 4-Door Hardtop and 4-Door Sedan." The LTD Country Squire is shown, but not mentioned.

The 1960 Country Squire V-8 sold for $3,080 and weighed 4,122 pounds. The 1969 LTD Country Squire (V-8 only) sold for $3,644 and weighed 4,202 pounds. You can see there wasn't a great deal of change in the Country Squire in the 1960s. One innovation was the two-way tailgate of 1966. It could open sideways, like a door, or drop down like a pickup truck tailgate. By 1969, the wheelbase had gone up two inches and it was about three inches longer. Bigger, more powerful engines were added over the decade, but the top-of-the-line station wagon stayed much the same.

The 1960s trends toward prestige models and increased sales of options helped the upscale Country Squire. Early in the decade, the wagon had model-year runs in the 15,000 to 25,000 unit range. By the middle of the decade, the Country Squire was contributing close to 50,000 deliveries per year. By 1966, the total was over 75,000. The 1968 LTD Country Squire had 91,770 builds while the 1969 version zoomed to almost 130,000 and the more expensive, more profitable 10-passenger accounted for 82,790.

1963 Ford Country Squire station wagon **Tom Glatch**

1964-1969 Oldsmobile Vista-Cruiser

GM designers added a "skylight" to the rear of a mid-size wagon to create the Vista-Cruiser. They stretched the wheelbase by five inches, making it Olds' biggest wagon. The elevated roof resembled a Greyhound Scenicruiser bus. *Old Cars Weekly* editor Keith Mathiowetz says the "skylight" made the interior brighter. A college buddy drove his parent's Vista-Cruiser. Memories of it brought a smile to Keith's face. "There were special sun visors in the rear," he recalls. "The car looked cool, but the raised roof didn't add a lot of room."

Olds advertised the new model as a "see-all carry-all." Two- and three-seat versions were marketed for just under and just over $3,000. Base engine was a V-6, but V-8s with up to 290 hp were available. Only 14,000 Vista-Cruisers were made in 1964, but somehow Olds' new "sky's-the-limit" model hung on through 1972. With a special "10-foot" wheelbase, the Vista-Cruiser provided 100 cubic feet of cargo room. In the three-seat model, the rear seat faced forward, so a sun visor was needed for the Vista-Roof's "windshield."

The first full selling season was 1965 and production climbed to 31,985. In 1966, a Chevy 250-cid in-line six became standard. A 330-cid 250-hp engine was base V-8. The best seller was the Custom nine-passenger with a $3,278 price. "You'd expect a wagon this big and beautiful to cost a bundle more, but that's Oldsmobile's Vista-Cruiser for you. Full of surprises," said an ad. Styling changes for '67 gave more of a "Toronado" appearance. Walnut-grained vinyl trim on the lower body sides and under the tailgate window was optional.

1960s "Solid Gold"

1964 Oldsmobile Vista-Cruiser
Custom station wagon

6	5	4	3	2	1
$ 608	$1,824	$3,040	$6,840	$10,640	$15,200

Estimated values in today's marketplace taken from the 2006 Standard Guide to Cars and Prices.

The '68 Vista-Cruiser was completely restyled. It had a one-inch longer wheelbase and eight-inch-longer overall length. A new tailgate could drop or swing open. Production-wise, it was the best year yet, with 36,143 Vista-Cruisers leaving the factory. In 1969, the "11 window" Vista-Cruiser was pretty much the '68 model with a new split grille. Production was 33,387 units.

Olds Vista-Cruiser: Keeps a sharp lookout with 11 windows.

It's easy to see why Olds value is way ahead of its price.
Take a look: Over 100 cubic feet for storage. 2- and 3-seat models—and all seats face forward. Tinted Vista Roof. You can order a luggage rack for it. And a tailgate that drops or swings. You'll see youngmobile thinking in its new styling. Rocket 350 V 8 engine, GM safety features, too. Get a new view on wagons—at your nearest Olds dealer s. **Escape from the ordinary.**

1969 Oldsmobile Vista-Cruiser station wagon

1966 Oldsmobile Vista-Cruiser station wagon

1964-1969 Buick Skylark Sportwagon

The Sportwagon was Buick's counterpart to the Vista-Cruiser and also bowed in mid-1964. It shared the 10-foot wheelbase of the Olds, but unlike the case at its sister GM division, the Sportwagon was not the largest Buick wagon. That distinction belonged to the LeSabre wagon. The Sportwagon was merchandised in two- and three-seat standard and Custom models. At Buick, the observation window was called a "Skyroof" rather than a "Vista-Dome." Prices for both brands were nearly identical and first year sales were close, too. Model-year production for 1964 was 13,654 and the standard model sold best. Base engine in the Sportwagon was the same 225-cid 155-hp V-6 used in the Vista-Cruiser, but Buick V-8 options were different. The base V-8 was a 300-cid 210-hp with a two-barrel carburetor. A four-barrel version made 250 hp.

Full-year production of Sportwagons for '65 climbed to 28,356. This was again less than the Vista-Cruiser, but it's important to remember that Buick buyers interested in a wagon had more options than an Olds buyer with the same focus. Sportwagons came with durable all-vinyl upholstery. Custom Sportwagons had plusher upholstery, full-length exterior body side moldings and carpeted lower door panel sections. Options included load area carpeting, a second seat with a divided seat back and an instrument panel pad.

In 1966, Buick Specials got a new body with more sculptured sheet metal and the Sport Wagon took on a similar appearance on its longer wheelbase. Buick's 340-cid 220-hp V-8 became the standard engine for Sport Wagon models. Custom Sportwagons had satin-finished lower body moldings, a Deluxe steering wheel and tailgate lamps. Custom padded seat cushions and Custom interior trim were used. Production was 21,600.

A new grille set off the carryover Sportwagon body in 1967. The same models were offered and model-year output dropped below 20,000. High-performance buffs with a family gravitated towards the Sportwagon with optional 340-cid 260-hp four-barrel V-8.

Specials got a sweeping "S curve" on the body sides in 1968. Sportwagons wore the new look very well, especially when the lower body sections carried "woodgrain transfers" (simulated wood paneling), which was also repeated on the tailgate.

The Sportwagon was again a V-8-only series and for those wanting more power the GS 400 engine with 340 hp was optional. Business got a little boost to 22,888 units for the model run. The 1969 models had a minimum of change for another year, though standard models were dropped. Only 20,670 Sportswagons were built in this final year of the 1960s.

1964 Buick Skylark Sportwagon **John Berkowicz**

1960s "Solid Gold"

1966 Buick Sportwagon Custom two-seat station wagon

6	5	4	3	2	1
$ 740	$2,220	$3,700	$8,330	$12,950	$18,500

Estimated values in today's marketplace taken from the 2006 Collector Car Price Guide.

1968 Pontiac Executive Safari two-seat station wagon **Phil Hall Collection**

1967-1969 Pontiac Executive Safari

In 1966, Pontiac decided the Star Chief (which dated to 1954) was getting a little long in the tooth. So the company's "middle" full-sized car became the Executive Star Chief. This was a neat package – a Catalina with Bonneville-style trimmings. But there was no station wagon in the series that year. Wagon buyers had to settle for a Catalina in either six- or nine-passenger configuration or move up to a more expensive three-seat Bonneville.

This was corrected in 1967, when the Executive ("Star Chief" was dropped) line gained six- and nine-passenger wagons. You could still get a smaller, plainer, cheaper Catalina or a more expensive Bonneville, but the Executive had its own niche and seems a bit more collectible due to its luxury touches and added rarity. Only 5,903 two-seat editions and 5,593 three-seat editions were built. That compares to 18,305 Catalina two-seaters, 11,040 Catalina three-seaters and 6,771 Bonnevilles. In 1967, only wagons with wood grain paneling – like Executives—got to use the famous Safari name. All big wagons had a 121-inch wheelbase and Executives used the 400-cid 290-hp V-8.

In 1968, full-size Pontiacs had a unique ship's prow nose with a Pinocchio-style split bumper-grille. The instrument panel and the taillights were reworked. Executives had all Catalina features plus a deluxe steering wheel, extra moldings, deluxe wheel discs, additional lighting and "Executive" front fender badges. The Safari had the fake wood paneling below the belt line. Pontiac put together 6,195 with two seats and 5,843 with three seats.

A major revamp in 1969 gave big Pontiacs a unique split bumper-grille, revised roof lines and ventless side windows. Wagons had a new two-way tailgate and wood-grained dash. Executive Safaris featured wood-grained exterior panels with simulated teakwood molding trim, vinyl floor mats and a concealed luggage locker. The six-passenger listed for $3,872 and 6,411 were made. Slightly more popular was the $4,017 nine-passenger with model-year assemblies of 6,805. Three versions of the 400-cid V-8 were available with up to 340 hp. The 428-cid big-block V-8 could be had in 375- and 390-hp editions.

A memory of children raised in the 1960s is the rear-facing third seat like the one found in this 1968 Pontiac Executive Safari station wagon. **Phil Hall Collection**

1960s "Solid Gold"

1967 or 1968 Pontiac Executive Safari three-seat station wagon

6	5	4	3	2	1
$ 680	$2,040	$3,400	$7,650	$11,900	$17,000

Estimated values in today's marketplace taken from the 2006 Standard Guide to Cars and Prices.

Pontiac literature showed both two- and three-seat 1967 Executive Safari station wagons. **Phil Hall Collection**

1960-1969 Mercury Colony Park

The use of the Colony Park on Mercury wagons started in 1957 when the name was used to identify the automaker's fanciest and most luxurious of six station wagons. The Colony Park had four-door hardtop styling with vent windows and rich-looking simulated wood exterior panels. By 1960, the Country Cruiser station wagon series was down to a pair of four-door six-passenger models, the $3,127 Commuter (the base model) and the $3,837 Colony Park. A friend of mine's family won a Colony Park in a raffle at our local church.

After using a huge 126-inch-wheelbase chassis to support those '60s dune buggies, Mercury switched to a trim 120-inch wheelbase for its glittery 1961 cars. The Colony Park was priced at a more affordable $3,118 and weighed more than 400 pounds less. This didn't help business much, as production rose from 7,411 in '60 to just 7,887 in '61. For '62, there was a new grille and taillights and a new nine-passenger model. Production rose a bit to 9,596. In '63, both Colony Parks continued as part of the same Monterey Custom series. Model-year production included 6,447 two-seaters and 7,529 three-seaters.

In 1964, Mercury used the Monterey name on its entry-level cars. The matching wagon was the Commuter. The Colony Park had trim upgrades shared with the pricier Montclair/Park Lane models. Mahogany-toned paneling decorated the body. Production dropped below 10,000. In '65, the wagons used a one-inch-shorter wheelbase, but had a four-and-a-half-inch longer body. The Colony Park came only in six-passenger format. It cost $3,364 and 15,294 were made. Modest changes were made in 1966 when production rose to 18,894.

Lee Iacocca came to Mercury in 1965 and began a push to emphasize the Lincoln connection. While styling

changes along these lines were planned for 1969, the '67 and '68 models continued to offer 119-inch wheelbase wagons. Both Commuters and Colony Parks were offered in two- and three/four-seat models. In addition to wood-grained exterior paneling, the fancy wagon had plush fabric-and-vinyl upholstery, an electric clock, a spare tire cover, extra lighting and deluxe body insulation. The 1967 model saw 18,680 assemblies, while the '68 had 21,179. By this time, most sales were going to Colony Parks with added seating. Buyers could go for the nine-passenger job with a rear-facing third seat or a 10-passenger configuration with dual center-facing rear seats.

For 1969, new Mercury Marquis and Marquis Brougham models replaced the Montclair and Park Lane. Station wagons got a two-inch longer wheelbase and a four-inch longer overall length. Both Commuters and Colony Parks had full-length body moldings and chrome-trimmed wheel housings. The Colony Park also had plank-style wood-grain appliqués and a dual-action tailgate. The Colony Park was merchandised as a six-passenger model for $3,760. A rear-facing third seat was a $126 option and dual center-facing rear seats were a $95 option. A total of 21,179 Colony Parks were built in 1969.

1960s "Solid Gold"

1960 Mercury Colony Park Country Cruiser station wagon

6	5	4	3	2	1
$1,040	$3,120	$5,200	$11,700	$18,200	$26,000

Estimated values in today's marketplace taken from the 2006 Standard Guide to Cars and Prices.

1967 Mercury Colony Park station wagon

1966 Mercury Colony Park station wagon

1963 Mercury Colony Park station wagon   **Phil Hall Collection**

1966-1969 Dodge Monaco

1968 Dodge Monaco station wagon **Phil Hall Collection**

it had only a two-door hardtop designed to compete with cars like the Pontiac Grand Prix.

The 1966 Monaco went from a one-model line up to six models, including six- and nine-passenger wagons. Actually, the original Monaco hardtop became the Monaco 500 hardtop with bucket seats. The five other models were just Monacos. The wagons were priced at $3,539 and $3,604. Production was 4,984 for the sixer and 6,632 for the niner. Both in 1966 and '67, the Monaco used the Polara body with added trim and other upgrades like foam rubber seats and fancy wheel covers. Get your pencil out again – wagon production dropped to 1,890 six-passenger and 2,390 nine-passenger.

A larger 122-inch wheelbase adopted in 1967 was used again for 1968 Monacos. The wagons riding this platform were 220 inches long. A modest facelift greeted buyers of the 1968 models. Production went to 3,572 for the two-seater and 4,329 for the three-seater. Base price on the latter was $3,809.

A complete restyling for 1969 gave the Monaco station wagons the "airplane fuselage" look that was smoother and more rounded than in the past. A 112-inch wheelbase was used under all Polaras and Monacos and station wagons were 220.4 inches long. In the pricing department, the more expensive model cracked $4,000. At $3,917, the six-passenger version wasn't far behind.

At the beginning of the 1960s, the fanciest Dodge wagon was the Polara. It was a full-sized car with a 122-inch wheelbase and a 214.8-inch length. The Polara was not Dodge's *biggest* wagon. While regular passenger-car models in the Dart series had a 118-inch wheelbase, Dart wagons used the Polara wheelbase. The '60 Polara wagons were in the $3,500-$3,600 price range (more for the nine-passenger model). These wagons were rare. Brand new research reveals that model-year production was 1,235 for the six-passenger and 1,767 for the nine-passenger. In 1961, Dodge facelifted its wagons and put the fins on, but little else changed in a basic sense. This year the six-passenger had a run of 912 units and 1,137 nine-passengers were made.

In 1962, Dodge introduced a new top-of-the-line Custom 880 series. It was essentially a Chrysler with Dodge styling and badges. The Custom 880 became the 122-inch wheelbase model and the Polara moved down-stream to a 116-inch wheelbase (essentially the Dart platform). The Custom 880 was aimed at the luxury market. The series included a full range of models including six- and nine-passenger wagons at $3,292 and $3,407, respectively. Dodge made 1,174 of the first and 890 of the latter. You rarely see them today.

Big Dodges went to a squarer look for 1964 and the 880 was no exception. This year the "luxo" Dodge came in 880 and Custom 880 versions with two wagons in each car-line. In the 880 series the six-passenger was built 1,727 times and the nine-passenger 907 times. For the Custom 880, the corresponding numbers were 1,647 and 1,365. Engines went up to a 413 with dual four-barrel carbs on a cross-ram manifold and 390 hp. A 1966 facelift didn't change much. The four 880 wagons had runs of 1,908, 1,082, 1,639 and 1,796.

In '65, there was only a Custom 880. By this time the wheelbase was 121 inches and wagons were 217.1 inches long. The six-passenger had a 4,499-unit run and the nine-passenger a 5,923-unit run. While wagons were not part of it yet, a new Monaco series was the real news. For '65

1966 Dodge Monaco station wagon **Phil Hall Collection**

1960s "Solid Gold"

1966 Dodge Monaco station wagon

6	5	4	3	2	1
$ 512	$1,536	$2,560	$5,760	$8,960	$12,800

Estimated values in today's marketplace taken from the 2006 Collector Car Price Guide.

The 1963 Studebaker Lark Daytona Wagonaire introduced the sliding steel roof for more load potential.

1963-1966 Studebaker Wagonaire

The Wagonaire introduced by Studebaker in 1963 was one of the most unique station wagons of the decade. This car was a part of the Lark Daytona model range. In 1964 and later, the Daytona name was used and Lark was dropped. Industrial designer Brooks Stevens, of Milwaukee, Wisconsin, created the Wagonaire. Wagons had a 113-inch wheelbase and 187-inch length.

According to production total compiled by General Motors, Studebaker made 8,762 Model P8 Lark Daytona station wagons in 1963. Of these, 5,684 were six-cylinder cars, including 2,780 six-passenger versions. The other 3,076 were V-8 powered, including just 616 nine-passenger jobs.

Studebaker made 8,762 Model P8 Lark Daytona wagons in 1963. Of these, 5,684 were six-cylinder cars, including 2,780 six-passenger versions. The other 3,076 were V-8 powered, including just 616 nine-passenger jobs. Studebaker made 1,075 Lark Daytona station wagons in 1964. All were six-passenger V-8s. In 1965, only 1,824 wagons were built. Production of all Studebakers ended in March 1966. Only 940 wagons were made the final year.

A unique feature of the Wagonaire was the manually-operated sliding roof. With the roof in the open position, you could haul a refrigerator, a Christmas tree or a long package standing upright in the back of the vehicle.

In 1963 and 1964, the engines used were the 170-cid 112-hp overhead-valve six or the 259-cid 180-hp V-8. After 1964, Wagonaires built at the Studebaker plant in Hamilton, Ontario, Canada came with V-8 engines manufactured by the Canadian GM engine plant at McKinnon. These engines were also used in Canadian Pontiacs. They were similar to the venerable 283 found in American Chevys and had the same 9.25:1 compression cylinder heads used on 1964 Corvettes. With a two-barrel carburetor, the "Studebaker" 283 produced 195 hp.

The 1964 model was the last Studebaker Daytona Wagonaire to be made in the South Bend facility.

1960s "Solid Gold"

1966 Studebaker Wagonaire station wagon

6	5	4	3	2	1
$ 420	$1,260	$2,100	$4,730	$7,350	$10,500

Estimated values in today's marketplace taken from the 2006 Collector Car Price Guide.

Chrysler New Yorker and Town & Country

It is anyone's guess why Chrysler marketed station wagons. The production of these models was always so low that it didn't seem to make good business sense to tool up for them but they did. Maybe it was considered a company tradition, since the wood-bodied Town & Country wagon brought Chrysler so much attention. Even more amazing, Chrysler made wagons in both low and high-trim versions. We are going to stick to the fancy ones here, though they're all pretty rare. For instance, the 1960 picture looked like this: Windsor six-passenger – 1,120; Windsor nine-passenger – 1,026; New Yorker six-passenger – 624 and New Yorker nine-passenger – 671.

Windsors had a 122-inch wheelbase, while New Yorkers were substantially more impressive with their 126-inch stance. The New Yorker wagon was a big 220 inches long – that's over 18 feet! It cost more than $5,000. For power, it had a 413-cid V-8 with a four-barrel carb and 350 hp.

In the late 1950s, Chrysler had adopted tail tailfins to compete with Cadillac. By 1962, it was time to shave them off. This gave the styling a kind of a "split personality." When you saw the front end, you expected fins at the rear, but there were none. Due to a scandal, Chrysler was going through a management shake-up and the fins seemed like a link to the past. All things considered, '62 was not a banner year and a mere 1,521 New Yorker wagons left the assembly line. Of those, 793 were nine-passenger jobs.

The 1963 is one of my favorite Chryslers (because I once owned one), but even I have to admit that the styling is somewhat unusual. That didn't keep New Yorker wagon production from "zooming" to 2,194. If you think that's not zooming, look at it as a 44 percent increase! The 1964 Chrysler was the "evil twin" to the '63 and the wagon was now dubbed the Town & Country again (though it lacked the wood paneling of the classic version). It was another "big year" with 2,793 made, including 1,603 nine-passengers.

The 1965 Chrysler was more rectangular and "slabbier," but not flat. The body side were sculptured. Overall, a much larger appearance resulted, although the Town & Country's 121-inch wheelbase was actually an inch *shorter* than the 1963-1964 stance. Overall length was 218.4 compared to 219.7 previously. Prices had settled down to $4,751 for the six-passenger model (1,368 made) and $4,856 for the nine-passenger (1,697 made). Minimal styling revisions were done for '67, but the New Yorker series no longer included a wagon. Availability was limited to the Newport series that now offered both versions under the Town & Country model name. Chrysler made 9,035 of the $4,177 six-passenger and 8,567 of the $4,283 nine-passenger.

Since the Newport Town & Country seemed to make much more sense than separate Newport and New Yorker wagons, Chrysler kept things like that in 1967 and 1968. Prices rose a little each year. In '67 production was just under 15,000 and in '68 it was just over 22,000. The wagon's went to a one-inch-larger (122 inches) wheelbase. Base engine was a 383-cid 270-hp two-barrel V-8. a four-barrel option raised output to 325 hp. Also optional was a 440-cid 350-hp V-8. Wood-grain paneling was part of the T & C package.

When the "fuselage"-bodied 1969 Chryslers arrived, the wagons went into their own separate series. They were no longer identified as Newports or New Yorkers. Instead, they were simply called Town & Country models. A New Yorker grille was employed and simulated wood-grain panels were on the body sides. The six-passenger sold for $5,193 and had a run of 10,108 units, while the nine-passenger retailed for $5,279 and saw 14,408 assemblies.

1969 Chrysler New Yorker Town & Country station wagon **Phil Hall Collection**

Town & Country 2-Seat Wagon in Antique Ivory

1961 Chrysler New Yorker Town & Country hardtop station wagon

1964 Chrysler New Yorker Town & Country hardtop station wagon

1960s "Solid Gold"

1965 or '66 Chrysler Town & Country six-passenger station wagon

6	5	4	3	2	1
$ 720	$2,160	$3,600	$8,100	$12,600	$18,000

Estimated values in today's marketplace taken from 2006 Standard Guide to Cars and Prices.

1960-1969 Rambler

1960 Rambler Custom Cross Country station wagon
Phil Hall Collection

In 1954, Hudson and Nash-Kelvinator joined together to form American Motors Corporation (AMC). My father bought my mother a Kelvinator dishwasher a few weeks before the merger. The machine never worked properly and the warranty was worthless. In our family, this was a point of contention for years. Nash and Hudson cars worked fine and through 1957 they kept on making a few of them. Then, in mid-1958, the new company hit the jackpot. It brought back the small "Rambler" it had first sold in the early 1950s. It was renamed the American and it sold like hot cakes because the country was in a recession and needed a compact car.

In model-year 1959, nearly 100,000 Americans were put together. That was a big number for a small automaker and AMC zoomed to fourth place in car sales. Total production of Americans, Ramblers, and Ambassadors was 374,240.

All AMC products were aimed at the average car-buying family man. Ads of this era were comic strips that explained in simple terms the great value these cars delivered. It's true that AMC offered a Rebel V-8 version

of the Rambler and a somewhat fancy Ambassador, but it was the bread-and-butter American and Rambler Six models that really helped AMC earn a record profit of $60,341,823. As the chart below shows, the station wagon was a very important body style for AMC. Its offerings included a hardtop wagon called the "Cross Country." The company made about a tenth as many two-door sedans as Ford, about a quarter as many four-door sedans as GM and about a tenth as many four-door hardtops as Chrysler. But when it came to station wagons, AMC was close to – or even ahead of – the so-called "Big 3."

In 1961, AMC offered 14 separate lines of cars and 19 different station wagons. Deluxe, Super and Custom versions of the American wagon were available and all came with a choice of two or three seats. Things were about the same in the Rambler Six line, except that the low-priced Deluxe station wagon came only in two-seat format. A new Rambler Classic Eight line replaced the Rebel series and it included Super and Custom wagons in two- or three-seat versions. The three-seat version was a five-door wagon with a side-opening rear door instead of

1960 MODEL YEAR BODY STYLE PRODUCTION

STYLE	GM	FORD	CHRYSLER	AMC	S-P	%
2D Sedan	353,020	479,379	77,092	44,187	35,397	16.4
2D Wagon	14,663	59,803	5,123	28,813	4,973	1.9
2D Hardtop	422,169	178,931	106,306	--	7,234	11.9
2D Convertible	189,703	66,329	18,685	--	8,571	4.7
4D Sedan	992,380	646,134	489,043	234,455	51,427	40.2
4D 2-Seat Wagon	218,526	181,613	106,394	128,161	18,195	10.9
4D 3-Seat Wagon	54,516	50,888	34,087	17,568	--	2.6
4D Hardtop	549,164	75,411	57,290	5,657	--	11.4

1967 Rambler Rebel "Mariner" station wagon **Elton McFall**

a lift gate and tailgate arrangement. The Ambassador line aped the Rambler Classic Eight as far as wagons went.

Of all AMC station wagons, the Ambassador models were the rarest. For example, in 1962 the company built 27,268 American wagons, 109,477 Rambler Classic wagons and just 12,069 Ambassador wagons. The American station

1967 Rambler Rebel station wagon

wagon did not remain a hot-selling car as the decade unfolded. After the national economy rebounded from the recession of the late-1950s, it grew quite healthy and buying patterns shifted back towards large cars and especially sporty and prestige type models. By 1965, AMC was building only 17,539 American wagons annually. That year the company was down to 10 lines of cars and just seven station wagons. The Rambler Classic line still accounted for the most wagons (61,826). Only 12,513 Ambassador wagons were made.

By the mid-1960s, AMC had new management and was searching for a new direction. Ads stressed the AMC corporate identity and the cars were promoted as AMC products, rather than Americans, Ramblers and Ambassadors. In '66 there were eight lines of cars including Marlin and only six station wagons: American 220 (3,647 built including 72 V-8s), American 440 (7,007 built including 286 V-8s), Rambler Classic 550 (9,953 built including 920 V-8s), Rambler Classic 770 (25,636 built including 7,423

V-8s), Ambassador 880 (4,791 built including 2,783 V-8s) and Ambassador 990 (8,854 built including 7,759 V-8s). All were six-passenger jobs.

An entirely new line of larger cars was introduced for 1967, as AMC began to take aim at the youth market and tried to catch up with the trends of the 1960s in general. Again there were six station wagons. Those formerly known as Rambler Classics were called Rebel 550s and Rebel 770s. There was a special "Rebel Westerner" station wagon with wood-grained body side panels. Only 43,168 wagons were built in all lines. AMC was down to four station wagons by 1968 and production fell to 37,777 units. In 1969, the American station wagon was discontinued, but there were still four left as one new one was added to the Ambassador line. AMC built 8,569 Rebel wagons, 9,256 Rebel SST wagons, 8,866 Ambassador DPL wagons and 7,825 Ambassador SST wagons. That totaled out to 34,516 and reflected how times had changed.

1962 Rambler Classic 400 station wagon

1960s "Solid Gold"

1965 Rambler Classic 770 station wagon

6	5	4	3	2	1
$ 284	$ 852	$1,420	$3,200	$4,970	$7,100

Estimated values in today's marketplace taken from the 2006 Standard Guide to Cars and Prices.

1960-1969 Plymouth Fury

Of all the Chrysler brands, Plymouth clearly made the most station wagons. Plymouth was, in fact, famous for introducing one of the first all-steel station wagons in the early postwar years. It was called the Suburban and this name stuck as the name for Plymouth wagons for many years. The company's fanciest 1960 station wagon was the Fury Sport Suburban, which came as a six-passenger wagon for $2,989 or as an eight-passenger wagon for $3,099. The factory rolled out 3,333 of the standard model and 4,523 with the extra seat.

I have a "Christine" like reaction to this car, though it has nothing to do with the movie. Father Forrester, our local priest, drove a red Fury Suburban with a white roof. When we saw that car coming, we knew our man of the cloth was cruising for kids to help him deliver church bulletins, so we ran the other way. He probably had a three-seater so kids could hop in. This was the year that Plymouth lost the third spot in industry sales to AMC and the low production of the Fury Sport Suburban certainly didn't help matters.

In 1961 and '62, the big Plymouths went from looking a little weird to downright — well let's just say "unique." The fancy station wagon (called "Sport Suburban" in '61 and "Fury Station Wagon" in '62) suffered with production dropping to 5,932 the first year and 4,763 the latter year. By 1963, Plymouth went a little more conventional with its

1960 Plymouth Sport Suburban station wagon
Phil Hall Collection

design work and came up with a pretty package that really clicked as a station wagon. The Fury version accounted for production of 6,672 units — not a lot, but at least headed in the right direction. The up trend continued in '64, when 8,128 were built.

1960s "Solid Gold"

1964 Plymouth Fury
9-passenger station wagon

6	5	4	3	2	1
$ 444	$1,332	$2,220	$5,000	$7,700	$11,100

Estimated values in today's marketplace taken from the 2006 Standard Guide to Cars and Prices.

From Fury and Sport Fury lines in 1964, Plymouth went to four series in '65. There was no Sport Fury station wagon, but that body style did come in the Fury, Fury II and Fury III lines and accounted for a big rise in production. The Fury six-passenger-only version was built 13,360 times. In the Fury II line, production included 12,853 six-passenger wagons and 6,445 nine-passenger jobs. In the Fury III trim

1969 Plymouth Fury Sport Suburban station wagon

level, the totals were 8,931 six-passenger and 9,546 nine-passenger. Never before had Plymouth turned out anything like 51,135 Fury wagons (plus 17,540 Belvedere wagons and 16,955 Valiant wagons). The general picture was the same in '66, though the numbers tapered off a bit.

Plymouth dropped the Valiant station wagon in 1967. The Belvedere wagon was restyled and reflected that series move towards the youth/high-performance market with squarish lines and an aircraft look. The Fury remained a big car with a 119-inch wheelbase and the Fury wagon was even more of a monster with a three-inch longer stance and 216-inch-plus overall length (216 inches for the six-passenger and 217.3 inches for the nine-passenger). The arrangement of models was the same as in 1965 — one in the Fury I line, both in the Fury II and Fury III lines. Production was 44,255.

For wagon mavens, the one to look for arrived in 1968 when a Fury VIP wagon was added in both six- and nine-passenger form. The low-selling Fury I wagon was gone, as was the Fury II nine-passenger. All of these moves were good ones and total production hit a record of 56,208 Fury station wagons, with a higher percentage of sales going to pricier, more profitable models. Size-wise these were the same as the 1966s and the styling was cleaned up slightly.

After the way things went in 1968, it is hard to guess why Plymouth dropped the VIP station wagon in 1969 and re-instituted the Fury I wagon as well as the Fury II nine-passenger. It's not that things went bad with 54,318 assemblies of Fury wagons for the model year, but the one-inch longer '69 wagon with its new "airplane fuselage" styling would have made a great VIP!

CHAPTER SEVEN

The 1960s . . . Trucks

As the 1960s dawned, the market for trucks in the U.S. was far different than today. Where I lived on the East Coast, it was rare for anyone to own a truck of any type. The local gas station operator, the TV repairman and Con Ed workers drove trucks. Most people I knew had never been in a truck in their lives. Except for Jeeps, Dodge Power-Wagons and the new Scout, a four-wheel-drive truck was a rarity. The term SUV hadn't even been invented yet. Except for some far-out British models and an Isetta owned by the local shoemaker, there was no such thing as a mini truck. And the term van meant a cargo truck.

A total of 1,190,313 trucks of all sizes were made in calendar-year 1960. Only a robust export market and 12.6 percent jump in demand for light-duty trucks made the number go up from 1959. That compared to 6,696,108 passenger cars. By the end of the decade, truck production was at 1,963,099 and car production was 8,219,463. Over the 10-year period, truck production increased by 65 percent while car production increased only 27 percent. It wasn't exactly the light-duty truck revolution, but it was the start of a trend that would lead to market upheaval in the 1970s and later decades.

Of the trucks made in 1960, 6.5 percent had four-cylinders, 69.7 percent had six cylinders and only 23.8 percent had eight cylinders. The six-cylinder power plants included 95,000 V-6s made by GMC. It is doubtful if any light truck built in 1960 had air conditioning, power windows or power seats. Car stereos had not yet been invented, much less a tape or CD players. Many trucks had running boards, but tonneau covers, camper shells, bed liners and such accessories were in the future. An innovation was the release of a Ranchero based on Ford's new Falcon.

The best year for truck sales in the U.S. had been 1955 when 1,200,000 were built. That made 1960 the second best year up to that point. In 1961, the count stopped at 1,127,554, but there was a bright note. Production of four-cylinder trucks topped 100,000. The new-for-1961 IHC Scout probably contributed to the record. Also, the Corvair Greenbrier and Ford Econoline had a good first year. Corvair and Econoline buses, counted as cars, dented Volkswagen bus sales.

By 1966, the Jeep Wagoneer was a popular choice for many needing a tough, versatile wagon. **Elton McFall Collection**

In 1962, American makers shipped a record 1,254,220 trucks from their factories. Ninety-six percent operated on gasoline and two out of three of those had a six-cylinder engine. The number of trucks with a V-8 under the hood grew 18 percent. The truck market was bustling, with no end in sight. In 1963, factory shipments shattered an 11-year mark and calendar-year output surged to 1,427,002 trucks. For the 17th year in a row, more than one million trucks were produced.

Ford built 64,000 Econolines in 1963. Jeep shipments rose to 98,000, from 65,000 in 1962. In 1963, Kaiser-owned (since 1953) Willys Motor Company changed its name to Kaiser-Jeep Corporation. The Willys name vanished in 1965 when Kaiser-Jeep discontinued Willys wagon and truck production. Gas engine trends changed, too, as 92,000 trucks got a four-cylinder power plant, 863,400 got a six and 422,200 relied on a V-8. The five leading truck makers were Chevy (483,100), Ford (424,700), IHC (164,300), Dodge (111,000) and Jeep (110,500).

The entry of Chevy (Chevy Van), Dodge (A 100) and GMC (Handi Van) into the front-engine compact-van market was news in 1964, when factory truck shipments hit a record for the second straight year. In the calendar year, 1,509,644 trucks rolled off the assembly lines, a 5.8 percent gain from record year 1963. Buyers moved toward the V-8, which went into 523,400 trucks (up from 417,600). Six-cylinder installations rose from 762,200 in 1963 to 776,600 in 1964. The four-cylinder engine had a slight drop in popularity (89,400 vs. 91,800). Ford put V-8s in 56 percent of its trucks compared to 28 percent for Chevrolet. This was the year that the El Camino was re-introduced as a Chevelle-based mid-size model and it was the last year that Studebaker trucks – including postal Zip vans -- were made.

In 1965 Chevrolet began installing air conditioning in its light- and medium-duty trucks. You could also get it, for the first time, in Ford's Ranchero. This was a sign of the changing role that trucks were playing in the American lifestyle. This year 624,300 trucks – 37.1 percent of total production – had a V-8 engine. Sixes were used in 57.4 percent and fours in the rest. For the fourth year in a row, total calendar-year production headed upwards, hitting 1,785,109. That included 619,691 Chevys, 547,427 Fords, 171,638 IHCs, 143,452 Dodges, 136,705 GMCs and 108,601 Jeeps. For the first time, light-duty truck shipments in the U.S. passed 1,000,000 units.

Truck production just missed five straight years of increases in calendar 1966, falling short by 20,000 units. Chevy was number one (621,417), Ford was number two (526,408), IHC was number three (170,385), Dodge was fourth (153,139), GMC was fifth (127,294) and Jeep was sixth (99,624). Again, V-8 usage increased to 717,200. The number of six-cylinder trucks built fell to 887,600, the first decline in the decade. Four-cylinder installations also decreased to 49,900. Ford built its last Falcon Ranchero this season and also introduced the original Bronco.

In 1967, truck production fell to 1,585,481 calendar-year units, an 11.1 percent decrease. Industry rankings remained the same. Ford moved the Ranchero to the Fairlane platform to compete with the El Camino. V-8 engines were used in 41.2 percent of all new trucks. This was the first time in postwar history that more trucks (735,601) were built with V-8s than sixes (715,574). Chevy and GMC trucks were restyled.

More than one million trucks with V-8s were produced in 1968, when total production hit 1,950,713 units for the calendar year. Starting in 1965, trucks made

The new compact Ford Falcon car was accompanied by a new Falcon-based version of the popular Ford Ranchero like this 1961 version **Tom Glatch**

by GM, Ford and Chrysler outpaced the number built by independent makers like IHC and Jeep. This continued in 1968 when the smaller firms built only 324,694 units—down by 11,981 units from 1967. The Big Three were gobbling up all the industry growth. Important developments included restyling the El Camino and introducing a Dodge Custom Sports Special called the Adventurer. It had a plush interior and a high-performance V-8. This was the last year for the military-style Power-Wagon.

American truck makers were hoping to break the two-million production barrier for 1969. They missed, but managed to build more trucks than in calendar 1968. A record 67 percent of them had a V-8 under the hood. Total production of 1,963,099 included 683,694 Chevys, 639,948 Fords, 165,133 Dodges, 160,255 IHCs, 150,180 GMCs and 93,160 Jeeps. Struggling-to-catch-up IHC redid the Scout in a futile attempt to fight the Big Three. Chevrolet launched the Blazer as the SUV wars heated up. This was the final season for the Kaiser-Jeep name, as the old "war horse" would gallop into the AMC stable in 1970.

We'll bring a brand new SCOUT right to your door

just tell us where you live

Trying hard to sell vehicles, I-H promoted its "Bring a Scout to Your Door" ad in 1965. **Elton McFall Collection**

1966 Chevrolet El Camino

1960 and 1964 to 1969 El Camino

The 1960 Chevrolet El Camino was based on the full-size Chevrolet.

with a new oval-shaped grille and more angular wings at the rear. A total of 14,163 were built in 1960.

There were no 1961 to '63 El Caminos. In 1964, the El Camino became a boxy, truck version of the mid-size Chevelle. Standard ($2,380) and Custom ($2,461) trims were offered. Buyers could add many Chevelle options, but hi-po V-8s were not yet offered. About 35,000 El Caminos were made annually. The 1967 El Camino had a few changes like a new grille and front bumper. The 396 big-block V-8 was offered, but there was not yet an SS 396.

When Ford cut the back of the roof off its 1957 station wagon to make the Ranchero pickup, it caused a sensation. In reality, the coupe-pickup truck was similar to the "Utes" that had been sold in Australia since the 1930s. Chevrolet answered the Ranchero with its "More than a car . . . More than a truck" 1959 El Camino, a Ute-type vehicle based on the full-sized Chevrolet. Extensive updating brought the full-size El Camino into the 1960s

The completely restyled 1968 El Camino rode the 116-inch wheelbase of four-door Chevelles. A new SS 396 greeted performance buffs. SS emblems and simulated hood scoops were included on this model. A flat-black grille carried a 396 emblem. All SS 396s featured six-inch-wheels and Red Line tires. Production was 41,791 including 5,190 SS 396s. After its big 1968 changes, the '69 El Camino was little changed. Production hit a record 48,385.

1969 Chevrolet El Camino **Phil Hall Collection**

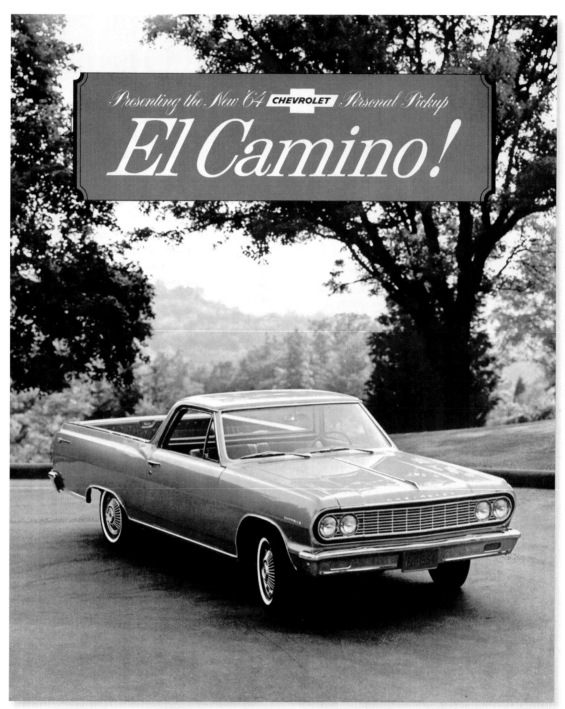

In 1964, the Chevrolet El Camino was reintroduced, this time based on the new Chevelle.

1960s "Solid Gold"

1967 Chevelle El Camino Custom Sport

6	5	4	3	2	1
$ 920	$2,760	$4,600	$10,350	$16,100	$23,000

Estimated values in today's marketplace taken from the 2006 Collector Car Price Guide.

1961-1964 Corvair 95 Trucks

The 1961 Corvair 95 Rampside pickup (top) had a small tailgate in back but everyone remembers its side-opening ramp.

Chevrolet introduced its Corvair as a 1960 model designed to fight off the "import invasion." In 1961, the Corvair 95 line of trucks was added. The "95" designation denoted the short wheelbase of these rear-engined, van-type trucks. Did anyone say "Volkswagen Bus clone?" VWs and the 95 were similar. New was the Corvan, the Greenbrier wagon and two pickups. The pickups came

with or without a swing-down side ramp that gave the one model its Rampside name. Loadside was the other pickup's name. "You've never had a choice like this," said a Chevrolet advertisement. "High-capacity — light-handed maneuverability — a totally new kind of truck."

Corvair 95s were designed for light, bulky loads. As Chevy put it, "The driver's up front, the engine's in the rear and all the rest is load space — a cavernous 191 cubic feet of it in the Corvan." Chevy saw the 95s as a replacement for the El Camino, but not for the conventional "like-a-rock" 1/2-ton pickup truck. In 1961, prices were $2,079 to $2,280. Chevy built 15,806 Corvans, 10,787 Rampside and 2,475 Loadside pickups. Greenbriers were built to carry people and their production was counted with that of cars

For 1962, Corvair 95 models were unchanged. Prices increased a bit and assemblies dropped considerably. The Corvan was still the most popular model and 13,491 were made. Rampside production fell off to just 4,102 units and a mere 369 Loadside pickups left the assembly line. Chevrolet sold its 8 millionth truck in 1962, but it was clear the Corvair 95 would never hit that level. Slow sales knocked the Loadside off the models list in 1963 when 11,161 Corvans and 2,046 Rampsides were built. The next year the corresponding numbers were 8,147 and 851. By then, the Chevy Van had been released, as well as the mid-sized El Camino. There was no one left to buy the Corvair 95s.

The 1963 Corvair Greenbrier Deluxe wagon was an economical family mover.

1960s "Solid Gold"

1961 to 1965 Corvair 95 Rampside pickup

6	5	4	3	2	1
$ 620	$1,860	$3,100	$6,980	$10,850	$15,500

Estimated values in today's marketplace taken from the 2006 Collector Car Price Guide.

1961-1967 Econoline Pickup

1967 Ford Econoline SuperVan

Jeep pioneered the compact, forward-control truck in 1957 offering pickup and stake models, but industrial designer Brooks Stevens designed a van version, of which two were made. Jeep dropped the ball by not mass-producing this beautiful truck. In 1961, Ford picked the ball up and ran with it and the result was its amazingly popular Econoline series. Of the various body types offered, the pickup is the one the collectors prize. This model first sold for $1,880. Its weight was in the 2,555-pound range. Ford made 11,893 standard Econoline pickups and 3,000 more with fancier Custom trim.

By 1962, more than 80,000 Econolines were being built. With their modest prices, these trucks had big appeal. Only 8,140 of the 1962 models were Custom Pickups. That's one reason that these trucks are so rare today. As in '61, the only engine was a 144-cid 85-hp in-line six. The trucks had a short 90-inch wheelbase and were only 168.4 inches long. Like Corvair 95s, the early Econolines were best suited to haul light, bulky loads. Custom-trim versions had large body side moldings and wraparound style quarter windows.

1960 Ford Econoline pickup

The Econoline pickup used a concept similar to the Volkswagen pickup and Corvair 95 Rampside/Loadside models, but avoided the use of an air-cooled engine mounted at the rear and other "radical" engineering. Their conventional Ford Falcon drive train made the buyers more comfortable in buying a Ford. This meant that the Econoline had little direct competition until the Dodge A-100 pickup arrived in 1964. An Econoline clone, the Dodge version sold for $1,927. Very few were built. One of the most famous was Bill "Maverick" Golden's dragster called the "Little Red Wagon."

Even with some new competition from the Dodge, the Ford Econoline pickup held its own in the marketplace. With nothing but modest changes, the pickup model survived for six years. It was a winner for FoMoCo. In February 1968, a completely new Econoline arrived as a 1969 model. It was on a larger 105.5-inch wheelbase and also available was a Super Van version with a 123.5-inch wheelbase. Instead of a flat front, these trucks had a hood of sorts. This design did not lend itself to a pickup truck model and none was offered.

1964 Ford Econoline pickup

1961 Ford Econoline pickup **Tom Glatch**

1960s "Solid Gold"

1961 to 1966 Ford E-100 Econoline pickup

6	5	4	3	2	1
$ 920	$2,760	$4,600	$10,350	$16,100	$23,000

Estimated values in today's marketplace taken from the 2006 Collector Car Price Guide.

1963-1969 Jeep Wagoneer

The Wagoneer was a new design and more glamorous image for Jeep in 1963. **Phil Hall Collection**

The Jeep Wagoneer replaced the classic all-steel Willys station wagon. It was designed to update Jeep's image and help the company compete. The new model took three years and $20 million to create. It was offered in two- or four-door styles with rear-wheel or four-wheel drive. Buyers could also choose between a tailgate or rear doors. An OHC six powered the Wagoneer.

Jeep described the Wagoneer as "the first station wagon to provide complete passenger car styling, comfort and convenience in combination with the advantages of four-wheel drive." While having a fresh look, it retained some traditional motifs. When you saw a Wagoneer, you knew it was a Jeep. A Custom trim package included stainless window trim.

No changes were made in the 1964 Wagoneer's looks or specs, but air conditioning was available, along with a less powerful "economy" engine. A V-8 option – Jeep's first – was new in 1965. The 327-cid V-8 produced 250 hp. You could get it with the standard three-speed transmission or with an optional GM Turbo-Hydra-Matic. A four-speed manual was added during the 1965 model run. A 232-cid AMC six also replaced the old 230-cid OHC six.

America's first luxury SUV arrived in 1966 with a "Super" nameplate on each rear fender. It included courtesy lights, a tilt steering wheel, front bucket seats, vinyl door panels, padded sun visors, a padded dash, a day/night prismatic mirror and retracting seat belts. Air conditioning, Turbo-Hydra-Matic Drive, power steering, power brakes,

a power tailgate window, tinted safety glass, styled wheel covers, 8.45 x 15 white sidewall tires, a chrome roof rack, an external rear view mirror, the 327-cid four-barrel V-8 and a push-button radio were all standard. The Super had a special full-width chrome grille.

After 1968, Wagoneers came only with four-wheel drive. A new four-door Custom V-8 was introduced. It featured carpeting, chrome dash knobs, a color-coordinated deluxe steering wheel, courtesy lights, a vinyl cargo area floor covering, bright metal body side moldings and full wheel covers. In 1969, the two-door models were dropped along with the Super Wagoneer and a commercial panel truck model. The 145-hp "Hi-Torque" six was still the standard engine, but a 350-cid Buick V-8 replaced AMC's 327 as the V-8 option.

In 1969, Jeep added more options and called it the Super Wagoneer. **Phil Hall Collection**

1967 Jeep Wagoneer **Phil Hall Collection**

1960s "Solid Gold"

1963 Jeep Wagoneer Custom four-door station wagon

6	5	4	3	2	1
$ 444	$1,332	$2,220	$5,000	$7,770	$11,100

Estimated values in today's marketplace taken from the 2006 Collector Car Price Guide.

1960-1969 Suburban

Chevrolet and GMC Suburbans are clones, except for badges and trim (and engines in some early models). The station wagon-like Suburban Carry-All with an all-steel body was introduced in 1935. Major changes were made in the 1940s and 1950s. Boxy "jet-pod" body styling and a low-profile grille characterized the new 1960 Suburban. It had a wraparound windshield. The Chevy version had a bow-tie emblem between the pods. The "Jimmy" said GMC in large block letters across the grille. An in-line six powered the Chevy version. A new 305-cid 150-hp V-6 was standard on the GMC model. For 1962, the Chevy Suburban got a new flat hood and single headlights, while the GMC stuck with dual headlights, although it used the new hood.

The Chevrolet Suburban was a versatile performer in the great outdoors.

Chevy Suburbans used straight sixes, but GMC offered only the V-6. Both brands sold two- and four-wheel-drive models. In 1963, a coil-spring front suspension greatly improved riding comfort and control. Chevy adopted a 230-cid 140-hp six and an optional 292-cid 165-hp version. A new egg-crate grille graced the Chevy. In 1964, the front windshield pillars were changed from a forward slant to a rearward one. The dash was also redesigned. Styling was unchanged in '65, but an optional 327-cid 220-hp V-8 was offered by Chevy. Another new option was air conditioning. Only trim changes were made in 1966, but a milestone was reached in March when the 500,000 V-6 truck was built.

GM's light-duty trucks were restyled in 1967, with cleaner exterior lines, more attractive interior appointments and a broader line of engines including new 307- and 396-cid V-8s. The much sleeker Suburban had a broad-shouldered appearance. The body was slightly longer than before. There were two doors on the passenger side

1969 Chevrolet Suburban

GMC suburban and panel

1961 GMC Suburban **Phil Hall Collection**

1962 Chevrolet Suburban Carryall

and one on the driver's side. At the rear, buyers got a choice of a tailgate or panel-style doors. The similar 1968 models had new safety equipment to meet recent government regulations.

The 1969 grille had a wider horizontal centerpiece. A foot-operated parking brake replaced the former hand brake. V-8 options included a new 350 with 255-350 hp and a 396 with 310 hp and more torque than the smaller V-8s.

1964 GMC Suburban

1960s "Solid Gold"

1960 to 1966 Chevrolet Suburban

6	5	4	3	2	1
$ 708	$2,124	$3,540	$7,970	$12,390	$17,700

Estimated values in today's marketplace taken from the 2006 Standard Guide to Cars and Prices.

1960 to 1966 GMC Suburban

6	5	4	3	2	1
$ 680	$2,040	$3,400	$7,650	$11,900	$17,000

Estimated values in today's marketplace taken from the 2006 Standard Guide to Cars and Prices.

1960-1966 Jeep FC-150

Jeep literature shows the original FC-150 series and the longer wheelbase FC-170 series for 1963. **Phil Hall Collection**

In Jeep terminology the prefix FC stands for "Forward-Control." That means the driver sits in the front of the vehicle above the drive train. After Kaiser bought Willys-Overland Corporation in 1953, it soon decided to discontinue Willys passenger car production in North America and concentrate on the Jeep market. At that point, Kaiser had the four-wheel-drive market virtually to itself and was seeking new applications and new product ideas.

Forward-control trucks like the Volkswagen Kombi were making inroads in Europe as both commercial vehicles and passenger buses. Such vehicles got good exposure in American car magazines of the early 1950s. Kaiser was planning a new line of Jeep vehicles for 1956. One was a forward-control truck with four-wheel drive. It was called the FC-150 for "Forward-Control 150-inch length (even though it was actually 147-1/2 inches long). Rated at 5,000 pounds, the FC-150 used an 81-inch wheelbase and had a 78-inch-long cargo bed. Power came from a 134.2-cid 72-hp L-head in-line four. (A similar, but larger FC-170 model with a 10-foot bed was introduced the next spring.)

Business Week covered the "FC" Jeep in its December 8, 1956 issue. Features and benefits of the new models included a larger payload capacity with the cab moved up over the engine, increased visibility (improved 200 percent over conventional trucks of the same size) and the power and maneuverability of Jeep four-wheel drive on a short wheelbase.

Industrial designer Brooks Stevens, of Milwaukee, Wisconsin, played a major role in the design of the FC-150. Stevens had done design work for Willys-Overland as early as 1942. In 1957, Stevens did a full-scale clay model of an FC-150 passenger van. Two or three prototypes were built by the German company Reutter of Stuttgart. One of these was kept for many years at Henry J. Kaiser's estate in northern Michigan and may still exist.

There was nothing else quite like the 1959 Jeep FC-150, a design that would last well into the 1960s **Jim Allen**

A Pennsylvania fire brigade has preserved this 1965 Jeep FC-170. **Pagsanjan Fire Brigade, Pennsylvania**

On November 29, 1956, Kaiser used a closed-circuit TV broadcast to introduce the FC-150 to dealers across the country. The new model debuted at the New York City Automobile show that December. In 1957, Kaiser-Willys sold 9,738 of these trucks. When the FC-170 arrived, FC-150 sales dropped considerably. NADA guides listed the FC model through 1966, although some sources say production halted in 1964. The 1960s models looked just like the 1950s models. The FC models were heavily used by the military and in commercial applications such as construction work, oil well drilling, fire fighting and farming. With the combination of low production and hard, industrial use, surviving examples are hard to find, especially in good condition.

1960s "Solid Gold"

1960 Jeep Forward Control 4 x 4 ½-ton pickup

6	5	4	3	2	1
$ 536	$1,608	$2,680	$6,030	$9,380	$13,400

Add 3 percent for six-cylinder trucks. Add 5 percent for custom two-tone trim.

Estimated values in today's marketplace taken from the 2006 Collector Car Price Guide.

Studebaker Champ

Studebaker always did a lot with a little and this talent served the South Bend, Indiana company's truck business well in the early 1960s – before the end came. Profits from strong sales of Lark automobiles, introduced in 1959, gave the Studebaker Truck Division a little money to work with. This was invested in a redesign of the 1/2-ton and 3/4-ton models. Borrowing a concept from its handsome coupe-express trucks of the late-1930s, Studebaker took the Lark body, chopped it off behind the door and converted it into the front end and cab of a truck. A beefier Lark-style grille and bumper were used on Champ trucks.

At the rear, the Champ used the pickup box and fenders from the 1959 Transtar pickup. The result was what you might call a successful merger and because the Lark automobile was riding the wave of compact car popularity, some of that public acceptance was transferred to an affection for the new light-duty trucks (heavier Studebaker trucks continued using the Transtar body). Both six-cylinder and V-8 engines were available in the Champ, as they were in the Lark car. That gave truck buyers options up to 210 hp, which was great in 1960. Two wheelbases of 112 inches and 122 inches were offered. Production delays and a steel strike held up the introduction of the Champ until spring.

In 1961, Studebaker released a 170-cid overhead-valve six for the Champ trucks. A more modern looking pickup truck box replaced the Transtar style. This was made from old Dodge tooling purchased by Studebaker and was basically of Dodge Sweptline style with a flatter, squarer character. Studebaker called it a "Spaceside" box and it gave the Champ a more up-to-date appearance. However, it did not boost production of Studebaker trucks, which fell by about 700 units to 7,841. Buyers could still get a 1961 Champ with the old-style box, but the new one was considered "standard equipment."

Things continued on the same track between 1962 and 1964, by which time Studebaker was on the ropes and past the point of no return. Prices were cut slightly to

It was natural that Studebaker used its successful Lark car design in the 1960 Champ pickup truck.

encourage sales, then had to be raised as the company ran out of money. In a last ditch effort to drum up business, Studebaker offered Service Champ models with special fiberglass utility bodies for plumbers, electricians and so on. Service Champs came only on the longer wheelbase. While Studebaker continued building the "Common Sense Car" in Canada in 1965, it was no longer listed in *Ward's Automotive Yearbook* under trucks.

1960s "Solid Gold"

1963 Studebaker Champ pickup (slab side, short wheelbase)

5	4	3	2	1
$ 575	$1,975	$5,075	$7,400	$10,650

1963 Studebaker Champ pickup (fender, short wheelbase)

5	4	3	2	1
$ 550	$1,900	$4,875	$7,125	$10,250

Note: The 2006 Collector Car Price Guide lists the 4E1 series pickup prices, the 1959 predecessors to the Champ series. The Champ prices above are taken from the VMR database, the statistical services for Edmunds Used Car Price Guide. They use a five-point rating scale.

BIG NEW WIDE BOX

NEW EXTRA-WIDE SPACESIDE PICKUP BOX
IN BOTH 6½' AND 8' LENGTHS—½ OR ¾ TON

A full 70¼" wide inside and sand tight. Pile in up to 2115 lbs. of payload—well over a ton. All steel floor has built-in skids, while body sides and tailgate are reinforced for rugged work. 1¾ feet of extra width makes for faster loading and unloading. Bigger cargo capacity means lower truck costs per mile, cuts trips and labor time.

A CHAMP FOR EVERY KIND OF JOB

CHAMP DOUBLE WALL PICKUP BOX

In 6½' and 8' lengths. Has 51½" width of clear floor space—no wheel wells—and carries up to 2065 pounds of payload. Double Wall steel sides and ribbed steel floor make it the strongest box made—and inside dents won't show on the outside. Safety taillight swings away under impact to avoid breakage, automatically resets to original position.

CHAMP STAKE BODY

8' length, full 78" in width with 30½" stakes. Available in both ½ Ton and ¾ Ton Champs. Steel channel section main sills, pressed steel cross sills and rub rails. Stake holes are metal reinforced. Removable stakes are of heavy gauge reinforced steel. New low level chassis suspension lowers lifting height helps loading. Individually removable floor boards are interlocked and protected by heavy rolled steel skid strips.

PLATFORM BODY ALSO AVAILABLE

The 1961 Studebaker Champs came in choices that included a wide box, narrower box with fenders and a stake body. **Phil Hall Collection**

1963 Studebaker Champ **Elton McFall**

1961-1969 International Scout

The original Scout was created as a competitor to the Jeep. Its 1961 introduction made that one of the most significant years in International Harvester Corporation history. The new model was developed and brought to the assembly line in less than two years—a remarkable feat in the 1960s. It bowed to the public on January 18, 1961 and created an immediate sensation.

The 1961 Scout was available in both two- and four-wheel-drive versions. The engine was a 93-hp four with a floor-shifted three-speed manual transmission. Pickup, station wagon and open roadster models were available, but the wagon with four-wheel drive was the big seller. By the end of the abbreviated model year, more than 28,000 Scouts were delivered. Roll-up windows were optional in 1962. Prices for the five-foot pickup started at $2,132. There were few changes in the product between 1961 and 1964 although prices increased and a special '64 Champagne Edition model was released.

Scout 80 was the designation for 1961 to mid-1965 models, which had slider windows, the Commanche Four, a folding windshield, vacuum-operated high-mounted windshield wipers and an IH logo center grille logo. The Scout 800 was marketed from late-1965 to mid-1971. The Scout 800 had a new car-like grille and a new windshield that reduced rain leaks. There was also a new Easy View instrument panel. Standard equipment included bucket seats and windshield wipers located at the bottom of the windshield.

A luxurious new "Sportop" was added in 1966 and a few Scouts got a turbocharged version of the Commanche III engine with 111 hp. In 1967, the first Scout V-8 was built. This 266-cid engine produced 155 hp. Other options ranged from a 196-cid four to a 232-cid V-8 and a 304-cid V-8 in 1969 and newer models. Scout sales through the 1960s exceeded the sales of all Jeep models.

The Scout remained a fixture throughout the decade like this 1969 version.

The 1965 Scout options included the memorable Sportop hardtop version. **Phil Hall Collection**

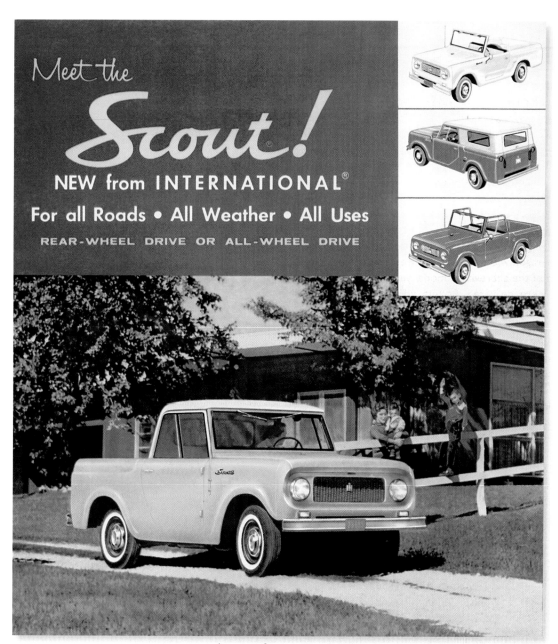

Longtime farm equipment and truck maker International-Harvester (I-H) introduced the versatile Scout in 1961. **Phil Hall Collection**

1960s "Solid Gold"

1961 to 1964 I-H Scout Series 80 ½-ton (4 x 4 version)

6	5	4	3	2	1
$ 396	$1,188	$1,980	$4,460	$6,930	$9,900

Add 5 percent for vinyl Sport-Top and add 4 percent for steel Travel-Top.

Estimated values in today's marketplace taken from 2006 Standard Guide to Cars and Prices.

In 1968, the Ranchero made its third appearance, this time on a Fairlane/ Torino platform, as the Ranchero GT and Ranchero 500. **Phil Hall Collection**

Ford Ranchero

A car with a pickup truck box was not a totally new thing when Ford introduced the Ranchero in 1957. Hudson, Studebaker and other companies produced models with the same concept. As did small-car makers like Bantam and Crosley. In Australia, a similar vehicle called the "Ute" had been made since the 1930s. You might be safe saying that Ford was the first to bring this concept to America in a model aimed at the volume-production market. Whether the Ranchero was a "first," it was a first-class, good-looking truck.

The big 1957 through '59 Rancheros were based on the full-size Ford Fairlane. A wide range of engines including the "Thunderbird Special" V-8 could be ordered. There were several fancy interior trim options. Standard and Custom trim lines were offered, the latter including bright metal body side moldings, more accessories and the richer upholstery choices. Two-tone paint schemes in contrasting bright hues were the rule, rather than the exception.

In 1960, Ford released its first compact car, the Falcon. The Ranchero model was transferred to the Falcon platform, where it stayed until 1966. The little car-truck

1964 Falcon Ranchero

was a great combination. It could haul 800 pounds of freight, deliver 30 mpg from its 144-cid six and provide dual-purpose "town and country" utility with its smooth, low-slung passenger-car styling. For Americans moving to the suburbs in big numbers, owning a Falcon Ranchero was a sensible choice. There was also a rare sedan delivery truck based on the Falcon running gear.

In mid-1963, the Ranchero got an optional engine. This 260-cid V-8 produced 164 hp. Sporty bucket seats, vinyl upholstery and a four-speed manual gearbox could also be ordered. The 1964 to 1965 Ranchero went to a

1960s "Solid Gold"

1960 to 1965 Falcon Ranchero ½-ton pickup

6	5	4	3	2	1
$ 600	$1,790	$2,980	$6,710	$10,430	$14,900

1966 Fairlane Ranchero Custom ½-ton pickup

6	5	4	3	2	1
$ 700	$2,100	$3,500	$7,880	$12,250	$17,500

1962 Falcon Rancheros (above), with boat and trailer, by **David Lyon** *and (middle) showing the cargo box area.*

squarer new Falcon body design. Ford's 289-cid small-block V-8 was offered in 1965. A rare two-tone paint scheme was available on Deluxe models. The 1966 Ranchero was a one-year-only Falcon/Fairlane hybrid. It went to the longer 113-inch Fairlane station wagon wheelbase, but had a Falcon-like body. Coil springs were used in front with leaf springs at the rear. Three engines were offered: a 200-cid 120-hp six, a two-barrel version of the 289 with 200 hp and a four-barrel 225-hp 289. Ford built 9,480 standard versions and 11,038 Deluxes.

In 1967, the Ranchero became a full-blown Fairlane with stacked dual headlights, a one-piece aluminum grille and rectangular taillights. The base pickup listed for $2,514 (a $300 increase) and 5,858 were made. Also available was the $2,611 Ranchero 500 pickup (9,504 built) and the $2,768 Ranchero 500 XL (1,881 built), which had plenty of extra bright metal body moldings. This car-truck came with all Ford engine options up to a 390-cid 320-hp V-8. This sporty truck is the probably the most collectible type of all the Rancheros made. It was basically carried over in 1968 when the 500XL became the GT.

GTs were all well-equipped with features like a standard V-8 and C-shaped body side stripes in coordinated colors. The '69 followed the same pattern, but replaced the 289 with a 302-cid 220-hp engine. Other available V-8 options included 351-cid 290-hp, 390-cid 320-hp and 428-cid 335-hp choices. The 428 engine package included a heavy-duty suspension, aluminum rocker arm covers, other bright engine parts, an extra-cooling radiator, an 80-amp battery, other special parts and "428" badges. In 1969, model-year production was 5,856 Rancheros, 11,214 Ranchero 500s and 1,658 Ranchero GTs.

1963 Falcon Ranchero

1969 Ford Bronco **Phil Hall Collection**

1966-1969 Ford Bronco

The Ford Bronco arrived in August 1965, introduced as a 1966 model. For years the Jeep had ruled the four-wheel-drive vehicle market, but in 1961 the International Scout came along to challenge the old soldier. By the late 1960s, the Scout's success was so compelling that the Big 3 wanted a chunk of the pie. Ford jumped in first with the Bronco. It was a "better Scout," but still very bare bones in nature. The line consisted of a door-less Roadster, a Jeep-like Sport Utility and Wagon body styles. The only engine was a 170-cid 105-hp six hooked "three-on-the-tree." However, the 289 V-8 was available by March. Ford built 18,200 Broncos in 1966. The company wouldn't stop there.

A Bronco Sport Package was introduced in 1967. It added a bright horn ring, moldings and window frames, a chrome-plated grille, chrome bumpers and guards and more. A bright trimmed hardboard headliner and vinyl floor mat were new in the Sport Wagon. A dual master cylinder and self-adjusting brakes were introduced. Back-up lights became standard. Prices were $2,417 for the Roadster, $2,546 for the Pickup and $2,633 for the Sport Wagon, each up about $400 from 1966. Ford built 16,100 Broncos in model-year 1967.

For 1968, the Bronco models got bumpers that now curved around the body corners and side marker lights. A heater and defroster were now standard equipment. Locking front wheel hubs, new inside door handles and soft window crank knobs were now extra-cost options. Prices climbed to $2,638 for the Roadster, $2,741 for the

Pickup and $2,851 for the Wagon. This was the last year for the 289 V-8 and the Roadster. Model-year production was 15,700.

Bronco production jumped to 20,956 units in 1969. The 302 V-8 replaced the 289. Two-speed electric wipers were a running change. The parking lamps now had amber lenses. Sport models featured aluminum door panel trim, a pleated parchment interior and a rear floor mat (if a rear seat was installed). The windshield no longer folded and the cowl section was beefed up to combat road noise. New doors were used. The Wagon body was beefed up, too, particularly around the door frames The roof was no longer detachable. There was fixed glass in the liftgate and on each side of the rear compartment.

1968 Ford Bronco **Phil Hall Collection**

1966 Ford Bronco U-100 Sport Utility or Wagon, 1/2-ton

6	5	4	3	2	1
$ 720	$2,160	$3,600	$8,100	$12,600	$18,000

Estimated values in today's marketplace taken from the 2006 Collector Car Price Guide.